Cracking the China Conundrum

Cracking the China Conundrum

Why Conventional Economic Wisdom Is Wrong

YUKON HUANG

OXFORD
UNIVERSITY PRESS

OXFORD
UNIVERSITY PRESS

Oxford University Press is a department of the University of Oxford. It furthers
the University's objective of excellence in research, scholarship, and education
by publishing worldwide. Oxford is a registered trade mark of Oxford University
Press in the UK and certain other countries.

Published in the United States of America by Oxford University Press
198 Madison Avenue, New York, NY 10016, United States of America.

Library of Congress Cataloging-in-Publication Data
Title: Cracking the China Conundrum: Why Conventional Economic Wisdom is Wrong / Yukon Huang.
Description: New York City : Oxford University Press, 2017.
Identifiers: LCCN 2016050471 | ISBN 9780190630034 (hardback) | ISBN 9780190630041 (updf) |
ISBN 9780190630058 (epub) | ISBN 9780190630065 (oxford online)
Subjects: LCSH: China—Economic conditions—2000– | China—Economic
policy—2000– | Regional planning—China. | China—Foreign economic
relations. | Fiscal policy—China. | Investments, Chinese. |
BISAC: BUSINESS & ECONOMICS / International / Economics. |
POLITICAL SCIENCE / Economic Conditions.
Classification: LCC HC427.95 .H843 2017 | DDC 330.951—dc23
LC record available at https://lccn.loc.gov/2016050471

9 8 7 6 5 4 3
Printed by Sheridan Books, Inc., United States of America

For my loving wife, Jing.

For my two daughters, Alison and Laura.

For my two grandchildren, Julia and Nate.

For my son-in-law, Jonathan Howe.

CONTENTS

PREFACE

Anyone following the economic rise of China will likely be confused by the differing views being expressed. Explanations vary among casual observers as well as acknowledged experts, whether in the United States or in China. I am part of that scene with biases shaped by my own heritage, education, and professional experiences.

I was among the first wave of Chinese who immigrated to the United States during and after World War II. My perspectives were shaped by public schools in Washington, DC, and then at Yale and Princeton for my education in economics. After teaching at various universities, followed by a stint with the US Treasury, I had a long career with the World Bank working in countries as diverse as Malaysia, Tanzania, Burma, Bangladesh, Russia, and finally China.

Until a few years ago, my thinking would have been characterized as Washington centric and typical of those working in international agencies such as the World Bank or International Monetary Fund. That might have been the end of my intellectual evolution, but I found myself by chance jolted into another direction after I joined the Carnegie Endowment for International Peace in Washington, DC, in the spring of 2010.

Carnegie was looking for an economist to write and stimulate debate on China for an international audience. I decided to give it a try, initially on a part-time basis because it was not clear to me—and no doubt also to Carnegie's management—whether I would be a good fit. Having spent most of my career working at a development bank operating on a confidential creditor-borrower relationship, I had not paid much attention to the concerns of the general public.

When I went to China in 1997 as the World Bank's first Beijing-based country director, China's economic policies were mainly a curiosity for those interested in how a large and very poor nation was transforming itself. By 2010, China's rise had become a hot topic with the media, academics, and financial community fascinated with every aspect of its development.

What differentiated China from other countries was the centrality of economic issues in shaping China's role as an emerging great power. And this resurgence was anything but normal in its manner and impact. The perspectives that I had developed in having visited each of China's thirty plus provinces and autonomous regions did not seem to mesh with the views being disseminated in Western capitals and business communities. Location clearly mattered, as did the orientation of institutions in shaping perspectives. But it went deeper than that.

Why did so many Sino-specialists see as a risk something that I saw as a non-issue and vice versa? Having worked on China for so long, I had come to recognize, as have others, its strengths and vulnerabilities. But global opinions tended to be more extreme, casting the country as either poised to take over the world or doomed to collapse.

Thus began a process of revisiting my own beliefs and the arguments made by others and, in the process, trying to "crack the China conundrum." Having spent the years before arriving in Beijing working on the former Soviet Union, I soon realized that the major reason why views varied so much among researchers came from the absence of any agreed-upon analytical framework for thinking about China's unique transition as it moved from central planning to more market-oriented systems while still retaining a major role for the state.

The contrasting views suggested that there was a perspective missing in much of the China debate, rooted in how one analyzed the country's economic and political transformation. I assumed initially that this was primarily a "Western" problem, but over time, I realized that it was also a problem for those in Beijing, including myself. All this forced me to question many of the principles that I had formerly accepted as conventional wisdom. In doing so, I had become both a skeptic and a contrarian.

The inspiration for my first article came from a point that I made at a seminar at the Carnegie Endowment in Washington, DC, in the summer of 2010. At the time, the accepted view was that China's currency, the renminbi, needed to appreciate given the country's persistent trade surpluses. But the ultimate objective was that its exchange rate needed to be market driven and that meant it could move either way. China was also experiencing massive inflows of capital as markets assumed the currency would continue to strengthen. In other words, the renminbi had become a one-way bet, and this was not sustainable. The challenge was to find occasions for it to depreciate and, with the collapsing euro, that time had arrived.

I wrote up my argument for the *Financial Times* which came out on June 10, 2010, as "China Can Let the Renminbi Depreciate." I then turned my attention to a point that everyone was making, that China was consuming too little and investing too much. Thus it needed a more "balanced" growth process. But I found it odd that the very factors which helped China grow so rapidly were now viewed as a problem. This became the basis of my next article in the *Financial Times* entitled "China's Unbalanced Growth Has Served It Well." Other articles soon followed, and the *Financial Times* asked me to be a regular contributor to their "A-List" section and more recently for "The Exchange."

I then began to seek other outlets to make my points, beginning with the *Wall Street Journal*, which is seen as taking a more free-market-oriented and critical view on China. Being a contrarian, however, did not mean that all is necessarily right in the middle kingdom. My first *Wall Street Journal* article in 2011 carried the title "Misinterpreting China's Economy," which argued that while China's statistics were misleading, its official numbers understated the size of the economy—even as most observers were suggesting the opposite. This was followed by an article on why restricting the residency rights for China's 250 million migrant workers—a seemingly purely domestic social issue—had major consequences for global growth and trade.

Over the past six years, some fifty articles of mine have been published in the *Financial Times* and twenty in the *Wall Street Journal*, followed by others in outlets with differing editorial positions such as *Bloomberg, Foreign Affairs, National Interest, New York Times, Diplomat*; journals sponsored by Cato, Aspen, and Johns Hopkins SAIS; and in China, in outlets aligned with the government such as *Global Times* and *China Daily*, and some that are more independent such as *Caixin* and *Sina.com*. This book draws extensively on my past writings.

But op-eds and journal articles cannot do justice to the complexity of the issues being debated. Only a book allows one to take a deeper and more holistic approach. The analysis here is that of an economist, but the topics include both relatively technical issues as well as more general concerns for those fascinated with China's emergence on the global scene. My intention is not to be comprehensive but to highlight points that affect broadly shared perceptions of China. I have long since realized, however, that one cannot expect to alter the many emotionally tinged views that many observers have adhered to for so long. But if I have managed to encourage some to think about them differently, then I will have met my aspirations.

ACKNOWLEDGMENTS

My views have benefited from discussions with the many World Bank colleagues that I have worked with over the years. I am especially grateful to Vikram Nehru, whom I had the privilege to work with both at the World Bank in connection with the *China 2030* report and later at the Carnegie Endowment. Others who have provided valuable insights from the World Bank's Beijing office include Bert Hofmann, Louis Kuijs, and Karlis Smits. Special appreciation goes to Fan Ying, Li Li, and Chen Tianshu, who have been strongly supportive of my work in Beijing over the past two decades.

Much of my rethinking on China issues stem from the in-depth studies done by the International Monetary Fund on the risks of China's unbalanced growth, which was also being elaborated on by many noted China analysts, in particular Nicholas Lardy and Michael Pettis. Eventually my views took a different path as discussed in Chapter 4 of this book.

The basis for my arguments came from ideas inculcated in me by my PhD thesis advisor at Princeton University, the late W. Arthur Lewis. His Nobel Prize-winning work on economic development with unlimited supplies of labor coincidentally mirrors the China experience and provides the basis for a major theme in this book—why rural to urban labor migration leads to rapid but also unbalanced economic growth.

My thinking was also influenced by working with Indermit Gill on a companion volume to his World Bank's 2009 World Development Report, *Reshaping Economic Geography*, which underscored the importance of spatial factors in development and why imbalances are part of the development process. I have also gained insights from the research of other former World Bank economists who are now associated with other institutions notably Homi Kharas, David Dollar, Pieter Bottelier, and Shahid Yusuf.

At Carnegie Endowment, my work has drawn on the work of others in the Asia Program, Douglas Paal and Michael Swaine in Washington and Paul Haenle in Beijing. This book and the articles that I have written for the media over the years could not have been completed without the help of a series of outstanding assistants and junior fellows at Carnegie: Alexander Taylor, Rachel Odell, Clare Lynch, Canyon Bosler, Michelle Winglee, Patrick Farrell, and David Stack.

This book has benefited from comments received from my presentations sponsored by the American and European Chambers of Commerce in Beijing and the Foreign Correspondents Club of China. Insights, both supportive and skeptical, flowed from my many discussions with investment banks and hedge funds in New York, London, Hong Kong, and Singapore and at forums hosted by think tanks and universities in the United States, Europe, China, and Asia.

Special appreciation goes to Eric X. Li, founder and managing director of Chengwei Capital and also a noted political scientist and commentator on China, for his support for Carnegie's work relating to China's economy.

Finally, I am especially grateful to the editors of the *Financial Times* and *Wall Street Journal* for their willingness to consider my views early on and in working with me over the years. This provided the platform for me to reach a much wider audience and to refine my thinking.

ABBREVIATIONS AND ACRONYMS

ADB   Asian Development Bank
AFC   Asian Financial Crisis
AIIB   Asian Infrastructure Investment Bank
ASEAN   Association of South-East Asian Nations
BIT   Bilateral investment treaty
Brexit   British withdrawal from the European Union
BRICS   Brazil, Russia, India, China and South Africa
CAFTA   China-ASEAN Free Trade Agreement
CDB   China Development Bank
CFIUS   Committee on Foreign Investment in the United States
EEZ   Exclusive economic zone
FAI   Fixed asset investment
FDI   Foreign direct investment
FSB   Financial Stability Board
FTAAP   Free Trade Area for the Asia Pacific
GDP   Gross domestic product
GFC   Global Financial Crisis
ICOR   Incremental capital output ratio
IMF   International Monetary Fund
IPR   Intellectual property rights
LGFVs   Local government financing vehicles
NAFTA   North American Free Trade Agreement
OBOR   One Belt, One Road
ODI   Outward direct investment
OECD   Organization for Economic Cooperation and Development
RCEP   Regional Comprehensive Economic Partnership
SDR   Special drawing rights
S&ED   Strategic and Economic Dialogue

SEZs	Special economic zones
SMEs	Small and Medium Enterprises
SOCBs	State-owned commercial banks
SOEs	State-owned enterprises
TPP	Trans-Pacific Partnership
TTIP	Trans-Atlantic Trade and Investment Partnership
TVEs	Township village enterprises
UNCLOS	United Nations Convention Law of the Sea
UNCTAD	United Nations Conference on Trade and Development
WMPs	Wealth management products
WTO	World Trade Organization

Cracking the China Conundrum

CHAPTER 1

Introduction

Few countries command the public's attention to the extent that China does. And few generate such widely varying views on its economic and political prospects. This book is about why there are such differences and why the conventional wisdom is so often wrong.

That China warrants so much attention is not surprising. Its remarkable economic performance is challenging the world's geopolitical balance of power and triggering debates on the virtues of state-led versus market-led capitalism. China's rise is seen positively in uplifting hundreds of millions out of poverty, but many also see it as a threat to the established international order and Western democratic traditions. All this is occurring at a time when populist pressures are raising concerns about the economic benefits of globalization and the capacity of institutions to deal with its social and political consequences. Against this background, the intentions of presidents Donald Trump and Xi Jinping to elevate the profiles of their respective nations and to champion differing views on globalization will increase tensions in the coming years.

Why perceptions about China's economy are so often wrong is not as easy to decipher. For China specialists, these differences stem from the lack of an agreed-upon analytical framework. For the public more generally, there are also challenges in drawing the appropriate conclusions about a country that is so big and regionally diverse in the distribution of its natural resources and economic activity.

For the economists and financial community covering China, the lack of an agreed-upon analytical framework makes it difficult for views to coalesce. Decades ago in the heyday of the Soviet Union and centrally planned Eastern European economies, universities routinely taught courses on socialist systems or "transitional" economies as an academic discipline. With the demise of the former Soviet Union and its economic links with Eastern Europe, this body of analysis faded away as a popular field of inquiry. The consequence is that many of the market-based principles used for analyzing the behavior of firms and macroeconomic aggregates for a typical developing country often fare poorly when applied to China. And because China's financial, fiscal, trade, and social welfare systems are more closely linked than those in market-based economies, it can be difficult to identify the fault lines when problems do emerge.

Unlike Russia's rapid economic transformation, China's reform process was more gradual in its systemic shifts. While market forces play a significant role in shaping China's economic outcomes, state-driven mandates often matter more. Western textbooks see competition as being driven by firms, but China's provinces and local administrative units also play a unique role in creating pressures for change. This phenomenon has no counterpart among other developing economies or the historical experiences in Eastern Europe.

And because China is a continental economy, regional and spatial factors shape economic outcomes in ways that traditional macroeconomic indicators do not easily capture. This creates a tendency for observers to simplify when a more holistic approach would be more appropriate. Moreover, sentiments are almost always clouded by emotionally tinged differences in ideology and culture between the West and China. Thus, aspects of China's growth process and structural transformation are easily misinterpreted, resulting in misguided policy prescriptions.

China's Rise Generates Conflicting Views

Usually, economic trends are a concern confined to financial institutions or academics. For China, even routine announcements such as last quarter's industrial production, a decline in imports or a modest 2 percent exchange rate adjustment, as occurred in August 2015, can end up as front-page news or grist in US presidential campaign debates.

Despite so much scrutiny, China is an abnormal economic power whose rise has mystified almost everyone. Over the years, one was as likely to read about the middle kingdom dominating the international economy as about a possible imminent collapse. Similarly, some observers see China's authoritarian system as its Achilles heel, while others see it as a major contributor to its impressive achievements.

Nobel Laureate Joseph Stiglitz writes about this being "the Chinese Century."[1] At the same time, predictions of China's demise can come from established economists such as Harvard Professor and former International Monetary Fund (IMF) chief economist Kenneth Rogoff, who has been warning for years of an impending debt crisis.[2] Among the more skeptical in the financial community is former UBS chief economist George Magnus, who has cautioned against China's rise being seen as inevitable given its weak institutions, aging population, and environmental degradation.[3] But Stephen Roach, the former chairman of Morgan Stanley Asia, continues to express confidence that China will be able to manage its economic challenges.[4] Many now see China's slowdown as a sign of a diminishing global influence, but given its size and still relatively high growth rate, others note that its role will only increase.[5]

Over the past decade, there have been a flood of media reports and in-depth studies establishing what has become the conventional wisdom about China's economic performance and prospects. Among the many popular beliefs are the following:

- "It is impossible for American firms to compete with China because its wages are so low." (Yet China's wages are now five times what they once were in the mid-1990s, and its $600 billion trade surplus in 2015 was six times that of a decade ago.)
- "American companies invest a lot in China and this is why jobs are being lost." (Yet only around 2 percent of America's foreign investment actually goes to China.)
- "Corruption has negative consequences for China's growth." (Yet spreading corruption has actually promoted rather than impeded growth.)

Typical of the economic arguments made in recent years are statements like these:

- "China's surging debt levels mean that a financial crisis is inevitable."
- "An over sixfold increase in property prices is a clear sign of a bubble."
- "China needs to rebalance its growth away from repressed consumption and excessive investment to escape the 'middle-income trap.'"
- "Official statistics are manipulated to give politically acceptable results."

The problem with these, and other, widely shared sentiments is that they are either misleading or wrong. If the analysis is off, then likely so are the policies that are being advocated.

China's Unique Economic Track Record

The context for this book is that China is at an inflection point in moving from its historic double-digit growth rates to a slower path whose dimensions are still to be determined. At the height of the Global Financial Crisis (GFC), China accounted for an astounding 50 percent of the world's economic expansion, yet today its slowdown is wreaking havoc on economies that previously benefited the most from its rise. Judgments about China's economic prospects have become more pessimistic, and this is also triggering concerns about its future political evolution. Markets are now questioning whether China can survive the threat of looming debt and property-market bubbles.

Much of the variance in perceptions stems from how one interprets China's remarkable economic history. China's economic performance after Deng Xiaoping opened up the economy in 1980 led to three decades of double-digit GDP (gross domestic product) growth, lifting some six hundred million from poverty—more than the entire population of Africa.

How exceptional is this performance when measured against other countries? As seen in Figure 1.1, China's growth rate over the two decades from 1991 to 2010 puts it in a class by itself. No other country comes even close. More recently, China's economic slowdown has generated widespread concerns about its prospects. Taking the average of the recent four-year period (2010–14) for which cross-country data are available (see Figure 1.1), China's growth rate of around 8 percent is still much better than all but a handful of countries and compares quite favorably with the global average of 3.4 percent.

China's exceptional economic performance is the result of a series of pragmatic reforms that encouraged more competition, made use of the country's advantages, and were sequenced to reflect evolving institutional capabilities and market opportunities. Its economy underwent three major transformations in the course of these reforms: from an agrarian to an industrial and services-driven economy, from a closed economy to a relatively open one, and from a totally state-dominated economy to one of mixed ownership.

What was different was the process that China used to reform its economy rather than the policies themselves, since the reforms broadly adhered to

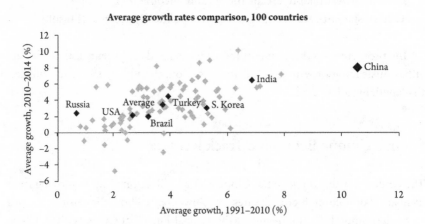

Figure 1.1 China GDP Growth Rate Comparisons. Source: World Bank World Development Indicators; author's calculations

mainstream prescriptions including liberalizing markets, diversifying ownership, and maintaining stable macroeconomic conditions. By pursuing reforms in a gradual, experimental way—often with second-best but practical approaches—and providing incentives for local authorities, the leadership was able to develop workable transitional institutions at each stage of development. These reforms made China's firms globally competitive without the need to embrace the mass privatization initiatives that took place in the former Soviet Union. China also grew rapidly because it was partially insulated from the swings in global economic cycles due to its capital controls and command over investment decisions.

For much of the period from 1980 to the early 2000s, China's performance was more of an academic curiosity regarding a growth experience that did not fit the usual norms. But that all changed after China gained membership in the World Trade Organization (WTO) in 2001. Its export prowess altered global trade patterns and ultimately geopolitical relations. China's trade surpluses soared to nearly 10 percent of GDP by 2007, unprecedented for such a large economy. Its surpluses were seen as globally destabilizing, contributing to the large trade deficits in the West, especially for the United States. After suffering through decades of financial weakness and shortages of foreign exchange, China's external reserves expanded twentyfold from less than $0.2 trillion in 2000 to nearly $4 trillion in 2014, before falling back more recently.

For most of this period, China's economic rise was largely seen as a positive outcome that buoyed up exports from commodity-producing nations in South America and Africa as well as Asian economies that specialized in high-tech components to be assembled in China for European and American markets. China became the major source of lower cost consumer goods for the world and helped support a protracted period of global economic expansion in the new millennium. For the most part, its success was seen by its neighbors as an economic opportunity and the process as harmonious regarding its impact on foreign relations.

But in response to the GFC in 2008, China's position both economically and geopolitically changed dramatically. China's policies to counter the financial crisis initially appeared to be a major success in keeping growth going at home when the economies in the West fell into recession. But subsequent cycles of credit expansion generated rapid debt buildup and excessive property construction. This has now raised widespread concerns that China would succumb to its own financial crisis. The combination of having to deal with mounting debt levels coupled with a maturation of its economy has led to a prolonged slowdown which as of early 2017 had yet to bottom out.

This contraction has generated worldwide concerns, because China still accounts for about a quarter of the increase in global output. The consequences have disproportionately impacted metal and energy prices, with ripple effects on financial markets. Commodity-exporting countries have felt this especially keenly, and prospects seem dampened for many formerly dynamic economies in East Asia.

Nevertheless, market watchers and the media have exaggerated the negative aspects of China's economic problems. Many of the uber-bears now point to China's recent problems as evidence of a flawed growth model or a precursor to a debt-driven collapse. Yet common sense tells us that no economy can grow at 10 percent annually forever, doubling in size every seven years. Cross-country experiences indicate that as an economy matures, growth moderates, just as it did for the other successful developing economies over the past half century. And while China's debt surge has gone on for too long and needs a more disciplined approach, it is still manageable.

China's GDP growth rate of 6.7 percent in 2016 hit a twenty-five-year low, yet it was still higher than any other major economy aside from India. And over the past decade and a half covering both the Asian Financial Crisis (AFC) and the GFC periods, China's growth record stands out in being more stable and robust than other major emerging market economies in East Asia or elsewhere (see Figure 1.2).

On the foreign policy front, China shifted from what had been seen as a largely passive stance on global and regional issues to increasing assertiveness regarding territorial claims in the South China Sea and similar frictions with Japan in neighboring waters. This has ratcheted up regional tensions and brought China into a more adversarial position with the United States, whose much-publicized

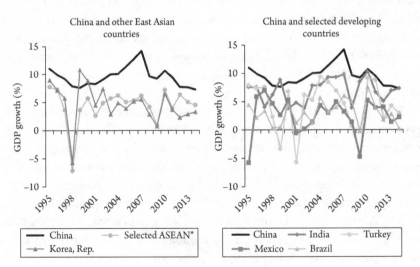

*Selected ASEAN include Philippines, Malaysia, Indonesia, and Thailand

Figure 1.2 Emerging Market Growth Comparisons. Source: World Bank World Development Indicators; author's calculations

"rebalancing or pivot" back to Asia is viewed by Beijing as a containment strategy. These days, security concerns in Asia are focused on the possibility of a conflict between a rising great power and the dominant one.

At the same time that China's external relations have become strained, its economic achievements at home are being compromised by widening income disparities, surging corruption, and worsening environmental conditions. The rapid shifts in China's prospects have spawned a growing debate about China's economic and political evolution and its domestic and foreign implications.

Differing Global Views of China

Differing perceptions of China begin with views about its position in the global economy. For many years, the majority of Americans and Europeans believed that China was already the leading economic power, yet the rest of the world—especially China's immediate Asian neighbors as well as China itself—felt strongly that the United States was still on top. Why is there such a dichotomy between the views of the developed and developing countries, which at first glance appears to be the reverse of what one might have expected? The answer lies in misunderstanding the importance of trade balances in determining a country's economic might (see Chapter 2).

Going beyond economic concerns, negative feelings about China have hit all-time highs in the United States. The same is true in Europe, although the depth of such sentiments varies considerably across nations. Many instinctively would guess that public opinions about China might be most negative in the United Kingdom, given tensions over Hong Kong, and more positive in Germany, given its strong economic and political relationships with China. Yet the reality is the opposite. Not recognizing and understanding the nature of such patterns makes it even harder to form effective foreign policy responses.

For the more ideologically inclined, China raises many red flags. Its economic ascendancy threatens the tenants of Western political liberalism—grounded in free markets, democracy, and the sanctity of human rights. China's impressive achievements challenge these principles. These concerns often surface as a debate between the roles of the state versus the market, or the priority to be accorded to individual liberties versus collective action. The debate has been caricatured as a battle between two systems, although the two may have more in common than differences regarding the problems that need to be addressed. This has nurtured sentiments that are likely to be harsher than the reality in judging China's economic situation.

Differing Views on China's Growth Model

The debate over whether a market- or state-led system is more growth enhancing became more serious after the AFC in the late 1990s, when China's growth
soared. It intensified further during the GFC in 2008 when the major Western
economies stumbled badly while China for a while seemed to be insulated. Many
believed that China would suffer in the aftermath of the AFC, even if it was not
among the most severely affected. They did not foresee the impact of three powerful drivers of growth that emerged with the new millennium: the dynamism
of an expanding private sector, a construction boom, and the emergence of an
Asian production-sharing network centered on China. These forces, along with
market liberalization, drove a surge in investment rates and rapid GDP growth
over the subsequent decade and a half (see Chapter 3).

Some of the hotly debated issues that emerged during this period found
support among both critics and believers in China's growth process. One such
theme is that China's growth model is excessively unbalanced as measured by its
extremely low share of personal consumption relative to the size of its economy,
with a commensurately high share of investment. This was seen as the major
reason for China's huge trade surpluses and a risk to its longer-term growth prospects. This led to many experts and institutions to recommend that for China to
escape the so-called middle-income trap it needed to have a more consumption
driven growth process.[6] This view, however, is misguided. Unbalanced growth is
largely a consequence of a successful growth process driven by urbanization and
regional differences rather than a weakness—even if these imbalances have been
pushed too far in recent years. Moreover, contrary to expectations, China's trade
surpluses moderated even as its consumption-investment imbalance widened
(see Chapter 4).

Part of the confusion comes from mixing up what economists call
"supply" or productivity-related factors that shape a country's medium- to
long-term growth process with the near-term cyclical problem of inadequate
"demand" to absorb what is being produced currently—which if unresolved
would dampen growth prospects. Thus most observers look to increasing
household consumption as the solution for inadequate demand caused by
depressed global trade and declining investment needs at home. Few realize
that given the nature of China's economic system, the problem can only be
solved by increased government expenditures largely in the form of social
services to supplement personal consumption as the source of more demand
in the future.

Since the GFC, China watchers have been fixated on the surge in China's
debt-to-GDP ratios and a looming property bubble. The doubling of equity
prices from 2014 to 2015, followed by a 40 percent collapse, have added to such

worries. Experts have warned that all economies that have incurred similar bubbles have experienced a financial crisis and there is no reason why China should be any different.

Yet China is different—not because it is immune to financial pressures, but because the structure of and interactions within its economic system are not the same as others. Most of China's debt is public rather than private, and sourced domestically rather than externally. China also did not have a significant private property market a decade ago, so that most of the recent surge in property prices is the consequence of market forces trying to establish appropriate values for land—whose value was previously hidden in a socialist system. China's equity bubble also differs in the sense that it was not driven by economic fundamentals but by flawed government policies (see Chapter 5).

The debt crisis has led most market analysts to focus on what they see as serious weaknesses in China's financial system as evidenced in the arguments that were being made after the GFC that China's interest rates were too low and that its banks needed to be better managed to moderate the surge in nonperforming loans. Yet the reality is that its interest rates have been too high rather than too low, and soaring debt levels are being driven more by weaknesses in its budgetary system than its banks. But there is a moral hazard problem since China's ambitious growth targets lead to excessive lending because the firms and banks involved can pass the costs of poor decisions on to the state. These concerns require attention, but the prospects of a near-term economic collapse are exaggerated. The solution lies in increasing productivity and overhauling China's fiscal system while strengthening accountability (see Chapter 5).

Differing Socioeconomic and Political Concerns

For many China watchers, worsening social tensions rather than the economy per se is the real risk. Income inequality has increased more rapidly in China over the past several decades than in any other major economy, and many see this as potentially destabilizing the system. Yet in one generation China has spawned hundreds of millions of new jobs for those leaving low-productivity agriculture, and growth in real wages has been multiples higher than in other countries. This paradox is explained by the spatial nature of China's growth process which can be characterized as a race to the top with urban incomes increasing faster than rural incomes (see Chapter 6).

On a more general level, the commonly accepted view is that economic and political liberalization go hand in hand and a market-driven form of capitalism is better than China's state-led version. Yet while the pace of economic liberalization in China has been impressive, political liberalization by the usual markers has been caught in a time warp. China also seems to be trapped in a spiral of ever-increasing corruption. Many assume that President Xi Jinping's highly publicized campaign against corruption, if successful, will lead to more rapid growth and a stronger role for the Communist Party, even though the opposite is likely to result (see Chapter 6).

Differing Views on China's Global Economic Relations

For the United States, trade tensions have dominated its economic agenda with China for much of the past decade. Most Americans believe that their country's huge trade deficits are closely linked with China's similarly large trade surpluses and that an undervalued renminbi is the reason. Yet the reality is that there is no direct causal relationship between China's surpluses and America's deficits, and much of the rhetoric surrounding the alleged manipulation of China's exchange rate and promoting more manufacturing jobs in the United States is similarly misplaced (see Chapter 7).

For those focused on global power shifts, a related issue of internationalizing China's currency is seen as signaling Beijing's desire to increase its stature in the world economy, possibly at the expense of the United States. Yet few understand that the economic rationale for internationalizing the renminbi is intrinsically weak and, given the structure of China's economy, the likelihood of this happening is very low. But this objective can play the role of a Trojan horse in supporting China's economic reforms and broader national security objectives.

The general public believes that American firms are investing heavily in China, leading to loss of American jobs. Yet contrary to popular perceptions, flows of foreign direct investment (FDI) between the United States and China are abnormally low. The standard view is that rich countries have excessive capital and invest in poorer countries that lack the necessary savings. Yet the United States and China illustrate the opposite situation, with China now investing more in the United States than the United States is investing in China. The nature of trade relations partly explains why this is the case, but political and security concerns also explain why the European Union's investment relations with China are so much stronger than America's (see Chapter 8).

Currently, the United States and European Union are both negotiating bilateral investment treaties (BITs) with China. Interwoven into the sensitivities of the discussion are concerns about technology transfer and intellectual property rights (IPR) theft as China's production process becomes increasingly more sophisticated and a direct competitor with the West. China has been pouring money into innovation, with surging levels of support for research and development, higher education, and strategic industries. Many in the United States see China as a potential threat as it moves up the value chain in production. Yet China is not really more innovative and technologically advanced for a country at its income level. Moreover given historical experiences, IPR theft is unlikely to be curtailed at this stage in China's development (see Chapter 8).

China's trade and foreign investment flows underpin President Xi Jinping's strategy to elevate China's regional presence and to gain more friends by strengthening links with Europe through his "One Road, One Belt" initiative, while the US "pivot to Asia" is an attempt to reassert itself in the region. The potential for conflict has increased because of the island disputes in Asian waters. These have also made it next to impossible for China to nurture warmer feelings with its neighbors. President Trump may take a harder position regarding these disputes even if the affected Southeast Asian nations seek options to lower tensions.

While China's economic reforms have nudged it to becoming a more "normal" market-driven economy, tensions are exacerbated because China has become an "abnormal" great power. It is the first great power that is a developing rather than a developed country, the first to get old before it gets rich. Its weak institutions and historical legacies mean that it has more insecurities than would be expected of a great power. Whether the result turns out to be destructive relations between China and its neighbors and the United States or a more conciliatory process that allows the region to remain stable and prosper is uncertain (see Chapter 9).

Explaining Why Conventional Wisdom Is So Often Wrong

How does one explain why there is such extreme variation in views and why conventional wisdom is so often misguided? The answer is that observers see China through multiple lenses (see Chapter 10). Geopolitical differences in values and inadequate analytical frameworks are part of the explanation, making it difficult or nearly impossible for both pundits and academics to approach issues in an intellectually validated or ideologically neutral way.

Policymakers in Beijing often complain that the Western media tends to "demonize" China and that judgments are impaired by unwarranted and ideological biases. But the more dispassionate observers will remind their friends in China that its discriminatory trade and investment practices and restrictions on the international media create the climate for stinging criticisms, as exemplified in the 2016 annual report of the bipartisan Congressional-Executive Commission on China which took a particularly harsh position on the government's human rights record.[7]

The issue is not whether one should be positive or negative about China's economy and its political and foreign policy implications but instead about fitting China into a framework that leads to a better understanding of the reality. Many experts inappropriately use the experiences of other countries to assess developments in China and in doing so their conclusions are often wrong. Some have argued that China does not follow the same economic and financial principles that apply to others—but while the principles might be correct, the assumptions might not fit China's mixed economy.

The problem is compounded by the opacity of China's economic and political system. Everyone thinks that China manipulates its statistics to give excessively positive outcomes, but the mystery lies in how such indicators are constructed and the implications of the rapidly changing structure of China's economy. Ironically, China's GDP growth rate measured over the long term has been under rather than overstated.

The media is under considerable pressure to convey an easily digestible message to the general public that is in line with accepted values and norms. The result often fails to take into consideration China's size and geographic diversity, as well as the peculiarities of its governance structures and growth path.

Among the more analytically inclined, differing perceptions reflect how one views the many distortions in China's economy that result from blending market-based principles into a still centrally controlled system, leaving many of its economic institutions caught in a no man's land. The consequence is that analysis of what economists call "market distortions" in a transitional economy like China is more tenuous. The more pessimistic China watchers see these distortions as signs of a possible economic collapse. The more optimistic see potential for improved outcomes with reforms. Purists seek ambitious market-based solutions that might yield a hypothetical "best" outcome. The more pragmatic see the logic in pursuing "second-best" approaches and the merits of a more gradual path to get around vested interests.

More often than not, the China debate reflects a misreading of the role of the state in influencing economic decision making in China. The Western concept of an economy is based on competition among firms in open and free markets. Unique to China, local governments are also part of the competitive economic environment. Beijing sets the broad parameters, and policies are calibrated in ways that defy traditional thinking. Competition in China is not just the result of pressures generated by markets and firms but can also come from local government entities. Not incorporating these factors into the analysis leads to a misunderstanding of what has been happening in China.

At the geopolitical level, views are driven by the tensions that come from a rising power seen as threatening the position of the dominant power and rewriting the principles upon which the existing global order was established. Economic differences between nations can and do raise concerns, but ultimately their resolution does not have to be a zero-sum game but one from which both sides can benefit. A realignment of global power relations, however, is usually a zero-sum game that is more likely to distort perceptions and foster conflicts.

Book Outline

This book takes a critical look at China's economy through many perspectives. Chapter 2 covers global public perceptions of China's economy and the contrasting views shaped by economic and political considerations. Chapter 3 explains how Deng Xiaoping's opening up of the economy more than three decades ago laid the basis for China's growth model which underpins the current debate about its economic challenges. Chapters 4 and 5 delve more deeply into China's growth process, focusing respectively on its unbalanced nature and more recent concerns relating to its debt and property problems. Chapter 6 elaborates on the social and political conflicts facing China and their relationship to economic developments. Chapters 7–9 discuss how China's trade and capital flows and foreign policies have impacted the global economy, particularly the United States and Europe. Chapter 10 provides an overview of China's current economic prospects and a framework for helping the reader crack the China conundrum.

CHAPTER 2

Differing Global and Regional Perceptions

Whether one is a casual observer of China, a keen investor, or a concerned academic, one's views of China are influenced by biases shaped by location, values, and political-economic orientation. But even taken together, these factors do not fully explain why China's economy is so often misunderstood or viewed more negatively than the reality would warrant.

At the global level, a marked shift in power relations, coming from China's increasing economic might and willingness to exercise it, has shaken up the foreign policy community. Many see China's accomplishments as a laudable outcome that has revived latent strengths and benefited the world. But the majority of Americans see China's awakening as a threat to their country's global stature. Europeans are less preoccupied with power politics but share America's worries that Beijing may try to propagate its own style of development and values by privileging growth and a strong state over democracy and human rights. There is generally less apprehension in the rest of the world, but even among developing countries, views, influenced by proximity and colored by history, vary significantly.

Today's headlines are replete with prognosticators suggesting a possible financial crisis, even while others remain confident about China's future. No other country generates such contrasting views about its economic performance, inspiring observers to coin the phrase "Beijing Consensus" to describe its singular economic policies, as compared to the "Washington Consensus."[1]

Despite all this scrutiny, many focus on the wrong issues. They analyze minute changes in China's exchange rate to gauge China's commitment to reforms, while ignoring the more important fiscal weaknesses—in contrast to the politically charged attention being given in the United States and Europe to budget debates. And for the more idealistically inclined, should one have faith that rapid economic progress in China will eventually encourage more open political processes when the evidence thus far suggests otherwise?

The focus in this chapter is on the geopolitical factors that shape public opinions of China in the United States and Europe, among the BRICS (Brazil, Russia, India, China and South Africa) and China's neighbors in Asia. A short survey of the developments in China's political economy over the past two decades provides context for discussing evolving global perceptions of China. Better relations between China and the West hinge upon improved mutual understanding. This starts with recognizing how the views of society across borders can shape media perceptions and in turn a nation's foreign policies.

China's Opening Up and Evolving Global Perceptions

Deng Xiaoping's death in 1997 marked the end of an era, both economically and politically, and provides a convenient starting point for much of this discussion about public perceptions. What China is today originated from his reforms in the late 1970s, when he opened the country to the outside world and allowed the market and private initiatives to transform the economy (see Chapter 3). Politically, unification with Hong Kong—also in 1997—marked the onset of the "one country, two systems" policy intended to be a less threatening approach to its inhabitants that could also be applied to the delicate Taiwan situation.[2] But the key economic event in 1997 was the onset of the Asian Financial Crisis, which devastated many seemingly dynamic economies—such as South Korea—and raised alarm bells about China's prospects.

By 2001, China's double-digit growth rates had fallen for the first time in a decade to below 8 percent. Whether it would return to its former growth path or be pulled down like the other Asian economies became the concern for financial markets as well as academics. The Asian crisis years gave birth to a cohort of doubters who even today command considerable public attention.

The World Bank, accustomed to making long-term forecasts, issued its comprehensive study *China 2020* in 1997, proposing that GDP growth could be sustained at 7 percent for the decade 2000–2010, with the requisite reforms.[3] Many at the time considered this overly optimistic, coming as it did on the heels of collapsing economies in the region and given China's perceived economic vulnerabilities. Carrying such concerns to the extreme, the perennial doomsday predictor Gordon Chang warned in his 2001 book, *The Coming Collapse of China*, that the economy would tank by 2006 due to its excessive share of nonperforming loans coupled with its loss-making state enterprises and corrupt political system.[4]

Yet, by 2006 China's financial restructuring program had eliminated nonperforming loans as an issue and the percentage of loss-making state-owned enterprises (SOEs) had been cut nearly in half. Construction and export-related activities helped push China's annual GDP growth rate to 11 percent, much higher than the seemingly optimistic rates the World Bank had projected a decade earlier.

Why were both alarmists and staid institutions like the World Bank so far off the mark? As Chapter 3 discusses, China not only survived the AFC but even flourished. The pessimists misinterpreted what was happening in the economy and missed the potential growth drivers that emerged soon after the crisis in the form of an emerging private sector and a booming property market. Nor did the pessimists foresee the extent of the productivity gains unleashed with the reforms related to China joining the WTO in 2001. By tapping the potential that came with the regional production-sharing network, China became the assembly plant for the world.

During this period, China's rapid growth and adept use of "soft power" changed popular perceptions within Asia—especially among the ASEAN (Association of Southeast Asian Nations) nations. While many had been concerned that with success China would become more of a threat, sentiments became decidedly more favorable in the early 2000s.[5] This sense was reinforced by frustrations in countries with Islamic roots, such as Indonesia and Malaysia, that the United States had become excessively preoccupied with its war on terrorism after 9/11, to the neglect of its Asian interests.[6]

While East Asia benefited from the huge trade surpluses that the regional production-sharing network helped to generate, China's surging current account surpluses from 2004 to 2008 were mirrored in America's huge trade deficits, raising alarm about global imbalances. This generated a heated debate in the mid-2000s about how to deal with these imbalances. China was increasingly seen as the culprit for driving Western trade deficits, but during the GFC, keeping China on track economically was viewed as the only option for stimulating global growth. All this reinforced sentiments that China was primed to overtake the United States as the world's dominant economy.

These trends nurtured an environment that encouraged many China watchers to conclude that the country's "unbalanced" growth model was a liability. And given the persistent economic difficulties in the United States and Europe, this became a convenient rallying call. What followed was a flood of articles suggesting that "global imbalances" were linked to China's repressed consumption and obsession with investments.[7] Even Ben Bernanke, the Federal Reserve System chief, got into the debate with an influential article arguing that China's huge volume of savings invested in the United States—the result of its trade surplus—drove down interest rates, which then spawned America's housing bubble and triggered the 2008 GFC.[8] This shifted the blame for America's financial crisis from the shoulders of its own risk-seeking banks to the excessive frugality of Chinese households.

The IMF took center stage in many of these discussions with its many studies about global imbalances.[9] This generated a heated debate on the role of China and Asia in driving these global imbalances, with the bulk of attention focused on the many alleged distortions in China's economy, notably its repressed financial system, undervalued exchange rate, and unfair trade practices.

These issues elevated what would normally be a technical debate among economists into media highlights and congressional hearings. Even today these issues continue to be featured in the annual US-China Strategic and Economic Dialogue (S&ED), which was initiated in 2006 in response to China's increasing global impact.[10]

Predictions of China's potential collapse receded with its sustained growth and rising levels of international reserves in the mid-2000s. The pendulum swung 180 degrees as public concerns shifted to when China would overtake the United States as the world's largest economy. All this fed into exaggerated trepidations that Beijing would rewrite the rules of the game regarding global governance and displace Washington as the major seat of power.

Never before has a country at once been so large, developed so rapidly, and possessed a culture so foreign to the Western world, argued British journalist Martin Jacques, who predicted "the birth of a new global order" in his 2009 book, *When China Rules the World*.[11] Arvind Subramanian, taking an economist's approach, echoed these sentiments. Rather than a multipolar world by 2030, Subramanian predicted a unipolar one dominated by a China, who would account for close to 20 percent of global GDP and 15 percent of world trade. While this China would lag behind the United States in per-capita income, military might, and soft-power influence, its role as "the world's largest banker" would give it unique leverage to either supply financing or withdraw it.[12]

On the flip side of the coin, there were also doubters who argued that China's rise was far from given. They pointed to internal dysfunction, including corruption, local government debt, a weak financial system, an unsustainable growth model, and a lack of ability to reform or evolve creatively to move up the manufacturing value chain.[13] Meanwhile, this debate in its various forms was occurring around the world, with countries having to navigate competing relationships with both the United States and China.

The prolonged economic problems in the United States following the GFC and weakening trade markets in Europe showed that China's economy could not be insulated from events in the West. Despite a series of stimulus programs beginning in 2008, which initially kept growth too high (in retrospect) for a few years, China's GDP growth had been declining steadily to below 7 percent.

Over the past few years, the voices of the pessimists have intensified with warnings of an impending debt-driven crisis.[14] The economic slowdown, resentment over government corruption, and defaults resulting from the misallocated resources to underperforming SOEs, would add up to the perfect storm.[15] China's economy was on the "treadmill to hell" because of a property bubble, according to James Chanos, whose firm makes money by identifying cases of financial stress.[16] In addition to the end of export- and investment-driven growth, the rating agency Fitch pointed to off-the-book loans or "shadow banking" as a major risk factor.[17] Large swings in equity market prices in 2014–2015, followed by bouts of capital flight and—more recently—a surge in property prices and debt indicators, have generated additional concerns about whether Beijing's policymakers have lost control over the levers of economic management.

At the official policy levels in the United States and China, the debate has shifted to China's desire to move up the value chain. This has steered attention to China's alleged IPR violations, cybertheft, and promotion of indigenous technology, legally or illegally. More technical issues such as the inclusion in September 2016 of the renminbi in the IMF special drawing rights (SDR) basket of reserve currencies are also drawing media attention since some view China as a potential threat to America's dominance of the international financial system.

Economic and Security Concerns Drive Public Sentiments

China's economic rise has certainly generated strong feelings globally, particularly in the United States, given the shift in geopolitical power relationships. These events have influenced public opinions and how China watchers form their views on both general as well as more technical developments. Some 60 percent of Americans worry about China's increasing economic strength, and some two-thirds think the country is untrustworthy.[18]

The domestic political climate also sways opinions. Views about China featured prominently in the 2012 US presidential elections with both incumbent Barack Obama and his challenger Mitt Romney competing to be the candidate who would be toughest on China if elected. Not surprisingly, Pew polls showed that more Americans that year thought that it was important to get tougher on China (49 percent) than to build stronger relations with China (42 percent). But two years later, as politically driven emotions subsided, the sentiments reversed, with 51 percent favoring stronger relations and 43 percent arguing for getting tougher. The 2016 presidential campaign revived such emotions as candidates once again promised to take a more forceful position on China.[19]

Public perceptions have nurtured these positions. A majority of both Democrats and Republicans hold China responsible for the US trade deficits and outsourcing of jobs abroad, with Republicans significantly more negative toward China than Democrats. All this has encouraged both politicians and the general public to argue for punitive actions, including countervailing tariffs and claims with WTO that China's exports are being unfairly subsidized. These concerns also provided a rationale for the United States' now suspended major trade initiative, the Trans-Pacific Partnership (TPP), which notably did not include China (see Chapter 9). Ostensibly, China was not included because the TPP standards were too high for it to qualify, a perception reflected in the view that two-thirds of the American public believe that China's trade practices are unfair. These sentiments also fuel the annual exercise about whether China should be labeled a currency manipulator.

Interestingly, the Chinese people do not have such a negative view of the United States. Various polls show that they have considerable admiration for American ideas, customs, and scientific accomplishments. This reaffirms the major advantage that America has in projecting its soft power. Unless the concern relates to sovereignty such as Taiwan, China tends to place more weight on cooperation in addressing foreign policy matters than being tough, and its citizens are more likely than Americans themselves to rank the United States as the leading economic power.

The US-China relationship is unique because these perceptions have been influenced as much by game-changing economic trends as by political factors. China's elevation as a global economic power parallels its emergence as the world's largest trading nation. Its success is mirrored in America's relative economic decline over this past decade and a half as the latter's increasing trade and fiscal deficits coupled with excessively leveraged banks triggered the 2008 GFC. This was soon followed by Europe's budget crisis and prolonged economic stagnation, which together tilted the world economic order toward the emerging market nations even if this has been tempered by the recent problems among the BRICS and other developing economies.

All this made it easier for the West to see China as part of the problem, providing support for confrontational policies. The recent surge in China's outward direct investment (ODI) and sensitivities about theft of foreign technology have further exacerbated political tensions in the West despite the many voices championing the potential benefits that such links can bring. These sentiments are unlikely to dissipate unless America's concerns about jobs subside and growth rebounds in Europe. And when this does occur, it will be largely the result of the efforts of the Americans and Europeans themselves rather than due to what has been going on in China.

Evolving US Views on China

Figure 2.1 illustrates the shift in American perceptions as to who is the world's leading economic power as indicated in Gallup polls since the late 1990s in the aftermath of the AFC and Deng Xiaoping's passing. This is mapped against major

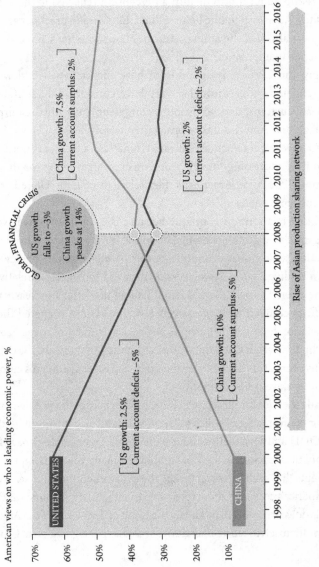

Figure 2.1 US Perceptions of Economic Power. Source: Gallup 2000, 2008, 2009, 2011–2014, 2016

economic events and trends over the past fifteen years. A majority of Americans since the GFC believe that China is the world's leading economic power, while a smaller share of around 30 to 35 percent see the United States as dominant— a sentiment broadly shared in Europe.[20] This was not the case in 2000, when only 10 percent of Americans named China as dominant, and 65 percent of Americans saw the US as on top.

This dramatic shift in perceptions reflects the contrasting economic growth paths that these two powers have taken over the past decade and a half since the AFC. China's growth rate for much of this period averaged 10 percent annually in comparison with America's 2.5 percent, with the former running large trade surpluses and the latter equally large deficits. The switching point regarding who is on top took place during the GFC.

This switch has contributed to the increasingly negative American sentiments toward China. Accustomed to being the world's dominant power, US policymakers and the general public have vacillated in their personal feelings about China's rise. Concerns about China's political system and positions on human rights have been long-standing issues. Some see a military threat in the making, but most realize that China is decades away from seriously challenging America's military superiority.

From a broader perspective, many do appreciate that the world is better off with a more prosperous China. This accounts for the positive ratings in the first half of the 2000s when the public was asked whether they have "favorable or unfavorable" feelings about China (see Figure 2.2). But by 2006, America's trade

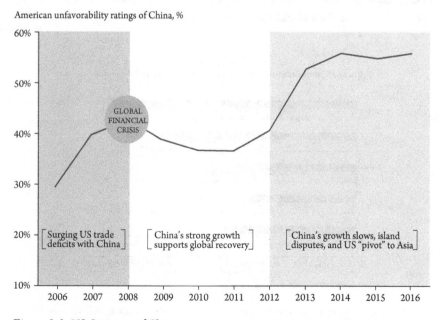

Figure 2.2 US Opinions of China. Source: Pew Global Attitudes Survey, 2006–2016

deficits and increasing complaints of unfair competition drove a decline in favorability ratings that bottomed out with the GFC in 2008. From 2009 to 2011, China's strong growth was again seen positively as propping up global demand while the West struggled with its financial problems. Sentiments turned and have remained strongly negative in recent years as the United States has reasserted itself in Asia and China has become more aggressive in challenging its neighbors over the island disputes in Asian waters (see Chapter 9).

Global Perceptions

With one regional exception, the rest of the world sees the United States as the leading economic power. Somewhat surprisingly, this view is stronger in Asia than in the other regions. The exception is Europe, which until 2016 viewed China as the leading economic power[21] (see Figure 2.3).

Is there a simple reason why the West (the United States and Europe) has been more inclined to see China as the leading economic power, while the developing world—including China itself—has felt otherwise? In part, this comes from the misleading impressions of a country's economic might as it relates to purely financial indicators such as trade balances or a country's size.

China has a huge trade surplus with the United States and to a lesser extent Europe, but it runs deficits with the rest of the world, most notably with commodity exporters and its East Asian neighbors. This generates considerable insecurities in the West about its competitiveness, concerns which are for the

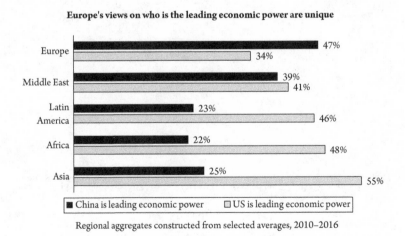

Europe's views on who is the leading economic power are unique

Regional aggregates constructed from selected averages, 2010–2016

Figure 2.3 Global Economic Power Perceptions. Source: Pew Global Attitudes Survey, Spring 2014, and Pew Research Center, June 2016

most part overdone. A country's economic power comes more from the strength of its institutions, its human capital base, and its technological prowess than from trade balances or the size of its population. With a per-capita GDP placing it around eightieth globally, China is far from ready to assume the mantle of being the leading economic power.[22] And given its relatively weak command of soft-power skills and underdeveloped alliances, it fares poorly regarding the usual criteria used to define great powers.

European countries are more conflicted than the United States regarding their general favorability perceptions of China. Overall, Europeans have been less negative than Americans, in part because there is no great-power rivalry. European feelings about China are also affected by their views of the United States, while American views of China are independent of their views on Europe. No European country, with the possible exception of Germany, sees itself as competing to be a global power, but many feel the need at times to distance themselves from American-led initiatives. But unlike the United States, European sentiments, although varying in degree, have not fluctuated as much over the years. Eastern Europeans, in particular, tend to have more positive views on China because they went through a similar economic transition away from central planning while also having to deal with the complexities of political liberalization.

Within Western Europe, official and popular perceptions can vary significantly as exemplified by Germany and the United Kingdom. The Germany-China economic and political relationship is seen as the strongest within Europe, since Germany is by far China's largest trading partner in the EU, and China is Germany's largest trading partner in Asia. Moreover, China has occasionally relied on Germany to get the EU community to take its concerns seriously. Even so, polls show that the German public has been more negatively disposed toward China than other Europeans—driven by an especially hostile media (see Figure 2.4).

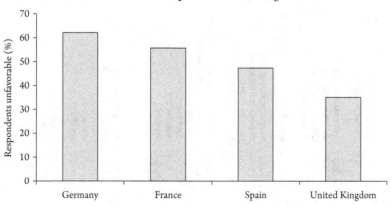

Figure 2.4 EU Opinions of China. Source: Pew Global Attitudes Survey, 2010–2016

Such differences in public sentiments are shaped by diverse reasons including culture, competitive pressures, and seemingly random coincidences. These range from heightened sensitivities that Germans have against authoritarian regimes and corruption and emotions arising from media coverage of the Chinese dissident artist Ai Wei Wei's family living in Bonn and the World Uighur Conference being headquartered in Munich.[23]

At the other end of the spectrum, many might think that British public opinion of China would be the most negative because of their feelings about Hong Kong and its much larger trade deficits with China relative to its continental partners, yet British views are the most positive. Such sentiments appear to be driven by the extensive person-to-person interactions between the British and Chinese people fostered by tourism and education exchanges as well as financial and services links that are seen as mutually beneficial. Thus it should not have been a surprise that the United Kingdom took the lead within the European Union in joining the China-initiated Asian Infrastructure Investment Bank (AIIB) in 2015 much to the discomfort of the United States (see Chapter 9).

Outside of the United States and Europe, views of China as reflected in Pew surveys vary by region and also over time. Two aspects are well recognized: Russia's and Pakistan's special relationships with China generate relatively favorable views among its citizens, and the historical frictions between Japan and China drive long-standing animosities (see Figure 2.5).

More generally in East Asia, views of China are less favorable today compared with a decade ago. During the AFC, China's decision not to depreciate its currency when others were doing so and to initiate discussions on a China-ASEAN free-trade agreement (CAFTA) and currency-swap arrangements were seen as providing support to struggling Asian economies when the West was viewed as

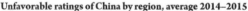

Unfavorable ratings of China by region, average 2014–2015

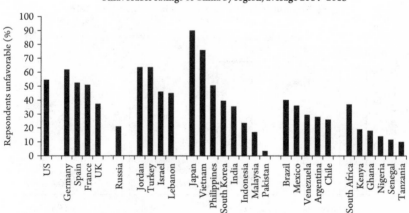

Figure 2.5 Regional Opinions of China. Source: Pew Global Attitudes Survey, 2014–2015

unsympathetic. China also generated considerable goodwill in the years after the Asian crisis by launching a "charm offensive" through a series of visits of its senior leaders throughout the region at a time when the US leadership was conspicuously absent because of its preoccupation with the instability in the Middle East.

Views vary considerably among the ASEAN countries. Malaysia and Thailand's views of China continue to be relatively favorable because of ethnic and cultural ties in addition to strong bilateral trade and investment links. Indonesia-China relations have improved steadily over the past decade in contrast to historical ethnic-based tensions, although the island disputes are beginning to affect feelings. Sentiments about China in Burma have shifted with its political evolution, while China's relations with Vietnam and the Philippines have deteriorated sharply (despite some recent softening) thanks to rising tensions triggered by the island disputes.

Within Asia, economic ties can be an important factor in shaping perceptions, but the impact of the production-sharing network is becoming more complicated. The network strengthened economic interdependence through trade links and associated FDI between China and other East Asian countries, but it has also nurtured tensions. China became the major trading partner for nearly all the Asian economies. Yet low-income ASEAN economies worry that China is not providing enough space for them to compete in more labor-intensive production. And China is now threatening its North Asian neighbors—South Korea and Japan—in manufacturing more sophisticated components.

Stronger economic ties between mainland China and Taiwan over the past decade have not generated improved people-to-people sentiments. This is due in part to perceptions that the economic well-being of the middle class in Taiwan has not improved despite closer economic links. A more decisive blow to cross-Strait relations came from the 2014–2015 "Occupy Central" protests in Hong Kong in revealing the extent of dissatisfaction with the "one country, two systems" policy. Faltering relations with China were a key factor in Taiwan's elections in 2016.

In South Asia, India has had long-standing concerns about China, while Pakistan's position has been the reverse. Less well noticed is the highly positive feelings that Bangladesh has toward China, in part influenced by its being a possible counter weight to India.

Elsewhere, China's rise is seen more favorably because it has helped to buoy emerging markets in Latin America and Africa, and it acts as a more independent spokesman for their interests. Many third-world countries favor a more multipolar world and thus are supportive of China's increasing economic strength. According to recent Pew Global Attitude surveys, every African country responded that China's growing economy had a more positive than negative impact on their country. The same held for Latin America.[24] African favorability ratings toward China reflect an appreciation for the financial support that China has provided for local infrastructure projects, as in Tanzania.[25] China is seen more favorably among those countries running significant bilateral trade surpluses relative to those running deficits.[26] Nevertheless, there are still the underlying concerns that the influx of cheap Chinese products might hurt domestic industries and that its foreign investments are not sensitive enough to local interests and environmental and social standards.

The Middle East tends to be favorably disposed toward China, though Turkey, with its historical links to the Uighur community in Xinjiang, frictions over the competition in the textile industry, and history of mistrust during the Cold War period, stands as an outlier.[27]

The BRICS grouping warrants special attention given its potential for influencing geopolitical relations, despite questions about the cohesiveness of the grouping. The newly created BRICS New Development Bank is seen as a potential competitor or collaborator with the World Bank and IMF and is motivated in part by the opportunity to check the dominance of the G7 (Group of Seven) in the global financial architecture. But also worth noting is that these countries differ significantly in economic circumstances, cultures, and political thinking despite sharing a desire for less G7-dominated global governance structures. Excluding Russia, the others do not necessarily see themselves as natural allies with China regarding foreign policy issues but more as economic competitors. This shows up in the Pew Global Attitude surveys (see Figure 2.6), which indicate that within their respective regions of Latin America (Brazil), Africa (South Africa), and South Asia (India), the BRICS countries, motivated in part

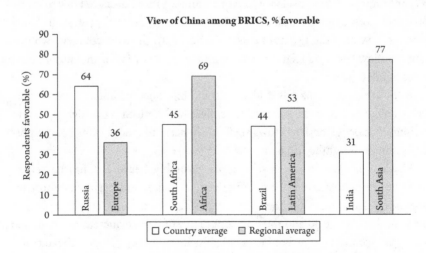

Figure 2.6 BRICS Opinions of China. Source: Pew Global Attitudes Survey, 2014

by worries about being unable to compete with China in the global trade arena, tend to perceive China more negatively than their neighbors.

In each region of the globe, public perceptions of China's influence are being shaped by a combination of economic and security concerns. While nearly half of the Americans surveyed see China as a military threat compared to about a third in Europe, the Chicago Council on Global Affairs poll shows that the American public overwhelmingly—by a measure of 77 percent to 23 percent—feels that China's economic strength rather than military might determines its power to influence global events. Nevertheless, more attention these days is being given to security-related issues because of the tensions surrounding cyber-security attacks, the island-related territorial disputes, and maritime incidents. Risks have also increased because of growing nationalism in China and among its neighbors. All this has driven China's neighbors to welcome the United States playing a stronger role in the region, including a more visible military presence.

Understanding the Past and Divining the Future

Policy wonks now worry and argue about how to deal with a more assertive China buoyed by its increasing economic prowess. These concerns are intensified by strongly held beliefs that an authoritarian regime cannot be trusted. Indeed, as an emerging and abnormal great power, China defies precedents, and this contributes to the wide variance in perceptions about both China's foreign policy intentions and its economic prospects.

Even as China moves closer to becoming a more "normal" market economy, it is not seen as a responsible global stakeholder in an international arena that largely reflects the values of Western nations. This dichotomy is sharpened by concerns about the pace and direction of its political evolution. Moreover, the apparent mishandling of its financial markets over the past year is triggering for the first time questions about the quality of China's economic management. These and other factors shape the topics addressed in subsequent chapters.

CHAPTER 3

Origins of China's Growth Model

As the newly anointed Party chairman in the post-Mao era, Deng Xiaoping's most celebrated achievement was to set China on a path of "reform and opening," a path that ultimately lifted an impoverished nation to the status of an economic power. Beginning around 1980, his actions allowed market forces to reshape incentives and encourage industrial activities to concentrate and develop along China's coastal provinces. Zhu Rongji—initially as vice premier and later as premier under President Jiang Zemin—accelerated the growth momentum from the early 1990s to 2003 by overhauling the major economic institutions. These reforms led to GDP growth averaging 10 percent annually over the three decades prior to 2010—a duration that is unprecedented in modern economic history.

Both Deng Xiaoping and Zhu Rongji exemplify what some scholars have called "policy entrepreneurs." Through their ideas and actions, they were able to overcome vested interests—in this case, the Communist Party and bureaucracy.[1] Successful change is about finding ways to alter incentives and transform institutions to realize a dramatic improvement in living standards. In doing so, these leaders and others around them were bold in taking risks and launching new initiatives, but they also took a gradual approach, using local experimentation and trial and error to test the feasibility of reforms before rolling them out nationwide.

During those years, some commentators were critical that China was not taking more of a "shock" approach similar to what happened during the fall of the former Soviet Union in the early 1990s. In retrospect, this line of reasoning failed to appreciate the political differences and benefits of phased interventions that co-opted vested interests that might have blocked change and avoided any sharp decline in economic activity.

The achievements of Chairman Deng and Premier Zhu have been widely recognized in the literature, but many of today's concerns about China's growth process, its debt problems, and trade frictions with the West originate from a transformation process that did not keep pace with the changing environment.

Progress on the reform agenda slowed in the years after Premier Zhu left office as China's continued rapid growth up to the GFC lulled the new team of President Hu Jintao and Premier Wen Jiabao into a false sense of confidence.

This chapter summarizes the economic origins of the concerns that have led to such conflicting views about China's economy. Much of the debate depends on how one treats the vast regional differences and the unique challenges of transitioning from central planning to a more market-based system. Deng's policies in promoting development initially along the coast and relying on financing from the banking system laid the basis for China's rapid growth, but they also generated imbalances in macroeconomic aggregates. The unbalanced nature of China's growth and rising debt levels underpin the concerns expressed in recent years about the sustainability of China's growth model. (Appendix A provides a more detailed discussion for those interested in China's historical development experience.)

Deng Xiaoping—the "Unbalanced" Reformer

Scholars have highlighted a number of unique features that characterized Deng's approach.[2] He established at the outset that his priority was economic liberalization and that political change was an issue for the future. He managed to reshape incentives to establish rapid growth without regard to near-term equity considerations. Despite his revolutionary credentials, he was pragmatic in not letting ideology restrict his policy choices. Deng was said to be the source of many quotable phrases—his oft-cited message that "it does not matter whether the cat is white or black as long as it catches mice" signaled a willingness to consider all policy options, and his mantra that "to get rich is glorious" made it acceptable to be entrepreneurial in a socialist economy.[3]

He encouraged market forces with "Chinese characteristics" to reshape the location and nature of economic activity while fending off interest groups keen to preserve the purity of communist philosophy and the role of the state. The key difference between China and other countries is how the state interacted with market forces to promote competition and growth. This was done by putting in place a "regionally decentralized competitive system" whereby local authorities were motivated by growth objectives but subject to competitive pressures so that the usual inefficiencies of central planning were kept within tolerable limits.[4]

In terms of reform episodes, three phases are worth emphasizing: liberalizing agriculture through the "household responsibility system," which allowed peasants to produce and sell freely without threatening the interests of urban consumers; industrializing through township village enterprises (TVEs), which represented a convenient partnership that co-opted the interests of local authorities to work with private entrepreneurs; and establishing special economic zones (SEZs), which allowed market forces to erode the rationale for the controls that benefited well-placed local authorities and reoriented production in favor of expanding trade.

In all three phases, Deng encouraged "private" or nonstate interests and market forces to begin driving growth, while avoiding resistance from Party ideologues by not formally abandoning socialist principles. These initiatives paved the way for future reforms because they benefited not only the masses but also the vested interests within the system that were adverse to change. China's financial, fiscal, and exchange-rate systems evolved in a piecemeal fashion in line with needs. They were restructured later by Premier Zhu to support the growth process, often in ways which deviated from standard textbook prescriptions.

Deng should be seen as a visionary who transformed China's economic landscape, but he can also be described as the consummate "unbalanced" reformer regarding the spatial and macroeconomic consequences. He deliberately promoted a regionally unbalanced growth process targeted to the coastal provinces and a shift in macroeconomic aggregates which is reflected today in China's unusually low share of consumption to GDP and commensurately high investment share. This also led to the rapid increase in income disparities distinguished by its regional dimensions. All this went against Mao-era principles encapsulated in the supremacy of "balanced regional development" and equity before wealth creation.

This strategy of promoting coastal development through exports supported by foreign investment transformed China from a largely stagnant agricultural economy to a highly competitive manufacturing-led exporting nation. But its success also fed into the global trade imbalances of the mid-2000s and exacerbated tensions with the United States about whether China has been "manipulating" its exchange rate.

Today's headlines about China's debt problems and property bubbles also have their roots in the approach taken decades ago by Deng to fund the country's investment priorities from bank loans rather than through the budget. This approach remained a feature of the Zhu period despite the fiscal and financial reforms that he initiated in the mid-1990s, and they became even more pronounced during the Hu-Wen decade because of various credit-supported stimulus programs in response to the GFC.

Nevertheless, China has managed thus far to avoid any major financial crisis and has never come close to falling into a recession. And despite the Deng-era emphasis on developing the coast, regional disparities eventually began to moderate in response to the natural evolution of the economy and regionally targeted investment policies. In sum, contrary to expectations, the actions of these reformers show that an unbalanced growth process can lead over time to more balanced economic outcomes in the form of sustained and widespread increases in living standards.

Spatial Transformation Drove China's Growth Process

Characterizations of China's economic performance tend to gloss over the implications of its huge size and regional diversity and thus are often misleading. It would be inaccurate to try to characterize America's strengths and weaknesses based on a few indicators or examples, given states as varied economically as California, Ohio, and West Virginia. Similarly, with over 1.3 billion people spread across thirty-one ecologically and economically varied provinces and administrative units, China offers a valuable case study of the importance of geography in shaping economic and social outcomes (see Box 3.1).[5]

In 1950—after half a century of economic decline—China was an unevenly developed country with industries concentrated in the Yangtze Delta, the Northeast provinces, and a few pockets inland. In the pre-reform central planning era, a deliberate policy of more "balanced" industrial growth took place via the establishment and transfer of large industrial complexes to the inner provinces,

---

Box 3.1 **China's Economic Geography—Key Facts**

China's geography has been fundamental in shaping five thousand years of recorded economic history and influencing settlement patterns. Although its land mass is large by global standards, 80 percent of the population is concentrated on 20 percent of the land in the more fertile central plains and major river valleys and along the more urbanized coast. The western region of twelve provinces, with large tracts of uninhabitable mountainous terrain and deserts, is less suited to commercial activities and home to the majority of China's ethnic minorities. The central region, with eight provinces, has large concentrations of population centered along prominent river basins and accounts for a large portion of agriculture production. Finally, the coastal region of eleven provinces is home to China's major industrial and commercial activities and historically linked to the outside world through trade and external migration. China's population is divided roughly equally across these three regions.

(Source: Yukon Huang, "Reinterpreting China's Success through the New Economic Geography," Carnegie Endowment, Asia Program, No. 115, November 2010)

irrespective of their less favorable locations relative to domestic and external markets.[6] By 1980, after decades of Mao's economic mismanagement—notable failures include the "Great Leap Forward" and the Cultural Revolution—China was still a desperately poor, but by international standards a remarkably equitable and regionally balanced, economy.

With this disheartening experience in mind, China's masses took a wait-and-see attitude to Deng's launching of his "unbalanced" growth strategy. This began with a series of reforms in the early 1980s which, in opening the country to the outside world, also coincidentally followed the principles underpinning two Nobel Prize-winning growth models that help explain how spatial factors can alter a country's development path.[7]

One was W. Arthur Lewis's model of economic development with unlimited supplies of labor. Put simply, the Lewis model shows how the transfer of "surplus" labor from rural activities to urban industries can lead to higher productivity, increased investment, and sustained rapid growth. The other was Paul Krugman's principles of the "new economic geography," which showed how the concentration of labor and economic activities in urban areas and regions could generate "agglomeration economies" or the additional productivity gains that come from specialization and economies of scale which then lead to rapid trade expansion.[8]

Both models turned out to be surprisingly accurate in predicting what would happen in China as it embarked on reforms. Both explain how regional or spatial factors can drive structural economic change and how this can alter key indicators such as the shares of consumption and investment relative to GDP, trade balances, and measures of inequality. In doing so, these models also explain why unbalanced growth should be seen as the byproduct of a largely successful growth process rather than the generally assumed vulnerability (see Chapter 4).

By taking this approach, Chairman Deng transformed China into the world's most efficient assembler cum exporter of a wide range of manufactured goods. He foresaw that the benefits would initially be concentrated along the coast but over time would spread to the interior.[9] Thus he warned the Chinese people that for the country to succeed, the priority initially had to be on developing the coast and not the interior where the bulk of the population actually lived. But he also predicted that there would eventually be a turning point when the transformation would reverse itself. This has indeed been happening in recent years with the interior growing more rapidly than the coastal provinces. Along with a decline in trade surpluses, the resulting changes will help harmonize the impact of China's growth internally by moderating regional disparities and externally by softening China's trade tensions with the West.

Understanding these forces helps to answer several major economic policy questions that dominate the current debate over the future of China:

- Will growth continue to be unbalanced and what will be the relative roles for exports, investment, and consumption?
- Can China avoid a financial crisis and establish a more sustainable growth path?
- Will trade and exchange-rate concerns and technology transfer disputes continue to exacerbate tensions with the West?

The answers lie in the nature of the spatial and structural transformation process that has shaped China's success and how these shifts are likely to evolve in the future.

Reshaping China's Economic Geography

The story of China during the quarter century after Deng opened up the economy revolves around trial and error and a series of pragmatic reforms, which worked with rather than against the country's geographic and inherent advantages. These policies had three distinct consequences: (1) they reshaped the spatial dimensions of development; (2) they broke the gridlock in terms of the internal mobility of labor, capital, and goods across provinces and between urban and rural areas, and externally between China and the rest of the world; and (3) they set in motion forces which increased regional disparities. In the process, China emerged as an exceptionally competitive and trade-oriented economy, having realized the productivity benefits from urbanization and regional specialization.[10]

With the advent of economic reforms, China experienced unusually high growth rates interrupted only by the Tiananmen protests in the late 1980s. The growth record, however, is marked by considerable regional variations, as the eastern (coastal) provinces began to grow much faster than those in the central and western regions (see Figure 3.1).

The major factors underpinning this performance have been well documented. Growth increased sharply in the 1980s, as China turned away from state farms and collectives and relied more on private household farming. In encouraging this, Deng had to deal with populist interests that were keen to ensure cheap food for urban consumers and tap agriculture surpluses as a source of revenue for the state. The new "household responsibility system" mandated that farmers still had to provide a minimum amount for the government, but they could freely market anything in excess. This led to major increases in agriculture

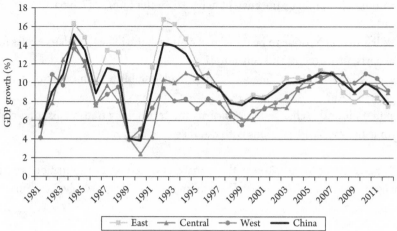

Figure 3.1 China GDP Growth by Region. Source: National Bureau of Statistics of China, Statistical Yearbook

productivity and liberated much of the surplus rural workers for other activities, as depicted in the Lewis model.

In the early 1990s, the formation of TVEs sowed the seeds of a rapid industrialization process which provided formal wage-based employment for the largely redundant workers previously tied up in farming. These TVEs, as discussed in Appendix A, began as associations between local authorities, who had access to the land and financing, and private entrepreneurs to establish new commercial activities. As with the agrarian reforms, the trick was not to offend those interested in protecting the role of the state but to use a largely trial-and-error approach through mixed partnerships between state and private interests to spur industrial development.

This industrialization cum urbanization process was influenced by the uniqueness of the transition from a planned to a market economy. The transition was supported initially by an open-door policy that strengthened the investment climate along the coastal provinces by providing incentives and opening them up to foreign investment. Rather than trying to override directly the vested interests in the provinces, this policy began with the establishment of the first SEZs in 1980 in four cities in Guangdong and Fujian provinces (Map 3.1). Variants were extended over time to the other coastal provinces, eventually reaching all the provincial capitals during the 1990s.

In 1992, Deng Xiaoping's famous southern tour gave a strong boost to the Chinese economy in reasserting his open-door policy and giving formal status to a spatially prioritized "gradient development model." This approach considered coastal, central, and western regions as three ladders of economic growth, and gave the coastal region priority access to resources as well as large benefits as first-movers of reforms.

Map 3.1 Location of Special Economic Zones. Source: World Bank, "Reshaping Economic Geography in East Asia," 2007

This was supported by a strategy of "big inputs, big exports," entailing importing components and raw materials to the coastal region to stimulate assembly trade and attract foreign investment. Foreign trade and investment provided the coast not only with capital but also advanced technology and management expertise, which enhanced productivity. Until recently, the coastal region accounted for over 80 percent of the foreign investment and some 90 percent of the total exports and imports. With the natural advantages from geographical location supported by preferential policies, major commercial centers in the eastern region took-off while the western region lagged behind.

Securing the Financing for Public Expenditures

The open-door policy was supported by shifting fiscal policies which, although far from meeting modern needs, did early on selectively provide the coastal provinces of Guangdong and Fujian with the incentives to experiment with reforms. This was reinforced by incentives favoring allocation of public investment to provinces with greater financing capacity. As a result, the share of public capital expenditures going to the coastal provinces increased from about 50 percent in the mid-1980s to nearly 65 percent by the mid-1990s.

But these budgetary resources could provide only a fraction of the resources needed for what Deng had in mind. Rather than trying to tackle all the vested interests that prevented the fiscal system from playing its accustomed role, Deng opted for tapping the resources of the banking system, which held the bulk of China's huge stock of household savings. This involved what economists call "financial repression," or the use of administered interest rates and capital controls to ensure that these savings would be made available for state-mandated needs. Because many of these loans went to local governments and SOEs for infrastructure and social programs with no immediate commercial returns, a portion would not be repaid. The consequences were hidden fiscal deficits, which periodically surfaced in the form of nonperforming loans and triggered concerns about a possible debt problem and financial crisis—the same concerns being raised today.

Infrastructure Investments Transform the Location of Industries and Labor

Much of the increased financial resources supported a major expansion of transportation and communication networks, initially along the coastal areas and then gradually inland. This sharply reduced the effective distances between major commercial centers and allowed competition between provinces to reshape interprovincial industrial links. Cutting transport costs as a percent of the final price of goods helped connect production centers to internal and external consumer markets.

China has been spending over 5 percent of GDP annually over the past several decades on transport infrastructure—unprecedented by global standards in relation to the size of its economy.[11] In the early-1990s, special attention was given to upgrading logistics services in the coastal cities to improve links with the outside world. Under Premier Zhu, more priority was given to infrastructure investments in the western and central regions as reflected in their expansion in highway mileage by 45 percent between 1999 and 2004, compared with 30 percent for the coastal region.

These investments narrowed the large regional differences in wages and prices previously nurtured by artificial provincial boundaries and vast distances. As markets became integrated, provincial industrial structures became more specialized. The more service-oriented or higher technology industries concentrated along the coastal urban areas, while resource-based and domestically oriented industries spread more widely across the country.

Urbanization drove this process by attracting vast numbers of agrarian workers into formal industrial employment. With urban wages several multiples of what could be earned in agriculture, a large migrant labor population now estimated at around 250 million concentrated in the major commercial centers around the Pearl River Delta (Guangzhou and Shenzhen), Yangtze River Delta (Shanghai), and Bohai Delta (Beijing/Tianjin), see Map 3.2.

The concentration of economic activities and influx of migrant workers spurred a spatial transformation of industrial production. Market integration encouraged specialization and economies of scale, contributing to increases in productivity as Paul Krugman's model predicts. As the coastal cities became linked to the global economy, the benefits became more obvious, exemplified by rapid employment creation, pressures on enterprises to compete, and surging profitability.

For much of the Deng era, China operated a multiple-exchange-rate system with differential rates depending on purpose. Rather than rely on movements in the exchange rate to promote exports, China, like many other East Asian countries, used a complex set of fiscal and institutional incentives to promote trade. During this period, the renminbi was significantly overvalued rather than undervalued, as evidenced by the rates in the "unofficial market" which offered a premium for US dollars. These premiums disappeared only with the emergence of China's large trade surpluses around 2005—well after the AFC and China's WTO accession in 2001.

China's "Regionally Decentralized Competitive System"

Central to the success of China's growth process was the state's role in promoting competition.[12] As described by Xu Chenggang, the system of incentives

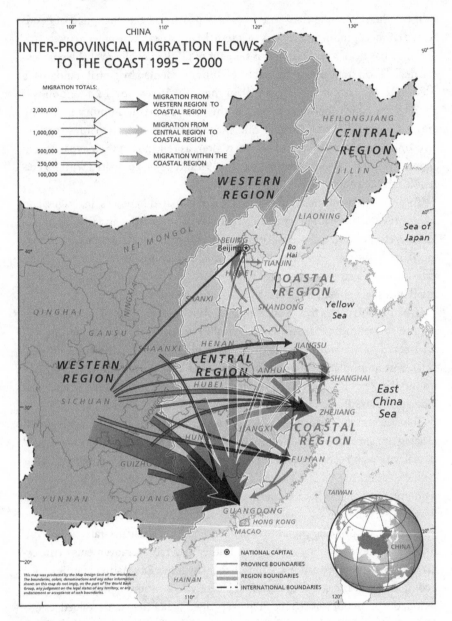

Map 3.2 Labor Migration to the Coast. Source: World Bank, "Reshaping Economic Geography in East Asia," 2007

provided to local authorities and the appointment and promotion policies encouraged jurisdictions to compete fiercely against each other.[13] They competed for their relative economic positions, and they also competed to build new institutions as China moved from a centrally planned to a more market-driven economy. This competition was the primary force shaping China's growth. The role of government in supporting this process was to unify the system to concentrate on the sole objective of promoting growth without allowing vested interests to divert resources.[14]

The prospect of promotions and prestige of presiding over large and dynamic jurisdictions motivated officials to encourage more investment and streamline procedures. In doing so, the more entrepreneurial ones pushed the limits of risk tolerance and reform commitments of the central government and Party leaders. The resulting push and pull, experimentation and negotiation over policy initiatives and institutional development were the driving forces behind China's reform process. This has not changed much over time.

From an outsider's perspective this process may not appear to represent substantial reform and the actions taken may seem insignificant rather than path-breaking. Pronouncements can read like self-serving lists of accomplishments. But from the Chinese perspective, this is how momentum for reform is maintained, how interest groups are sidestepped, political and policy risk minimized, and new ideas tried and tested. China has institutionalized momentum for reform through this centrally guided regional structure to ensure sustainability of the growth process.[15]

Two elements incentivize behaviors—the promotion process within the system and having a tax base linked to production and rising land values, which local officials have substantial power to influence. The consequences can be both positive and negative. China's growth model has always combined both bottom-up and top-down pressures. The common view is that reforms come from the top, but what happens at local levels is just as important in steering the economy.

As market institutions increasingly took root and drove incentives, local officials and firms found their policy options becoming increasingly shaped by market forces. Because of the many interests vested in its continuation, this became a force for change in itself. The creation of corporations became an intrinsic part of the transition since a market full of competing firms is a motivating force for economic initiatives just as competition among China's local authorities is a force for policy initiatives.

When the state and market interact properly, the state enhances the market and ensures that the results of competition are largely positive. The consequences regarding increasing productivity and rising living standards can be impressive. But the state does not always enhance the market nor does it always create incentives ensuring that competition leads to desirable results. Sometimes the interaction between the state and the market leads to rent-seeking activities and socially unacceptable outcomes such as environmental degradation (see Chapter 6).

Zhu Rongji Uses the Asian Financial Crisis to Accelerate Reforms

The AFC in 1997 turned out to be an opportunity for new premier Zhu Rongji to push through many major initiatives.[16] The crisis devastated many seemingly dynamic economies, such as South Korea, and raised alarm bells about China's prospects. Western perceptions of East Asia shifted dramatically from the image conveyed by the "Asian Miracle" to one dominated by flawed institutions and the limits of export-oriented economies. Shortly after the crisis, China's double-digit growth rates fell below 8 percent despite a major stimulus effort. Whether it would fall further or return to its former growth path became a serious concern for the leadership.

As mentioned in Chapter 2, the crisis years also gave birth to a cohort of doubters about China's prospects. The pessimism extended to major financial media with *The Economist* reporting, "In the coming decade, therefore, China seems set to become more unstable. It will face growing unrest as unemployment mounts . . . Growth has relied heavily on massive government spending. As a result, the government's debt is rising fast. Coupled with the banks' bad loans and the state's huge pension liabilities, this is a financial crisis in the making."[17]

Yet by 2004, Premier Zhu's policies led to a financial restructuring program that eliminated nonperforming loans as an issue and cut the number of loss-making SOEs nearly in half. His program to privatize the housing stock triggered a decade-long construction boom that kept growth going so that the massive layoffs of tens of millions of workers and transfer of surplus workers out of agriculture did not destabilize the system. Rather than collapsing, infrastructure investment and net exports helped push China's annual GDP growth rate steadily up to 10 percent for the rest of the decade—in contrast to the earlier doomsday predictions.

Why were the alarmists so far off the mark?

Although the AFC brought down so many strongly performing countries, China's closed capital account—prohibitions against moving capital in or out of the country—insulated it from any panic-driven capital flight. Even more important, however, was that China's financial position was stronger than the other crisis cases thanks to its persistent current account surpluses, high savings rate, and low external debt. Thus, its growth rate experienced only a temporary dip buoyed by a series of mini-stimulus programs in response to deflationary pressures, the subsequent bursting of the dot-com bubble, and the SARS epidemic in 2002–2003.

China did not collapse but prospered as a result of structural reforms that paved the way for its strongest performing period since opening up its economy. Three reforms are worth highlighting.

First were the trade reforms that Premier Zhu had been pushing for nearly a decade and which led to China's membership in the WTO in 2001. The liberalization measures required for WTO membership were strongly criticized by less reform oriented officials at that time but were needed to push China to higher valued activities and to release workers for industrial production. All this supported China's progress toward becoming the largest trading nation. In the decade before WTO membership, the trade-weighted statutory tariffs declined from 40 percent in 1992 to an estimated 7 percent by 2001.[18] The reduction in tariffs along with WTO membership gave a boost to the East Asian production-sharing network, making China the center for final assembly and export to the United States and Europe.

Premier Zhu realized that China's rapid growth and increased export success provided the basis for popular support for further trade liberalization and other reforms. Principal among these was removing protective barriers in agriculture. This was possible because rapid expansion in urban employment opportunities reduced the pressures coming from rural interests. Eliminating the remaining barriers that had isolated China from the rest of the world led to a remarkable change in the degree of openness of the economy. This is illustrated by the increase in the ratio of trade to GDP from 10 percent in 1978 to nearly 65 percent in the mid-2000s, before moderating to about 40 percent by 2015.

As indicated in Figure 3.2, both exports and imports surged from the late 1990s onward, but a significant trade surplus only began to surface around

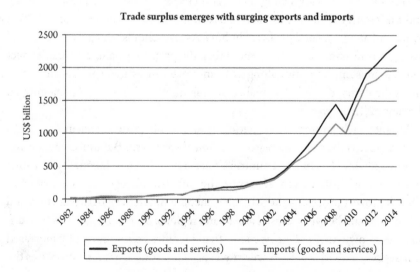

Figure 3.2 Exports and Imports Growth. Source: World Bank World Development Indicators

2004–2005. Thus, the process is more accurately described as trade-led rather than export-led in its early phases, which later evolved into huge trade surpluses driven partly by expansionary monetary and fiscal policies in the West and partly by the surge in savings rates in China.

Second, the restructuring of SOEs and the increasing presence of private firms led to steadily rising industrial profitability. China's enterprise sector bene-fited from Premier Zhu's strategy in the mid-1990s of closing or privatizing hun-dreds of its SOEs and putting pressure for improved performance on those that were retained under the mantra of "Grasp the large and release the small." This "dual-track" approach was a way to deal with vested interests that dominated the industrial sector given the political sensitivity surrounding concerns that the state's role was being eroded.

Even today, official commentary avoids using the term "private sector" but in-stead refers to "nonstate or mixed ownership." This approach sidestepped those interests intent on protecting state ownership of key resources and created space for private initiatives to gradually dominate activities that were seen as not being strategically important. That Premier Zhu was able to deal with the huge social costs involved in shedding some thirty million workers without being derailed by the kind of mass protests seen in other countries is remarkable. The conse-quences of shutting down underperforming factories and nurturing more com-petition were rapid increases in profitability for both private and state firms up to the GFC (see Chapter 5).

The third major reform, privatization of housing, was initiated in the late 1990s and allowed households to buy their homes at concessional prices with the option of eventually selling them. This created a market for private housing and explosive growth in construction that was only reined in beginning in 2012 by fears of an overheated property bubble. As households realized that they had been given an asset worth much more than the price they paid, the wealth effect spurred consumption and, along with increased investment in housing, pro-vided the demand needed to realize double-digit GDP rates as China entered the new millennium.

Despite such an impressive performance, an oft-made criticism of China's performance is the sharp increase in income disparities.[19] But unlike most other rapidly growing developing countries, the surge in income inequality in China was largely spatially driven, reflecting the unbalanced regional dimensions of China's growth process—the widening income differences between rural and urban areas and between coastal and inland regions. More recently, however, dif-ferences in ownership of assets rather than incomes compounded by increased rent-seeking activities have exacerbated social tensions. Chapter 6 discusses the nature of these widening disparities and their social implications.

Origins of Today's Controversial Issues

To sum up, the three most controversial economic issues being debated these days are the risks associated with China's unbalanced growth model; its current debt problems in the midst of an economic slowdown; and external policies relating to trade, exchange rates, and foreign investment. They all have their origins in the policies shaped decades ago by Deng Xiaoping and Zhu Rongji.

Soon after the onset of the AFC, the unbalanced nature of China's growth was elevated from a domestic to a global issue. This topic drew international attention because, summed across countries, trade surpluses must be matched by trade deficits. China's sharply rising trade surpluses beginning in 2004 were seen as driving the ballooning trade deficits in the West and thus became a convenient target for criticism (see Chapter 7).

China's current debt problems have raised concerns about a financial crisis and economic collapse in ways that are very similar to the sentiments raised during the AFC. But today many are unaware that this is not the first time that China has had to deal with a debt problem of such a magnitude. In the six years after the AFC from 1997–2003, China's debt-to-GDP ratio increased by about 50 percent and nonperforming loans a decade ago amounted to an estimated 30–40 percent of the outstanding loans of the major state-owned commercial banks.[20]

Implications for Subsequent Chapters

Although the debt burden measured by the share of nonperforming loans may not be as serious as it was during the GFC, prospects for growing out of the problem appear less favorable in the post GFC years. China has moved to a slower growth trajectory, and it can no longer count on robust growth in the West to pull up exports. This survey of China's performance up to the GFC lays the basis for subsequent chapters which delve more deeply into the nature of its unbalanced growth process, its current financial difficulties, growth prospects, and economic tensions with the West.

CHAPTER 4

China's Unbalanced Growth

Until a few years ago, China's GDP growth had been remarkably rapid as well as stable—fluctuating within a narrow range of 8–11 percent over the previous quarter century. Despite this impressive performance, China's growth process has been widely criticized for being *internally* unbalanced, defined by its exceptionally low share of consumption to GDP and comparatively high share of investment to GDP. Its growth was also seen until recently as *externally* unbalanced in the sense that China was generating huge trade surpluses reaching as much as 10 percent of GDP in 2005 to 2008 mirrored by potentially destabilizing trade deficits in the United States and Europe. Because there is a link between a country's internal and external balances, the argument was that if China consumed more but invested less—that is, rebalanced internally—it would generate a smaller trade surplus and the problem of global imbalances would be ameliorated.

Today, concerns about global trade imbalances have moderated. Yet the solution was not what many had envisaged. China's trade surplus is now around 2–3 percent of GDP, but its internal imbalances actually widened from 2000 onwards as the relative shares of consumption and investment to GDP became even more extreme before stabilizing more recently. Nevertheless, the vast majority of China watchers continue to argue that internal rebalancing is needed. This view has featured prominently in US policy discussions with China. As recently as the June 2016 US-China S&ED, the United States stressed the priority "to shift China's growth model to one driven by household consumption rather than investment and exports."[1]

Many theories have been advanced to explain China's "dual" imbalances, but none have highlighted the critical role that urbanization has played in shaping the process. If properly understood, China's internal imbalances would be seen not as a risk but as the unavoidable byproduct of a generally successful growth process that reflects rapid urbanization and regional specialization in production. Even a good thing can be overdone, however. State-driven investments have gone increasingly into unproductive activities as part of intermittent stimulus programs in recent years. Instead of artificially promoting investments or household consumption for the sake of rebalancing, the priority should be on raising productivity and increasing public funding for social programs to support demand. Done properly, rebalancing will evolve naturally over a decade or more as China reaches high-income status.

Unbalanced Growth and Trade Balances

The IMF has been at the forefront of these discussions, coming out with many studies on the need to rebalance and emphasizing that China's growth needs to be "accompanied by a decisive shift toward consumption-based growth."[2] The IMF is not alone in making these allegations. Many scholars and market analysts have argued that China's imbalances originate from policy distortions and institutional weaknesses ranging from misaligned exchange and interest rates to excessively high savings rates.[3]

The argument is driven by the basic national accounting identity showing the links between GDP (Y), consumption (C), investment (I), exports (X), and imports (M):

$$Y = C + I + X - M$$

Reworked, the identity indicates that a country's trade balance $(X - M)$ is equivalent to its so-called savings gap $(Y - C - I)$ or the difference between what is produced and what is consumed and invested.

$$Y - C - I = X - M$$

A lower trade surplus would require China to either increase its investment or consumption. Since China's investment rate of around 35–40 percent of GDP in the early 2000s was already judged to be high by global standards, it was argued that Chinese households needed to consume more to drive down the country's current account surpluses. This line of reasoning was also interpreted to imply that if its growth was more balanced, its longer-term growth prospects would be enhanced.

This premise reflected not only the US policy position concerning China's economy but also that of the European Central Bank, which noted that China's "export-led growth model . . . has produced domestic and external imbalances which are associated with economic inefficiencies, financial stability risks, social unrest and tensions with major trading partners. These imbalances include a share of investment over GDP which is too high . . . financial repression, rising income inequality and inefficiencies in the use of production factors—all features that cannot be redressed without a fundamental overhaul of the current growth model."[4]

Today, China's current account surpluses have moderated, but internal imbalances are greater than they were in the early 2000s. Why did most China observers get it wrong?

China's Unbalanced Growth Has Been Misunderstood

The policies launched by Deng Xiaoping and Zhu Rongji led to a spatially unbalanced growth process which sharply ratcheted up productivity and concentrated investment along the coast. This led to sustained increases in the investment-to-GDP ratio and a commensurate decline in the share of personal consumption. Personal consumption as a share of GDP in China declined steadily since 2000 from over 45 percent to 35 percent—the lowest of any major economy—while the investment share rose from 40 to 48 percent—correspondingly the highest of any major economy (see Figure 4.1). Thus, it is understandable that most observers believe China needs to rebalance its economy.[5]

Much of the public's attention has been on the low share of consumption rather than the high investment share. It is easier to convey a sense that something is amiss by alluding to consumption being repressed rather than pointing to a high investment rate, which is often positively associated with growth. Even former premier Wen Jiabao took this view in his oft-quoted statement at

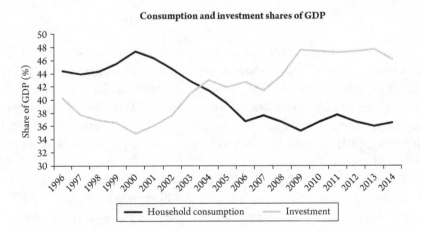

Figure 4.1 Consumption and Investment Shares of GDP. Source: World Bank World Development Indicators

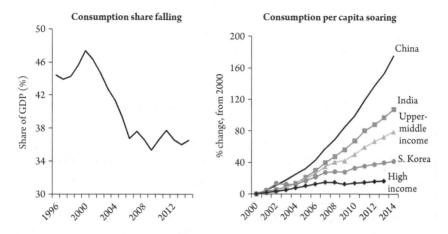

Figure 4.2 China's Consumption Paradox. Source: World Bank World Development Indicators; author's calculations

the March 2007 National Peoples' Congress Meetings that "China's economy is unstable, unbalanced, uncoordinated, and unsustainable."[6]

However, over the past decade and a half, China's economic growth has triggered record increases in consumption *levels* compared to other countries, even as the *share* of personal consumption in GDP fell. The paradox of one indicator suggesting repressed living standards while the other suggests the opposite holds the key to understanding the nature of China's growth process (see Figure 4.2).

Financial and Wage Repressions Are Wrongly Seen as Driving Imbalances

Changes in personal consumption are due to shifts in the incomes of households and their savings rates. Thus, if there is a sustained decline in the share of consumption to GDP, it should show up as a decline in the share of household income to GDP or an increase in the savings rate or both.[7] Both the decline in the share of household income in GDP and the increase in savings rates are largely the result of urbanization as workers move from rural to urban-based employment.

In contrast, those favoring a more balanced growth model have argued that policy distortions, namely low interest rates and repressed wages, have been the primary factors causing the share of consumption to fall. China's interest rates were deemed to be too low since there was a ceiling on how much banks could pay depositors. This result was seen as discouraging consumption and

Box 4.1 Were China's Interest Rates Too Low or Too High?

For most of the past decade, China's interest rates were deemed to be too low given the ceiling on deposit rates. This supposedly provided a subsidy for borrowers and encouraged households to save more because they had to earn a "target" level of interest earnings from their bank accounts. This then explained why China's growth was unbalanced in terms of repressed consumption and excessive investment. The ceiling on deposit rates was relaxed and eventually eliminated in late 2015, while lending rates had been freed up even earlier. If the argument was correct, these actions should have led to higher interest rates, but rates have actually declined in recent years.

How does one explain the decline? The original argument was flawed because it did not take into consideration the broader range of factors that shape interest rates when market forces are allowed to function. A country's interest rates are determined by a variety of factors including the productivity of capital, inflation, savings rates, exchange-rate expectations, and cross-border capital flows.

In the years after the GFC, the cap on deposit rates kept China's rate at 3.3 percent. Nevertheless, this was actually much higher than rates in other major regional financial markets where deposit rates were around 0.2 percent. Most other OECD (Organization for Economic Cooperation and Development) economies had a negative real deposit rate, while China's was positive. During that period, the renminbi was also expected to appreciate against the dollar, bolstering real returns even further. Thus the "real return" in China was about five percentage points higher than in other major economies.

The argument being made at that time assumed that if the controls were lifted on deposit rates, banks would set higher rates to attract more deposits. But this has more to do with distortions in the financial system than with how a liberalized financial market would price capital. With globalization and monetary easing elsewhere and less restrictions on cross-border capital flows, interest rates in China have moved closer to rates in other major financial markets. This is the consequence of investors pouring more money into China, and Chinese firms borrowing abroad at lower rates than available domestically, buoyed until recently by limited downside exchange risks. In sum, more market-determined interest rates mean removing restrictions not only on what banks pay for deposits but also on the supply of capital in allowing money to flow both in and out of China. Under such circumstances, interest rates in China have been declining until recently relative to major financial markets elsewhere.

(This box draws on Yukon Huang, "China's Interest Rates Are Too High, not Too Low," *Financial Times*, January 7, 2014.)

encouraging investment.[8] But whether interest rates in a truly market-driven system would have been higher is debatable (see Box 4.1). The argument about wage repression comes from the notion that wage increases have been less than the increase in labor productivity. This leads to a rising share of profits to GDP at the expense of labor and in turn a lower share of consumption to GDP. Both arguments, however, are flawed.

Practically all developing economies have used financial repression to secure savings from households to support government expenditure priorities.[9] But only a few experienced imbalances similar to China's, and these were the other East Asian success cases of Japan, South Korea, Singapore, and Taiwan (see Box 4.2). All these countries used a combination of "directed" lending to public entities, controlled interest rates, and restrictions on capital movements to promote growth. Some observers have in fact argued that financial repression served China well in the context of its transition to more

---

Box 4.2 **Why China Resorted to Financial Repression**

The argument in favor of using financial repression was even stronger for China than for other developing countries. Its policymakers simply did not have a better alternative to secure the resources to jump-start its development process given the institutions it inherited from the central-planning era. Under central planning, banks did not function as typical banks but as financing entities for centrally determined expenditures to complement the budget.

When Deng Xiaoping opened up the economy in 1980, China's fiscal position was precarious and its access to foreign resources limited. The legacy of the Mao years left the country with little useable capital stock and profitability of SOEs was plummeting. Budgetary revenues declined steadily to a low of nearly 10 percent of GDP by the mid-1990s from over 30 percent in the 1970s. The standard prescription for resource generation would have been higher consumption-based sales taxes. Income-based taxes were impractical given pervasive poverty and institutional weaknesses. Such taxes would have been difficult to collect and regressive, since lower income households would end up paying more than the wealthy. Raising the resources needed for investment by tapping household savings parked with banks provided an inexpensive and easy alternative, with the added benefit of being a "progressive" tax, forcing the rich to pay more thanks to their higher savings. Thus Deng's approach avoided a confrontation with vested interests which would have jeopardized the goal of jump-starting the economy.

market-appropriate approaches.[10] The benefits of continued financial repression, however, have diminished as China's economy has become more private sector oriented. China's public-sector financing needs should now be increasingly provided through the budget and non-bank capital markets rather than through bank loans.

Following the Growth Path of Other East Asian Economies

China's growth pattern resembles the handful of other successful East Asian economies that managed to move from middle to high income over the past half-century. All of them experienced steep declines in their consumption share of GDP and commensurate increases in their investment share during their high-growth periods.

This pattern fits the Lewis model in explaining how rapid growth comes from transferring surplus workers from agriculture to urban-based industries.[11] The model lays out the conditions for the so-called Lewis turning point, when labor shortages, rising wages, and appreciation of the exchange rate eventually lead to slower but more balanced growth.

Timing of this Lewis turning point in relation to China's current stage of development is a topic of much speculation among Chinese academics.[12] Some have argued that, given the rapid increase in wages, the turning point was reached in the early 2000s. Others have suggested that there is still a surplus in the sense that wages have not increased as rapidly as labor productivity. Moreover, there are still considerable numbers of workers in rural areas and smaller cities who could be reallocated to more productive jobs in major cities if restrictions on migration were lifted.

Still left to be explained is why the transfer of labor from rural to urban activities resulted in a decline in the share of personal consumption to GDP in China over the past decade and a half. The answer lies in decomposing consumption as a share of GDP into two components, namely the disposable income of households and their savings rates. As seen in Figure 4.3, disposable or household income (which serves as a proxy) as a share of GDP has been declining over the decade 2000–2010 before ticking upward more recently. The pattern raises two obvious questions: first, why did it decline, and second, why did the decline only begin around the year 2000? Combining the implications of this decline in disposable income with rising savings rates answers why consumption as a share of GDP has been falling over the past decade.

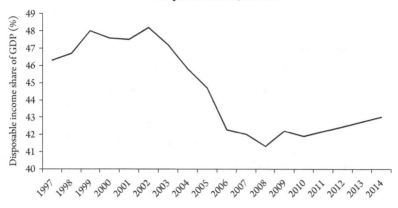

Disposable income, % of GDP

Figure 4.3 Disposable Income Trends. Source: National Bureau of Statistics of China; author's calculations

Urbanization Explains Why China's Growth Has Become Unbalanced

The explanation lies in the urbanization process. The transfer of workers from labor-intensive, rural activities to more capital-intensive, urban, industrial activities increases the share of profits in the economy and leads to higher investment levels and more rapid growth. But it also results in a reduced share of consumption to GDP even though the growth rate of consumption surges—hence the paradox of consumption.

This can be illustrated through an example of what has been happening in China. Assume that a farmer produces rice worth 10,000 renminbi a year. After paying for inputs, he then nets 9,000 renminbi as his disposable income, out of which he saves 2,000 and spends 7,000. In the national accounts, his activity translates into a consumption share of 70 percent of the value of agriculture production.

Now suppose that he moves to Shenzhen and gets a job with Apple to assemble iPods and is paid 30,000 renminbi a year, triple what he was formerly earning—and similar to what has been actually happening in China. Like most migrants, he saves half and consumes half—15,000 renminbi. Apple combines his labor with capital and imported components to produce iPods worth 60,000 renminbi. His consumption as a share of industrial production is now just 25 percent.[13]

As in Figure 4.4, this particular labor transfer shows up in the national accounts as labor's share of output declining from 90 to 50 percent and consumption as a

How does labor migration influence national accounts?

Farmer Huang
- Value of rice = 10, 000
- Huang's income = 9, 000
- 7,000 consumed, 2, 000 saved

Factory Worker Huang
- Value added of iPod = 60, 000
- Huang's wages = 30, 000
- 15,000 consumed, 15, 000 saved

Labour share of output goes from 90% to 50%
Consumption share of GDP goes from 70% to 25%

Figure 4.4 Migration and GDP Implications. Source: Author

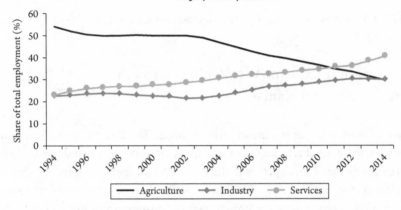

Employment by sector

Figure 4.5 Employment by Sector. Source: World Bank World Development Indicators

share of GDP going from 70 to 25 percent. This story has been replicated count-less times through the transfer of millions of migrant workers annually.

Various studies confirm this sketch of what has been happening. Drawing on household- and firm-level surveys, Chongen Bai and Zhengjie Qian, two Tsinghua University Professors, have estimated that labor's share of output is much lower in industry, at around 50 percent, compared with nearly 90 percent in agriculture (comparable to the pattern in other developing countries). There has been a sharp decline in agriculture's share of the labor force from around 50 to 35 percent and a commensurate increase in the share of workers in industry and services (see Figure 4.5). The movement of workers from agriculture to urban jobs in industry and services accounts for the bulk of the decline in labor's share of GDP and in turn leads to a decline of the share of consumption in GDP.[14]

But there is nothing sinister about this outcome, since everyone is better off than before. Migrant workers are earning, saving, and consuming multiples more than they used to. Firms are able to expand by hiring more workers and in-creasing investments. Meanwhile the country benefits from higher productivity, rising trade volumes, and double-digit GDP growth rates. This rural to urban labor shift is the primary reason China's productivity growth has been well above the norm for middle-income countries. Consumption as a share of GDP will eventually flatten out—that is, rebalancing will occur—but this process takes decades.

Rebalancing begins when the pace of rural to urban migration slows down and urban workers begin to get a larger share of the value of industrial production. This happens when labor becomes relatively scarce and wages are bid up as indicated in the Lewis turning point. It also occurs as urban workers move from jobs in manufacturing to jobs in services, since wages are a relatively larger share of the value added in services compared to manufacturing.

This is just beginning to happen in China. The services sector now accounts for a larger share of the economy than manufacturing. Coupled with a slackening in the pace of urbanization but continued strong growth in wages despite slower GDP growth, the share of consumption has risen slightly in recent years. However, if rural to urban migration picks up and wage growth moderates as the economy continues to slow down, this will dampen the extent of the rebalancing in the coming years.

Regional Dimensions of China's Unbalanced Growth

As shown in Figure 4.3, the decline in disposable or household income as a share of GDP began around 2000. Decomposing this decline by region helps to explain why imbalances intensified during this period. If imbalances were the result of repressed interest rates or an undervalued exchange rate, one would not expect the pattern to be different across regions since these rates are the same across regions.

However, a striking pattern emerges when the nationwide share is disaggregated by region as in Figure 4.6. This is consistent with the argument that the sharp decline in the share of consumption to GDP is due to the urbanization-cum-industrialization process and not to financial repression or distorted exchange rates.[15] Figure 4.6 shows that the decline in the share of household income to GDP has been minimal in the northeast and moderate in the east and central regions. The only region that has experienced a sharp decline akin to that visible in the nationwide pattern is the west. And because its decline was so great, it drove the decline for the country as a whole over the past decade and a half, even though it accounts for less than 20 percent of the country's total GDP. If low interest rates or exchange rates were the primary reason for China's unbalanced growth, as many China experts have argued, one would have expected the pattern of the decline to be similar across regions or that it would be more

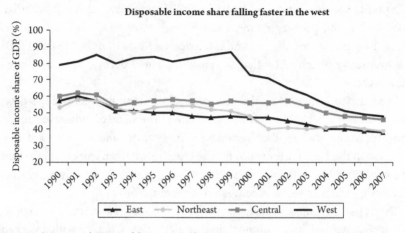

Figure 4.6 Regional Disposable Income Shares. Source: National Bureau of Statistics of China; Li Taocai and Chen Shi, Tsinghua University Center for China in the World Economy

pronounced in the coastal provinces given their major commercial centers and more rapid pace of development.

Clearly what has been happening is both location and policy event related. The sharp fall in household income as a share of GDP in the western region reflects the fact that its labor force was more rural based relative to the rest of the country, which explains its high household income share before 2000. But when Beijing launched its special "Develop the West" initiative in the late 1990s, the western region began to catch up rapidly with the rest of the country.[16] This initiative supported massive investments in infrastructure and urban-based activities in the twelve most underdeveloped western provinces and prompted a sharp decline in labor's share of production as workers shifted from traditional rural activities to industry and construction.

Because urbanization had taken off decades earlier along the coastal region, the decline in labor's share of production there was spread more gradually over a longer period. This is illustrated by the fact that the urbanization rate for the western region was increasing by 3 percent annually from 1999 to 2007 compared with 1.4 percent for the coastal region.[17]

These shifts in consumption patterns are mirrored in regional investment trends. In recent years, for example, gross fixed capital formation as a percentage of regional GDP ranged from 80 to 100 percent for western provinces like Tibet, Guangxi, Qinghai, and Inner Mongolia, while for coastal provinces like Shanghai and Guangdong, it was between 35 and 40 percent. A recent IMF study notes that "two-thirds of the rise in China's investment-to-GDP ratio and the entire decline in the private consumption ratio over the last ten years are attributable to the inland provinces."[18]

China's urbanization ratio is now around 56 percent, compared with 20 percent in the 1980s. As millions of workers moved from smallholder agriculture, where labor's share of the value of production is exceptionally high, to industry and services, where it is only half as much, the net effect has been to push down labor's share of GDP by some seven percentage points from 2000 to 2010.[19]

Consumption Decline Amplified by Surging Urban Savings Rates

The decline in consumption as a share of GDP, however, was even greater than the decline in household income would suggest since it was amplified by an accompanying rise in savings rates on top of already high savings rates. There is a voluminous literature on why savings rates have risen in China.[20] The reasons proposed include a precautionary motive due to China's weak welfare system and aging population; pressures that came from rising housing prices (and the need to save more to cover the down payment); increasing income inequality (as the rich have higher savings rates); and China's one-child policy, which has led to a shortage of females and forced males to save more to attract a spouse.[21]

To be valid, however, the explanation needs to be consistent with the fact that the increase in savings rates is largely an urban phenomenon. As seen in Figure 4.7, the increase in household savings rates is due to escalating urban savings rates. Rural savings rates have remained broadly unchanged or have fallen. Again, labor migration to the cities explains this pattern.

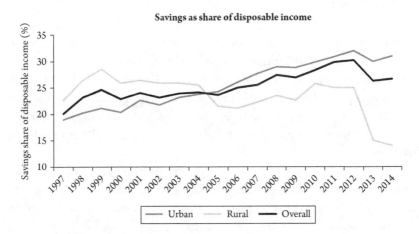

Figure 4.7 Urban vs. Rural Savings. Source: National Bureau of Statistics of China; IMF staff calculations

Because migrant workers are not eligible for the usual range of urban social services due to lack of residency rights (or *hukou*), they end up saving a much higher proportion of their income than established urban residents. A study covering twenty-two provinces showed that households without *hukou* consumed 31 percent less than other urban residents. Other studies based on household budget surveys show that migrant households save 40–80 percent more than normal residents.[22] This behavior can be seen as a more extreme version of the "precautionary motive," but its roots differ from other studies on this topic. Multiply this effect for each migrant by the millions of new migrant workers annually and the result is the surge in urban savings rates.

Determining the increase in savings rates for the overall economy means including what has been happening with corporate and government savings rates. Corporate savings surged over most of the decade prior to the GFC. This was driven by rising corporate profit rates and a preference for private firms to rely on internal funds given the underdeveloped capital markets. Net savings also rose in government, in part due to the more rapid increase in tax revenues relative to recurrent expenditures and the capitalization of pension and social funds which were established to put the welfare system on a more sustainable footing. The overall result was that national savings increased more rapidly than investment, leading to a surge in China's current account surplus that peaked in 2008.

Unbalanced Growth Leads to Higher Consumption per Household

Urbanization largely explains the decline in labor's share of income relative to GDP and also plays a major role in ratcheting up savings rates. Together, these two factors explain most of the decline in consumption as a share of GDP. Yet, far from being repressed, per-capita consumption has been growing by 8–9 percent annually in real terms over the past decade and half—the most rapid growth of any major economy—even as the share of consumption to GDP has been falling (see Figure 4.2).

Many observers arguing that China's growth process should be more consumption driven have not appreciated the fact that maximizing sustained growth in *consumption levels* over the past several decades may have necessitated a phase when the *share of consumption to GDP* declines. This allows for the growth of investment to exceed the growth in GDP, and if the productivity of investment is high enough, then the resulting rapid growth of GDP leads to personal consumption levels increasing steadily over time.

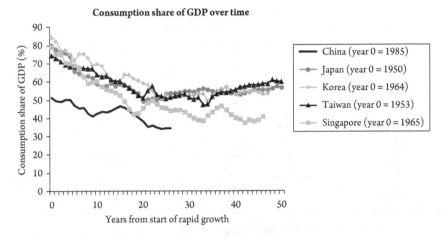

Consumption share of GDP over time

Figure 4.8 Trends in Consumption Shares. Source: World Bank World Development Indicators; National Statistics, Taiwan

China's unbalanced growth pattern mirrors other successful East Asian economies that went through similar structural transitions over several decades, although there is a difference in magnitude. The personal consumption share of GDP fell steadily, bottoming out at around 50 percent in Japan in 1970, Taiwan in 1986, and South Korea in 1988, at roughly similar PPP-adjusted per-capita income levels (see Figure 4.8).

After about twenty-five years of unbalanced growth, consumption as a share of GDP fell by twenty-nine percentage points for all three countries compared to eighteen percentage points for China (with partially offsetting increases in the investment shares) (see Table 4.1). But all four of the other countries started from much higher levels—in the range of 75–85 percent compared with below 50 percent for China as discussed in Annex B. The challenge for China today is to make its unbalanced growth process more efficient. And if successful, China's unbalanced growth phase will be extended rather than curtailed prematurely. If China follows the pattern of the other economies, significant rebalancing as measured by increases in the share of consumption to GDP will not occur for a decade or more, but GDP growth in the range of 5–7 percent annually could continue for many years to come (see Chapter 10).

Benefits from Rising Investment

The other successful Asian economies experienced a sustained increase in the investment share of GDP, peaking at nearly 40 percent. China's investment rate has been significantly higher. This is explained partly by the fact that real interest

Table 4.1 **Consumption and Investment Shares and Growth (%)**

Years	Change in C/GDP		Change in I/GDP		Average GDP growth	
	Japan, S. Korea, Singapore, Taiwan	China	Japan, S. Korea, Singapore, Taiwan	China	Japan, S. Korea, Singapore, Taiwan	China
0–25	–29.1	–17.7	15.7	9.9	9.0	9.9
25–35	–0.1		–3.3		6.4	
35–45	1.3		–3.3		5.0	

Japan base year = 1950; Taiwan base year = 1953; South Korea base year = 1964; Singapore base year = 1965; China base year = 1985

Source: Penn World Tables

rates during the past decade and a half have been significantly lower globally than during the high investment period for these other countries and partly by the fact that China began with a relatively much lower useable capital stock. The common thread linking all these successful East Asian countries is that widening imbalances are associated with sustained high growth rates that propelled these economies from middle- to high-income status and eventually to more balanced outcomes as they matured.

The process in East Asia was supported by an outward-oriented growth strategy that took advantage of rapidly increasing exports. Real export growth averaged 15 percent or more in Japan and Singapore during their two-decade takeoff periods, similar to China's experience, while Taiwan's real export growth was over 20 percent and South Korea's reached almost 35 percent.

Addressing the Recent Decline in Investment Productivity

With the steady increase in China's investment-to-GDP ratio, the popular presumption is that China has overinvested and productivity has declined sharply.[23] This is seen as the reason for China's current economic slowdown and debt problems. It is difficult to estimate the overall productivity of investment, and comparisons with other countries are often not credible. Moreover, given cyclical fluctuations and other distortions, such measures have little meaning over short time spans but can be informative in a longer perspective.

One measure of investment efficiency used by economists is the ICOR—incremental capital-output ratio—which indicates how much investment is

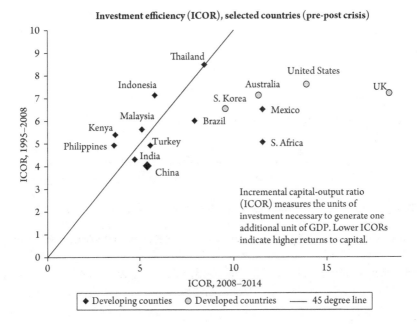

Figure 4.9 Investment Returns Comparisons. Source: World Bank World Development Indicators

needed to produce an additional unit of GDP. The *lower* the ICOR, the *higher* the implied returns to investment. Figure 4.9 plots the ICOR for selected countries split between two periods before and after the GFC: 1995–2008 and 2008–2014. The countries include other Asian countries, selected major emerging market economies, and some developed countries.

In this comparison, China's investment productivity is the best among all these countries in the earlier period (1995–2008), but after the surge in its investment rate since the GFC, productivity has declined to the levels of the others. This pattern is mirrored in the trend line for China's ICOR over the past decade. Figure 4.10 plots IOCRs for China and a sample of other major developing economies.[24] Up until the GFC, China's ICOR was declining, implying increasing productivity of investment. Relative to the others, its return on investment was generally more stable and also better. Since the GFC, however, diminishing investment returns have caused China's ICOR to converge to the levels of other emerging market economies.

Other indicators reinforce this bifurcated view. A comparison across countries undertaken by the Asian Productivity Organization for the period 2000–2010 showed that China's total factor productivity growth of around 4 percent annually compared quite favorably with the others.[25] But since 2010, total factor productivity has declined significantly—as has been the case for other countries. These

ICOR, five-year moving average

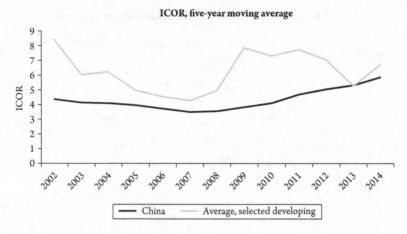

Figure 4.10 Investment Returns Trends. Source: World Bank World Development Indicators

indicators are also consistent with the steady increase in rates of return on assets for China's enterprises up to 2010 followed by a decline in the last several years.

Balanced Economies Are the Ones That Remain Trapped

While the East Asian success cases managed to move from middle- to high-income status over a multi-decade period, this has been rare for developing countries more generally. Hence, the literature has coined the concept of a "middle-income trap," a term that has been used most often to characterize several major Latin American economies who failed to narrow the gap with developed countries once they hit middle-income levels at around $10,000 in per-capita terms.[26] They became stuck at this income level when they could not shift to a growth process driven by increasing productivity. Yet the growth path of these "trapped" Latin American economies has been "balanced," with shares of consumption and investment remaining roughly constant over time—symptomatic of their relatively lackluster growth. This same balanced outcome can be seen in lagging East Asian performers like the Philippines and Indonesia.[27]

From 1960 to 1990, the growth of real consumption expenditures in "balanced" economies like the Philippines, Mexico, and Brazil was in the range of 3–4 percent. Conversely, real consumption growth in "unbalanced" economies such as China or South Korea over the same comparable period was far higher, averaging 7–9 percent (see Table 4.2). The premise that more balanced growth means faster growth in consumption is simply not true.

Those who have argued that wage suppression was a major reason for China's low consumption rates typically point out that wage increases lagged behind labor productivity increases. Economic theory tells us that wage increases will

Table 4.2 **Consumption Increases Faster with Unbalanced Growth**

	Average annual growth in real consumption (t to 30 years)	Change in C/GDP share
Korea	**7.0 %**	**−31.7%**
Taiwan	**8.8%**	**−13.4%**
China	**7.8%**	**−15.7%**
Philippines	3.7%	+4.9%
Mexico	3.9%	−4.9%
Brazil	4.3%	−4.3%

t = 1960 for Korea, Taiwan; t = 1970 for Brazil, Mexico; t=1980 for China, Philippines

Source: Calculated from World Bank Development Indicators and national sources

Table 4.3 **Growth in Real Wages in East Asia**

	2000–2005	2006–2010
China	**12.6%**	**12.1%**
Malaysia	3.5%	0.8%
Philippines	−1.1%	−0.4%
Thailand	−1.0%	1.7%
Taiwan	1.5%	−0.5%
Korea	4.4%	−0.5%

Source: Calculated from International Labour Office data base

mirror increases in productivity over time, but not during periods of either rapid or sharply declining growth. The combination of huge labor surpluses and massive investments during this rapid growth phase made it logical for wage increases to lag productivity increases. But this does not mean that such wage increases were too low in some normative sense; they were in fact quite high by historical standards and in comparison with other countries (see Table 4.3). Because the demand for labor exceeded the number of job seekers in China, salaries for migrant workers increased even more rapidly than average wages over this period.[28]

Eventually, growth in wages moderates as an economy matures and becomes more balanced. China is now at the tail end of the surge and wage increases will likely begin to decline before 2020, as was the case with the other Asian success cases as seen in their "peaked" historical wage trends (Figure 4.11).

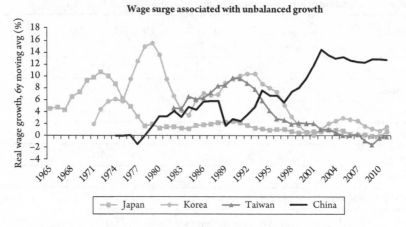

Figure 4.11 Wage Increase Patterns. Source: International Labour Organization

Urbanization and Services—Still a Long Way to Go for China

The relocation of workers from rural to urban areas is driven by a trade-oriented industrialization process that promotes the development of specialized manufacturing clusters and later on more sophisticated services. The shift of people slowed when the urbanization ratio reached 70 percent in the late 1980s for South Korea and Taiwan, and 75 percent in the early 1970s for Japan, indicating that the rebalancing turning point for these economies coincided with the leveling off of a rapid urbanization process (see Figure 4.12).

The experience of Taiwan, South Korea, and Japan also suggests that rapid urbanization is linked to the development of the service sector. Taiwan's increase is particularly pronounced compared to that of South Korea. For Taiwan, a deliberate policy to shift manufacturing to mainland China and liberalize entry of lower-cost foreign workers from Southeast Asia generated a surge in services growth from the late 1980s up to 2000. In contrast, Korea has been more inclined to keep its manufacturing activities at home, and it is likely that China will follow Korea's path.

Rebalancing occurs when household income and consumption shares begin to rise relative to GDP. This happens when the economy is close to becoming fully urbanized, and workers move increasingly into more skilled jobs in services where wages are higher. Successful countries are those with the right policy package to support this process, while those that fail often end up with a growing pool of underemployed urban workers living in slums.

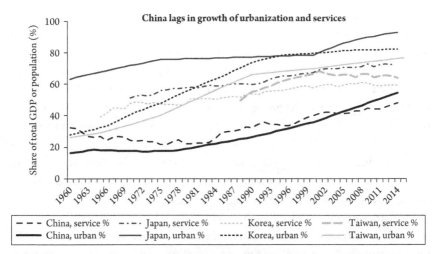

Figure 4.12 Urbanization and Services Trends. Source: World Bank World Development Indicators; United Nations World Urbanization Prospects; OECD National Accounts

China's impressive growth rates for consumption could have been even higher had its household registration policies (*hukou*) not retarded the speed of urbanization and encouraged discriminatory treatment of migrant workers. At 56 percent, China's urbanization rate is still below expectations for its level of development and resource endowment, indicating that large numbers of workers are still trapped in lower-productivity rural activities or less productive smaller cities. The service sector's share of output is also unusually low despite the recent rebound— and the experience of successful East Asia countries suggests that repressed urbanization may be partly to blame.[29]

Policy Implications

Misinterpreting the reasons for China's unbalanced growth leads to misplaced policy emphasis. Pricing distortions such as misaligned interest and exchange rates were not the primary reasons driving China's imbalances as most analysts have suggested. Thus recommendations that China's growth model should be more "consumption-led" is inconsistent with growth theory.[30]

For most of the past two decades, the unbalanced nature of China's growth process was a consequence of how unusually fast it was growing. But its huge stimulus program in response to the GFC and more recent bouts with credit easing has led to a surge in investment into less productive activities. The solution is not, as some have suggested, to support artificially driven consumption initiatives, such as tax incentives to spur purchases of durables. Instead, the answer lies in increasing productivity and fiscal reforms.

Nevertheless, there are distortions that make China's growth process more unbalanced than it should be. The major issue is its restrictive *hukou* residency policies. Without formal residency rights, migrant workers are unable to access social services in the cities where they work. Thus they save a much higher proportion of their income than those with *hukou* residency rights. If migrant workers were given such rights and consumed at the same rate as established residents, China's consumption shares would be a few percentage points higher in relation to GDP.[31] As a notable byproduct, this would reduce if not eliminate China's trade surpluses and in doing so address one of the major concerns of the United States and Europe, without getting into the more contentious issue of whether the renminbi is still undervalued (see Chapter 7).

The other priority related to rebalancing is to rationalize the regional distribution of investment.[32] This would mean curbing the tendency to overinvest in infrastructure in the interior provinces in favor of increased social and environmental expenditures. This is a politically sensitive policy issue driven largely by concerns over rising regional inequalities (see Chapter 6). It was given additional support by the huge reconstruction effort in response to the 2008 earthquake in Sichuan and then by the GFC-related stimulus, much of which led to increased infrastructure projects targeted toward the interior provinces.

Since the GFC, the focus on the interior became an excuse for local officials in those provinces to push for investments that went beyond providing core public services to creating new cities on the premise, "If we build them, they will come." The resulting ghost towns are now a common feature in some localities and illustrate why too much investment has been going to areas where employment growth has been limited or rates of return are lower.[33]

Over time, more resources might flow naturally to the central provinces. Development of high-speed rail has given the central provinces greater prominence as a logical hub for moving goods and people both east and west. As such, over time, less well known central provinces like Henan, Hunan, and Hubei, with populations ranging from sixty to one hundred million each, will play a greater role in an economy that is more focused on domestic demand than external trade.[34] However, there continues to be a politically powerful constituency supporting the development of the far west given geo-strategic reasons and this is likely to continue.

Waiting for 2020

Many observers who are monitoring growth trends take comfort that the economy appears to be rebalancing. This is confusing means with objectives. The modest rebalancing that has occurred merely reflects the fact that GDP growth has slowed. Since wages (household incomes) have not declined as rapidly, consumption as a share of GDP is increasing. Meanwhile lower corporate profits are leading to lower investment rates. There is nothing positive about this trend. This is a reminder that the objective is not to achieve a particular share of consumption to GDP but to support more sustainable growth in the level of consumption.

What is important for the global economy is whether China can maintain growth in the 5–7 percent range and create enough demand to produce widespread benefits. Whether that demand comes from investment or consumption should be less of a concern provided it is economically justified. Although markets are focusing on consumption, global balances would benefit more from robust investment demand, which is more import intensive and thus more likely to impact positively on other nations, especially commodity producers.

China's per-capita GDP has not yet reached the level at which the respective consumption shares of GDP in the other Asian success cases began to increase significantly. If investment productivity can be improved and urbanization remains on track, China could continue to grow at a reasonably rapid rate and would not reach the so-called Lewis turning point when rebalancing accelerates until well into the next decade.[35] While South Korea, Japan, and Taiwan had urbanization ratios closer to 70 percent at their turning points, China's ratio is more likely to be around 60 percent by 2020, given its larger size and geo-economic characteristics. Looking at the issue in terms of demographics and likely trends in the exchange rates, a recent IMF study also concluded that the Lewis turning point should occur sometime between 2020 and 2025.[36]

In sum, far from being a threat to China's stable development, its unbalanced growth was evidence of a generally successful structural transformation that helped to eradicate poverty. If China pursues the structural reforms needed to increase productivity and fosters a more efficient urbanization process, this will create the basis for a more sustainable growth path. Significant rebalancing will then occur later and naturally as the economy matures.

CHAPTER 5

China's Debt Dilemma

In recent years, attention has shifted from concerns over China's unbalanced growth and trade surpluses to anxiety about its rising debt levels and seemingly bottomless economic slowdown.[1] Many among the financial community have warned that China is headed for an economic collapse with headlines such as this: "The coming debt bust—it is a question of when, not if, real trouble will hit China."[2]

The argument typically begins by pointing out that China's debt-to-GDP ratio has grown rapidly since 2009, about double the buildup that occurred in the United States before the GFC and in Korea before the AFC. Others compare China to Japan's debt situation in the 1990s, that nation's lost decade. As these uber-bears argue, such debt indicators have led to a financial crisis in all other cases—so why not in China?

The argument that China is about to fall off a financial cliff is overstated. China's situation is different from the other crisis cases in many key aspects, the most important being that the debt problem in China is largely confined to the state sector whereas in the others it was largely between private agents. Comparisons with Japan's lost decade are also misplaced since the kind of equity or property market collapse Japan experienced is highly unlikely in China. Nevertheless, China's debt burden has been steadily increasing since the GFC and, if not stabilized within the next several years, will in due course dampen longer-term growth prospects. Thus the failure for the authorities to take more decisive steps so far is worrisome, even if warnings of an imminent crisis are overdone.

Although there are anecdotal but striking examples of financial stress in China, there is little evidence of widespread insolvency that could threaten the broader economy. But there are serious problems that need to be resolved among a narrower subset of construction and property-related firms, as well as others in the commodity and energy sectors dominated by stated-owned firms who often over spend since they can pass on any losses to the state. The risks of shadow banking, however, although warranting attention, are unlikely to destabilize the system. In all but the most extreme scenarios, the government has the flexibility in the form of discretionary fiscal and financial resources to bail out the most important distressed entities and to recapitalize major banks. This will ensure that any tensions do not turn into the sort of systemic financial crisis that could derail the economy, as was the case elsewhere.

The stabilization process, however, will be messy and costly as the economy slowly hemorrhages financial resources and throws good money after bad to keep growth in line with official targets. China's inexperienced new investor class also may react to market stresses in unexpected ways. Adjustments in an overbuilt property market will exacerbate vulnerabilities. And, the surge and then collapse of the equity market followed by a more recent surge in shadow-banking activity built on the issuance of weakly regulated wealth management products (WMPs) and lending between related firms have accentuated market perceptions about increasing risks.

These issues point to China's need for reforms to slow the growth of bad debt and encourage productivity growth. While most observers see the crux of the problem emanating from banking vulnerabilities, its origins come from China's weak fiscal system, which encourages local authorities to rely on bank loans including shadow-banking products for financing that should be coming from the government's budget. The financial stresses are actually symptoms of underlying fiscal problems.[3] In addition the moral hazard problem needs to be addressed. This means, for example, forcing SOEs to bear the full consequences of their borrowing decisions, including bankruptcies if necessary.

Enacting reforms and allowing for a period of subdued growth while the property market corrects could sustain medium-term growth of around 6 percent. This would keep China's debt burden manageable. The alternative would be continued weakening of the economy, which—given the government's considerable resources—would not manifest itself in a near-term collapse but would make it much more difficult for the leadership to reestablish a more sustainable growth path over the coming decade.

Understanding China's Credit Boom

Why are the pessimists wrong in predicting an imminent collapse?[4] In most countries that have experienced a financial crisis, the preceding credit surge has typically been the culmination of a long-term and broad-based deterioration in financial and fiscal indicators. China simply does not fit that pattern. It possesses a strong balance of payments position, modest fiscal deficits, and high household savings rates. Nor have the most vocal pessimists keyed in on the fact that

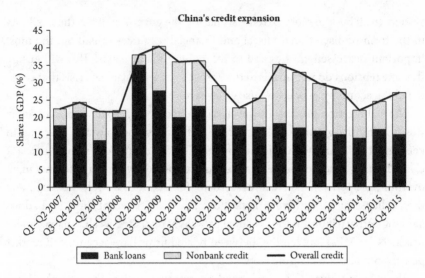

Figure 5.1 China's credit expansion. Source: CEIC; UBS Investment Bank; author's calculations

the dynamics of a debt crisis are different for financial systems in which the bulk of the debtors are SOEs borrowing directly or indirectly from state-owned commercial banks (SOCBs).

The country's debt problems are rooted in the government's November 2008 announcement of a 4 trillion yuan ($586 billion) stimulus package to counteract the effects of the GFC. Rather than being channeled through the government's budget, the stimulus took the form of an explosion in bank lending, predominantly to SOEs and local governments.[5]

By 2010, the worst of the crisis seemed to be over—GDP growth rebounded to double-digit levels—and the government scaled back bank lending by about a third. But shadow banking—nonbank lending through entities other than government institutions and informal channels—classified as nonbank credit in Figure 5.1, quickly emerged to fill the gap, and by 2012, nonbank credit accounted for 40 percent of the new credit—more than double its share before the crisis.

The riskier elements of shadow banking in the form of loans from trusts and informal sources were reigned in after 2013, but in 2015, nonbank credit soared again. This was the result of the large volume of bonds issued by local authorities to reduce their bank debt levels and the smaller banks relying on WMPs to fund loans since they lacked the household deposit base of the major SOCBs.

Altogether, the bank-credit stimulus and shadow-banking boom pushed China's debt to over 250 percent of GDP—higher than most emerging market economies but lower than most high-income countries and about the same as the United States (see Figure 5.2).[6] This intuitively seems about right, since

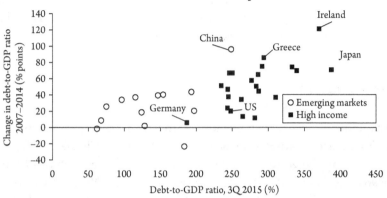

Figure 5.2 Debt Comparisons. Source: Bank for International Settlements total credit statistics; World Bank World Development Indicators

China is neither a developing nor a developed country. What has raised alarm bells, however, is that the speed of the increase in the period after the GFC was much higher than most other countries and by early 2017 some estimates indicate that the ratio is now over 270 percent. Only a handful of countries have experienced an increase in debt as a share of GDP of the same magnitude as China, and most of them—such as Greece and Ireland—experienced a financial crisis. Thus it seems reasonable to conclude that China will also suffer the same fate. But China is different in many critical aspects.

Though credit booms can bring new risks, they can also bring beneficial financial deepening and economic growth. An IMF report explains that only a third of these booms result in a financial crisis.[7] Further, countries that experienced credit booms between 1970 and 2010 saw 50 percent more growth in per-capita incomes over the same period than countries that experienced no credit booms.

What is more, while almost all financial crises are preceded by credit booms, China has none of the external vulnerabilities that often trigger a crisis, with a current account surplus of around 3 percent of GDP, external debt of only 10 percent of GDP, ample reserves in relation to external needs despite the recent decline, and a currency that is generally seen as appropriately valued.[8] In contrast, crisis countries are typically running significant current account deficits of around 3–5 percent of GDP, burdened with a large share of external debt, and lacking flexibility because of minimal amounts of foreign reserves and low household savings rates.

Similarly, China's banks are highly liquid and not particularly vulnerable to a US-style freeze of the interbank lending market. Loan-to-deposit ratios are not high, and the major banks are minimally dependent on large institutional accounts, drawing instead on a huge population of household savers. In short, aside from some of the smaller regional banks, China's banking sector is flush with deposits. Household debt has increased rapidly because of the rising share of mortgages, but it remains manageable relative to household incomes.

Corporate Debt

The clearest area of concern for China is corporate debt, and its size sets China apart from other countries. Over 80 percent of the rise in China's debt-to-GDP ratio can be attributed to the explosive growth of corporate debt, which rose from 96 percent of GDP in 2007 to over 160 percent of GDP in 2016. It is much more menacing than household debt and now makes up 60 percent of China's total debt. Even so, the risks associated with rising corporate debt in China are mitigated by the fact that much of it is concentrated in state-dominated sectors where government support is available. Moreover, industrial profitability, while declining, has remained broadly acceptable.

China's large corporate debt share also reflects relatively underdeveloped equity markets and the exceptional role household savings play in the banking system. Consequently, firms—especially the larger state enterprises and local governments—find it much easier to borrow from commercial banks than to tap bond and equity markets for financing. This holds true even for investments with long gestation periods, such as infrastructure.

Although corporate leverage in China has risen significantly, it is not clear that it has reached crisis levels. Despite the sharp increase, China's current level is still well below the median debt-to-equity ratios of the AFC countries in the year before the crisis.[9]

There is also little evidence that this overall rise in corporate leverage has led to widespread financial stress among firms. Wells Fargo analyzed the financial position of the industrial sector in 2013, which accounted for 60 percent of China's corporate debt, and found little cause for alarm.[10] Revenues have kept pace with debt accumulation in the industrial sector and, contrary to popular perceptions, interest expenses for most industrial firms as a share of revenues have not increased excessively.

An IMF study indicated that private firms had reduced their debt burden over time, but SOEs have increased their leverage.[11] These firms are concentrated in real estate and construction as well as mining and utilities, largely from borrowing to increase capacity as part of the GFC stimulus program. There is a high degree of concentration of debt among these firms. For example, only sixty firms, mainly state owned, accounted for two-thirds of the liabilities in the real estate and construction sector among the two thousand firms surveyed.

In a more recent study using data through the end of 2015, the research firm Gavekal estimates that the share of financially troubled and money-losing firms is around 10 percent, a ratio that is not unusual.[12] This compares with 7–8 percent in 2011, so there has been some deterioration with the slowdown, but the comparable number was over 20 percent in 1998 during the AFC, which at that time necessitated massive layoffs. In sum, there is still no indication that debt servicing has become an unmanageable burden as a general issue, and while profit margins have declined recently, they are not distressingly low.

Still, there are prominent pockets of weakness. The steel, cement, coal, aluminum, sheet glass, and shipbuilding sectors are not as productive as other sectors, as capacity utilization rates have fallen sharply.[13] Firms in these sectors account for 10 percent of industrial assets but only 2 percent of industrial profits, and their return on assets is less than half that of the industrial sector overall.[14] Utilities and raw materials producers have also become highly leveraged, and the solar energy sector suffers from similar issues of excess capacity and falling, if not negative, profits. Overall, there is a significant impact on financial indicators but less of an impact on GDP growth because the valued added in many of these sectors (which make up GDP) is relatively less pronounced than in other activities.

These sectors' struggles largely reflect the fact that they are dominated by SOEs, which are, as a class, highly leveraged and less commercially oriented. Given their weaker financials as a group and their dominance in high-risk sectors, it is likely that any financial stresses will be concentrated among SOEs and firms heavily involved in property development.

The debt-to-profit ratio of privately listed firms is 5 percent lower than in 2008, compared to a 33 percent rise for state-listed companies, with similar trends observed in other leverage ratios.[15] The contrast between the financial position of private and state companies becomes even sharper when you consider their cash holdings. According to Goldman Sachs, private firms had sixty cents in operating cash flows for each dollar of current liabilities, while central government SOEs had just thirty cents.[16] And as discussed later, SOE returns on assets have declined sharply over the past decade and are now only about half of that of private firms.[17]

These trends should not be surprising. In 2003, the newly installed Hu-Wen government put an end to the widespread privatization and shuttering of underperforming SOEs. This removed the threat of failure and left SOE managers with little reason to behave in a financially responsible manner. Any remaining incentives to behave prudently were eliminated by the postcrisis bank stimulus, when SOEs were charged with propping up growth.

Also providing a cushion for the SOEs—particularly the larger ones—is the fact that they are more likely to be bailed out, thus shifting the liability for their bad debts onto the government. While the government might consider allowing some minor players to go bust as a means of disciplining financial markets, it is very unlikely that it will allow many major players to fail. Yet it is precisely the firms most likely to be bailed out that are most likely to mismanage themselves into requiring a bailout.

Some studies have shown that the larger firms have been increasing their net debt-to-earnings ratios in recent years, while smaller ones have actually delever-aged since the financial crisis.[18] Even if the financial risks are not entirely con-centrated in SOEs, much of the bad debt is likely to land on the government's balance sheet in one way or another. The government has previously bailed out private firms that are seen as strategically important for localities.[19]

As in any emerging economy, there will be genuine defaults in the cor-porate sector that the government does not absorb. In the first half of 2016, defaults of a major SOE, Dongbei Steel, and a half dozen other companies shook the bond markets, causing prices to fall and new issues to be post-poned.[20] But studies have suggested that the actual numbers of bond defaults are likely to be only a couple percent of those coming due.[21] Such defaults are not out of the ordinary for a large emerging economy in the midst of structural changes, especially given the need to reduce capacity in some sectors. They are unlikely to be significant enough to jeopardize the financial system. What is more, most of these defaults will be well anticipated—and well-anticipated defaults rarely cause crises. Any spillovers that occur are likely to be limited to other financially weak companies in similarly excess capacity sectors. That is not an entirely undesirable outcome, since China needs a process to weed out nonviable firms.

Local and Central Government Debt

Government debt, which is incurred predominantly at the local level, is not as high as corporate debt, nor has it grown as dramatically. For these and other rea-sons, central and local government debt is unlikely to prompt a financial crisis, but its complex and opaque structure may hide unpredictable risks. As pressure is applied to instill more discipline in local financing, there will also be a signifi-cant fiscal contraction with negative near-term growth consequences as evident in a prolonged economic slowdown.

The strength of the central government's balance sheet on its own merits is uncontroversial: it had debt of just 29 percent of GDP in 2009, and it fell to around 25 percent at the end of 2014, according to IMF data. But this is an incomplete picture of the government's financial health, because it does not account for China's local governments, which take on the majority of the public debt while being implicitly guaranteed by the central government.

Unfortunately, accounting for local debt is easier said than done. Local governments in China have been prohibited from officially running deficits or issuing debt since 1994. This has forced them to take a more circuitous route to finance their expenditures. In particular, local governments rely heavily on local government financing vehicles (LGFVs). These are SOEs set up by local governments to conduct activities that would normally be undertaken directly by the governments themselves, such as building roads and power plants.

Local governments support LGFVs with cash injections or state land transfers, which LGFVs then use as collateral to borrow from banks and capital markets. LGFVs invest that cash in projects to develop the local economy, particularly via infrastructure or new housing developments. The distinction between LGFVs and other local government SOEs is blurred and controversial, but even under the conservative official definition there are more than ten thousand LGFVs active in the country.

The borrowing of LGFVs through bank loans and bond issuance is relatively transparent and easily tracked through periodic financial disclosures by the LGFVs or the banks that lend to them. Local governments also borrow through the less transparent shadow-banking system. Such borrowing is not regularly disclosed and is difficult to track, forcing observers to rely on rough estimates and sporadic audits.

However, in December 2013, the government announced the results of the most comprehensive audit of local government debt to date, which indicated that shadow banks and other forms of nonbank financing grew from $360 billion at the time of the 2011 audit to almost $1.2 trillion in June 2013. The audit results indicate that the expansion in local government debt is predominantly occurring through shadow banking and other informal arrangements, since generally the local governments are not allowed to borrow from the formal banking system for investment needs. According to the audit, local government debt by June 2013 stood at just over 33 percent of GDP, up from 27 percent in 2010.

Adding the audit's estimate of central government debt to the estimate of local government debt leaves China's total public debt at about 60 percent of GDP in 2016, which is not alarming compared with other major economies. This is still much lower than most developed countries, in line with the generally recognized prudent ceiling of 60 percent, and lower than the other BRIC economies of India and Brazil.

Moreover, unlike other countries, China can directly access valuable assets should it actually run into debt-servicing problems. According to the Chinese Academy of Social Sciences, China's foreign exchange reserves are roughly equal in size to China's expected government debt.[22] The government's land holdings are also valuable, although the usage rights for much of the land have already been allocated. Finally, the combined assets of China's 100,000 SOEs are worth roughly $13 trillion according to the Ministry of Finance. After accounting for SOE debt, the net asset value of SOEs is $4.4 trillion, or roughly 50 percent of GDP.[23] While it is true that many of these assets cannot be easily liquidated during a cash crunch, they can help finance a bailout over several years, and their mere existence can head off a sudden loss of confidence.

Local Government's Fiscal Problems

Although the government is clearly solvent, LGFVs and the localities that support them do face short-term liquidity challenges. Much of the debt they have incurred is in the form of short-term loans from banks or borrowing through the shadow-banking system with short maturities. As a result, many are experiencing liquidity shortages. Most LGFVs are strong enough to cover interest payments, so debts are likely to be rolled over. Although such rollovers tie up banks' working capital and prevent them from lending to more productive new projects, they represent a slow restructuring of local government debts rather than a crisis. In addition, nearly 4 trillion renminbi of bonds are being issued to replace some of the bank debt. With lower interest rates and longer maturities, this will also help moderate the servicing burden over time.

Beyond short-term liquidity challenges, there are at least three long-term vulnerabilities associated with local government debt: the misaligned fiscal system, incentives for local officials to overinvest, and the lack of transparency in local finances. Prior to the opening up of the economy in 1980, the government relied on the artificially protected profits of SOEs to pad its budget. When economic reforms were introduced, SOE profits plummeted and government's revenues fell precipitously to around 10 percent of GDP until the major fiscal reform in 1994 which introduced new valued-added and consumption taxes.

The restructured fiscal system has steadily increased government revenue, which is currently around 22 percent of GDP, but it has also created an imbalance between the central and local governments. While the local governments were left responsible for funding more than 70 percent of government expenditures, they only collect about half of the tax revenue.[24] Transfers from the central government address some of this gap, but this fiscal misalignment drives much of their reliance on borrowing and, more recently, land development. Giving local authorities access to more reliable revenue sources and a larger share of the fiscal pie is necessary to ensure their long-term financial sustainability.

At the same time, local officials were until recently evaluated almost entirely by their ability to produce economic growth. This incentive structure has been integral to China's economic success over the past three decades, but it has also come at the cost of creating a system that favors short-term growth over long-term financial, environmental, and social sustainability. Although much local investment is still necessary as China rapidly urbanizes and develops its transportation network, local officials' incentives are more closely aligned with investing heavily than they are with investing productively, leading to overinvestment and overindebtedness. In addition, local governments are highly exposed to rising interest rates because much of their borrowing has to be refinanced annually, and some are ill-prepared to manage risks.

Dealing with Fiscal Misalignment

These concerns have not gone unaddressed. The economic reform plan announced following the 2013 Third Plenum meeting of the Party leadership gave pride of place to reforms intended to better align the fiscal system.[25] A portion of spending on social services is to be transferred to the central government to lighten the burden on local finances, and local revenues are to be increased through the expansion of taxes that flow directly to local governments. The government also seems to recognize the need for more holistic assessments of local officials' performance, announcing in late 2013 that a variety of factors, including local debt levels, will be incorporated going forward.[26] This will hopefully encourage the development of better risk management systems and help to improve the structure of local debt.

While these steps are not a complete solution, they show that China's leadership understands the vulnerabilities posed by the structure of the fiscal system and local officials' incentives and that they are serious about remedying them. What is less clear is how the leadership intends to improve the transparency of local government debt. China's leaders have moved to use more local government bonds, which will help because bond financing involves rating agencies and formal audits. In early 2014, the government selected a few localities and cities to launch a pilot bond-financing program amounting to 3.6 trillion renminbi to supplement their revenue needs. This has been extended to other localities, but the local governments included thus far were specifically selected because of their relatively strong financial positions. This has left unresolved the problem of improving the transparency of the localities most in need of reforms.

The main cause for some optimism lies in the June 2014 decision by the Politburo to authorize comprehensive reform of the fiscal system by 2016.[27] The fiscal reform package aims to reduce these local budget deficits by expanding the value-added tax to include services and instituting new resource and property taxes. It also calls for the restructuring of local government debts and the elimination of loans backed by land. Multi-year budgeting may reduce incentives for off-budget revenue collection to meet short-term fiscal targets, and local officials will be assessed in part on how prudently they manage their debts. While much work is still needed to make intentions actionable, political support for this initiative is still tentative given differing interests at the various levels of government.

Implementation of the fiscal reform agenda will take years, but the more immediate concern is the impact of declining revenue growth as the economy slows down, combined with restrictions on local government borrowings and land sales which have provided a large share of their revenues in recent years. In the absence of increased fiscal support from the central government, a major fiscal contraction could lead to an even sharper decline in GDP growth than the government has indicated. To offset the fiscal contraction at local levels, there has been a significant increase in the budget deficits in excess of the government's announced intentions since 2015 along with increased funding from the policy banks such as the China Development Bank and greater use of private and public partnerships to support infrastructure needs.

Shadow Banking

Cutting across both corporate and local government debt is the issue of shadow banking. Broadly construed, shadow banking includes informal lending between individuals and companies, loans made by nonbank financial institutions like trusts and investment funds, and some common banking practices like bankers' acceptances. Some would even include bond financing, although for our purposes this is not counted. In China, there is no formal definition of what activities constitute shadow banking, leading many to simply refer to all lending activities that occur outside of banks or off of bank balance sheets as shadow banking.

The most useful definitions of shadow banking, from the perspective of financial stability, are those that include all systemically important activities while omitting marginal forms of lending as well as more institutionalized channels such as bonds. In particular, activities that are strongly linked to the formal banking sector, namely WMPs and bankers' acceptances, and those that are large relative to the size of the economy, namely trust products and entrust loans, are the key components of shadow banking. Minor activities, such as underground lending, are excluded here.[28]

Estimates that are in line with this definition place shadow banking at around 50–60 percent of GDP or around 25–30 percent of banking assets in China. These figures are not abnormal in international comparisons of shadow banking. The Financial Stability Board (FSB) estimates that globally, shadow banking averaged about 117 percent of GDP in the major OECD economies and 52 percent of banking assets, more than double the figures for China. In at least three other major emerging markets, shadow banking represents a larger share of banking assets than it does in China (see Figure 5.3).[29]

Opinions on the issue of shadow banking in China are divided. Many financial experts have noted that shadow banking is more responsive to the needs of private enterprises that have traditionally lacked access to the state-dominated banking system and that those enterprises have played a major role in driving productivity growth and employment.[30] The People's Bank of China estimates that half of all the firms it regularly surveys have accessed some form of shadow banking.[31]

Others are alarmed by the rise of shadow banking in China because it is widely perceived to be more risky than traditional bank lending, which is subject to more stringent oversight. As with the broader debt, concerns about China's shadow-banking system often focus on its rapid growth rather than its absolute level. Shadow-banking activities in China expanded dramatically since the end of the credit-fueled stimulus in 2009, accounting for roughly a quarter of the outstanding credit stock until recently.[32] Much of the growth in shadow banking was driven by the surge in property related financing. In 2014, shadow banking was scaled back significantly as the property market cooled off and local governments turned to bond financing to reduce their debt burdens. More recently, shadow banking has resurfaced in response to movements in the property market and a rise in WMPs being issued by the smaller banks as a means to secure funding to increase their loan-making capacity.

Regardless, rapid growth of shadow banking is not atypical of emerging markets in recent years. According to the FSB, seven major emerging market countries have experienced growth above 15 percent, and China's pattern is broadly

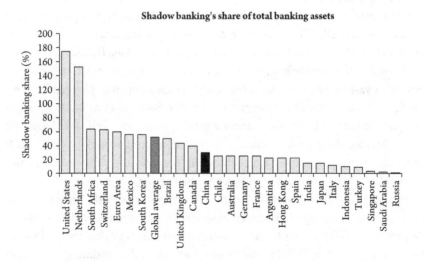

Shadow banking's share of total banking assets

Figure 5.3 Shadow Banking Comparisons. Source: Financial Stability Board; JP Morgan Chase

similar but more affected by property-related activities. Such growth rates should not be considered inherently problematic for countries developing their nascent shadow-banking systems from a very low base.

Risks behind the Numbers

While such aggregate numbers make for good headlines, they are not particularly helpful for assessing the risks associated with shadow banking. There is much more to the story. An implication of the term "shadow banking" is that diverse and distinct forms of nonbank credit can be grouped together under the same heading and thought of in the same way. In reality, each form of credit exhibits a dramatically different risk profile. Pointing to the riskiness of one form of shadow banking—as some of the most vocal critics do—and then citing the overall amount of shadow banking gives a misleading perception of the magnitude of the risks.

Broadly, there are two ways in which a shadow-banking sector can pose a risk. The first is direct: credit risk is increased by lending to financially weak borrowers. For this to become a serious issue, such lending must also be large in magnitude so that the potential losses are significant relative to the economy. The second form of risk comes when a shadow banking sector is strongly interconnected with the rest of the financial system. This channel was critical to transforming relatively modest losses on mortgage portfolios in the United States into a systemic financial crisis in 2008.[33] In China's heavily bank-based financial system, the primary risk comes from interconnectedness between shadow banking and the commercial banks.

Each form of shadow financing—entrust loans, bankers' acceptances, trust companies, and WMPs—should be analyzed regarding risks and on its own merits. Only a fraction of these activities are really risky (see Box 5.1).

Alongside the high-risk, high-return products that draw most of the attention are a vast number of relatively low-risk investments that play healthy and productive roles in facilitating economic activity. Some shadow banking activities pose no extraordinary risks: entrust loans cannot easily spill over to impair banks' balance sheets, and bankers' acceptances are not acutely risky. The real concerns are more narrowly concentrated in the activities of trust companies and banks' WMPs, although even here the risks can be overstated.

In reality, the much-discussed, high-risk components of the shadow banking system are overhyped. All forms of shadow banking amounted to a total of 84 percent of GDP in 2014. The high-risk components of shadow banking—concentrated among WMPs and trust products and accounting for about 18 percent of the total—are unlikely to have exceeded 15 percent of GDP or

Box 5.1 **Shadow Banking Components and Risks**

Entrust loans are a means by which nonfinancial corporations lend to each other. They are often portrayed as riskier than traditional bank loans, but in reality, as much as 80 percent of entrust loans are between related companies. As such, lending through entrust loans is arguably safer and more efficient than the average bank loan due to lower information asymmetries between companies that are familiar with each other. That means entrust loans pose virtually no direct threat to financial stability—even if the borrower is a high credit risk, the hit of a default will land largely on the company that did the lending, with minimal spillover to the wider financial system.

Bankers' acceptances are a form of short-term credit used to facilitate business activity by having the bank guarantee payment, obviating the need to evaluate whether a business partner is creditworthy. Most acceptances are at least partially collateralized by deposits and backed by underlying transactions, so the threat is modest.

Trust companies—a form of nonbank financial institution unique to China—surpassed insurance companies to become the second-largest type of financial institution in the country after commercial banks. Trust companies function in a way somewhat analogous to investment funds in the West and are authorized to manage assets for enterprises and individuals. But, unlike banks, they are prohibited from taking deposits. Instead of collecting deposits and issuing loans, trusts make loans, purchase securities, or invest in private equity, which they then sell to investors in the form of "trust products" that often offer high interest rates. Because their investment activities are generally riskier, this aspect of shadow banking warrants more attention and regulatory oversight.

Wealth management products (WMPs) are investment products created by banks, but they are often confused for a type of deposit. They are somewhat analogous to a money-market fund offered by a bank. While they may not have introduced additional credit risk, they have generated a variety of other vulnerabilities. What sets WMPs apart is their intrinsic connection to the banks, which creates large spillover risks. A loss of confidence in WMPs could pose significant systemic risk to the banks and the economy. WMPs have been one of the most rapidly expanding elements of the financial system with interest rates somewhat higher than that on bank deposits.

(This box draws on Yukon Huang and Canyon Bosler, "China's Debt Dilemma," Carnegie Endowment, September 2014.)

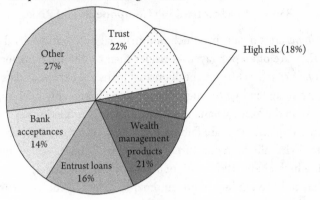

Figure 5.4 Components of Shadow Banking. Source: People's Bank of China; China Banking and Regulatory Commission; China Trust Association; author's calculations

about 6 percent of bank assets (see Figure 5.4).[34] However, the surge in the issuance of WMPs since 2015 to attract household savings has led to renewed concerns about the quality of the loans and assets being used to support the WMPs.

Granted, there are second-order financial risks associated with the shadow banking system, and potentially dangerous situations could arise, such as a vicious cycle in which the unraveling of some portion of shadow banking slows economic growth. Moreover, the authorities have not always been able to deal with such risks appropriately. The consequences could then damage the fiscal health of marginal borrowers, potentially leading to wider systemic consequences. A cascade of improbable events would have to take place for this scenario to happen on a scale that might lead to havoc, and as a whole, this is highly unlikely to occur.

The Workout

Of course, there is always the fallacy of the heap: each individual component of the financial system does not look overly menacing, but the combination of the various risks together could pose a threat. To assess whether the heap is truly more menacing than its individual components, there are stress tests and scenarios that should be explored.

A number of scenarios come from the past; this is not the first time China has faced serious debt strains. Throughout the 1990s, nonperforming loans at China's banks were steadily rising as a result of excessive lending to poorly managed SOEs. The official nonperforming loans of SOCBs reached their peak in 1999, when they accounted for more than 30 percent of loans and about

29 percent of GDP. Unofficial estimates ranged up to as much as 40–50 percent of total loans.[35]

China's current challenges may be more complex, but the financial situation in the late 1990s was more severe, and even then the difficulties proved manageable. The government created four asset management companies to buy up nonperforming loans at face value. The central government also injected substantial amounts of capital into the biggest SOCBs so they could write off many of the remaining nonperforming loans. By 2005, the total face cost of these and other efforts to restructure the banks had reached nearly 4 trillion renminbi, or over 40 percent of GDP in 1999.[36]

Although the direct cost of the bailout was immense, it allowed the banks to return to lending and allowed economic growth to accelerate over the coming decade. It is difficult to disentangle the effects of the bailout from other actions that were taken, but it seems likely that the bailout process was successful in forestalling any major growth slowdown and that reforms, along with China's accession to the WTO, were subsequently responsible for the acceleration of the growth rate after 2001. As the banks' balance sheets expanded with new and better loans, nonperforming loans as a share of total loans steadily declined to below 1 percent by the end of the decade.[37] All of this occurred in the context of a modest deleveraging between 2003 and 2008 when nominal GDP growth was outpacing credit growth and gradually pushing down China's debt-to-GDP ratio.

So what are the prospects of a repeat of this successful, if costly, cleanup of the financial sector? This time growth alone cannot solve the problem. The days of double-digit growth and strong external demand are gone. Nevertheless, one can be cautiously optimistic. Even the most pessimistic current estimates of credit losses fall far short of what was observed in the late 1990s and early 2000s, which passed by with no serious macroeconomic fallout.

Although the official number for nonperforming loans is less than 2 percent as of mid-2016, a number of comprehensive exercises of possible scenarios have been done assuming that actual nonperforming loans might be in the 10–15 percent range eventually.[38] These simulations suggest that credit losses might lead recapitalization costs amounting to 10–20 percent of GDP, which would not represent an unmanageable burden for the government.[39] China's financial and fiscal metrics simply do not point to a looming "Lehman moment," despite all the periodic warnings to the contrary.

The IMF's recent study on China's financial risks tries to develop a better estimate of potential nonperforming loans as a trigger to a financial crisis. To the official number of around 2 percent of the loans outstanding, the IMF adds a set of loans that are potentially at risk and concludes that possible losses might amount to as much as 7 percent of GDP. Nevertheless, the IMF says that "they are manageable given existing bank and policy buffers and the continued strong underlying growth in the economy."[40]

The IMF's views, however, have become more worrisome recently. Its 2016 monitoring report was less sanguine in noting: "The near-term growth outlook has improved . . . But the medium-term outlook is clouded by continued resource misallocation, high and rising corporate debt . . . and the increasingly large, opaque and interconnected financial system. The apparent challenges . . . add to concerns that China may exhaust its still-sizable buffers before the economy changes course sufficiently."[41]

Clearly, tough actions are needed to curb the borrowings of local governments by strengthening their revenue base and restructuring their debt burden by converting bank loans into longer-term and lower-interest bonds. Fortunately, the corporate debt problem, while large in magnitude, is concentrated among a few specific activities and a small set of the larger SOEs, most notably the steel and coal sectors. In 2016, plans were initiated to curb lending for new steel and coal projects that did not meet national objectives and for firms that could not service their borrowings.[42] The consequence is that some bankruptcies will need to take place and in that anticipation, new safety net programs have been created to assist the localities and firms with the costs.

Property Market Correction

Although financial woes are unlikely to bring China to its knees, an overbuilt property market can and is having a significant impact on short-term growth. Over the past decade, land prices in China have surged nearly fivefold in renminbi terms (about 6.5 times in dollar terms) according to the Wharton/NUS/ Tsinghua Chinese Residential Land Price Index while the construction sector has expanded from 10 to 13 percent of GDP (see Figure 5.5).[43] With such a dramatic increase in land and property prices and a glut of housing, this has understandably led to concerns that China may be experiencing a property bubble. These concerns were brought to a head by deteriorating sales figures and some price cuts in 2014, but from late 2015 into 2016 prices surged again in selected major cities with the latest round of monetary easing and an easing in ownership eligibility.

A correction will probably occur at some point, but the impact is less likely to manifest itself in sharp price declines than in a prolonged slowdown in construction-related investment, especially in China's second- and third-tier cities. Unlike other bubble-afflicted economies, growth in China's land prices coincided with the emergence of a real property market that did not exist until a process for privatizing housing was initiated in the late 1990s. Because of this,

Land prices increase fivefold

Figure 5.5 Land Price Increases. Source: Wharton/NUS/Tsinghua Chinese Land Price Indexes; author's calculations

the sharp rise in property prices is more indicative of the market trying to establish appropriate prices for an asset whose value had previously been hidden by the socialist system, a pattern also observed in Russia after the fall of the Soviet Union.[44] Although this does not rule out the possibility of a more "traditional" bubble, it does suggest that much of the rise could reflect the true underlying value of land. Further, it means that rapidly rising land prices alone cannot be interpreted as evidence of a bubble.

Further, there are strong fundamental drivers of urban housing demand that suggest China suffered from undersupply until a few years ago. Over the past decade China has been experiencing the largest population movement in history with an average of around twenty million migrants a year moving into urban areas, driving exceptionally strong demand for new housing.[45] Similarly, explosive growth of urban wages has increased the affordability of housing despite rising prices and has driven massive upgrading demand as households seek out more spacious and modern apartments. Even more demand comes from the need to replace old communist-era housing stock.

Thanks to a construction boom following the GFC, China's housing supply, however, has overshot the already substantial market demand in the post- GFC years. The oversupply of housing varies regionally, with the excess much more serious in the smaller cities than in the megacities.

Widespread distortions are also artificially inflating demand for property. For one, Chinese households have limited investment options; the closed capital account leaves few avenues for savers seeking returns higher than savings deposits can provide. Real estate is treated as an investment vehicle in China to fill the gap. According to the China Household Finance Survey, 18 percent of households own more than one home, suggesting that demand for property as an investment vehicle is substantial.[46] Moreover, the fact that China does not tax property, aside from ongoing pilot programs in Shanghai and Chongqing, means that there are lower costs to purchasing and holding unused property. Much of this activity had been curbed in recent years as the government has gradually tightened restrictions on multiple home ownership and improved mortgage standards, but these restrictions have been lifted and reinstated depending on the locality.

Overall, a correction is necessary, especially in the secondary and tertiary cities, and the investment incentives that fed the bubble curbed to encourage a continued decline in construction activity. It is difficult to evaluate the balance between the fundamental drivers of the expansion of the property market and irrational distortions, making a confident assessment of how severe the correction might be impossible. Still, there are some reasons to believe that the correction will not be financially destabilizing for either households or the banking sector.

First, the trends in land and housing prices in China are inconsistent with the typical pattern of a bubble. In a typical bubble, investors buy not because they see value in what they are buying but because they expect the price to continue rising. Thus, when prices show signs of falling (or even just slowing) growth, investors rush for the door and cause a collapse.

Prices in China have fallen in the past such as during the GFC and in 2011, followed by rebounds after the GFC and in 2012 and now again in 2016. These rebounds suggest that rising prices were being supported by something more real and persistent than "irrational exuberance." This also suggests that the 2012–2014 levels may represent a reasonable floor, implying that any correction is unlikely to be more than 10–20 percent depending on locality. Such a fall would not have serious economic consequences and is dwarfed by the 30–50 percent collapses in the United States and Japan.

The other reason to be relatively sanguine about the severity of a price correction is that China's property market is not highly dependent on leverage. Since down payments on property as a share of the purchase price are much higher in China than in the United States, it is less likely that banks will be drawn into a foreclosure process in the event of a major downturn.[47] The results of the China Household Finance Survey indicate that even after a 30 percent decline in prices, only 3 percent of households would be underwater thanks to high down payments and the equity accumulated over the course of their ownership.[48] The highly leveraged property developers that account for the other third of banks' direct exposure are more concerning. Although those developers have been building up large liquidity buffers, some will certainly default given a significant correction, although this will not destabilize the financial system.

The strength of the household balance sheets and its limited exposure to the property sector has led the Bank of China to estimate that even a 30 percent drop in real estate prices would have a negligible impact on banks' nonperforming loan ratios.[49]

While the likely price correction may not be a major issue, scaled-back construction is having a negative impact on economic activity. Construction and real estate have been gradually rising as a share of GDP over the past three decades (see Figure 5.6). As with property prices, these sectors have not exhibited the pattern common to other bubble economies during the AFC—such as Korea or Malaysia—of a very sharp increase in share over a short period. However, amounting to 13 percent of GDP as of 2013, construction and real estate have become important components of China's economy. And accounting for related industries, such as steel, cement, and construction equipment, would show that construction's contribution approaches 20 percent of GDP. This makes China's economy vulnerable to a construction downturn.

That downturn has been underway for several years already and will have likely subtracted two to three percentage points from GDP by the time it is over. But the actual impact of the correction on GDP growth is likely to be moderated because the entire correction need not occur in a single year and because increases in infrastructure investment are compensating for a portion of the decline in housing construction. Demand is also likely to rise as China's urbanization plan is further implemented, which will reduce the magnitude of the adjustment that must take place.[50]

As a result of these factors, it would be reasonable to expect GDP growth to decline to 6 or even 5.5 percent over the next year or two (2017–2019) as the property sector continues to work through the oversupply of housing. But the darker scenarios in which growth collapses to 3 percent or lower are highly unlikely.

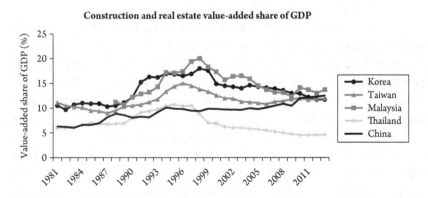

Figure 5.6 Construction Share of GDP. Source: CEIC; UBS Investment Bank; author's estimates

Many bears on China retort that even if the current situation is manageable, it is just a matter of time until China hits its debt constraint. Some argue that the only way China can avoid a financial crisis is for growth to collapse to the low single digits.[51] Similarly, the Fitch Ratings Report in 2013 elevated concerns about shadow banking and ever-rising debt levels.[52] The argument being made is that the only thing that has kept growth so high recently in China is the even faster growth of credit.

To the extent that growth has become solely dependent on credit-fueled investment with a sharp drop-off in returns, this line of reasoning is plausible. However, one need not be so pessimistic about the economy's potential to generate more productivity-driven growth. Nor should one overlook the role that credit has played in establishing market values for land-based assets whose true worth was blurred by poorly defined property rights in China's evolving socialist system.

Property Market and Investment Rates

The more pessimistic narrative misunderstands how credit is being used in China. Much of the credit surge has been financing rising prices for property and other assets, but such increases are not included in calculating GDP growth. If these asset price increases are sustainable, however, current concerns over the debt buildup are exaggerated.

Here, the definitional difference between fixed asset investment (FAI) and gross fixed capital formation (GFCF) becomes important. Both concepts are measures of investment, but FAI measures investment in physical assets, including land, while GFCF measures investment in new equipment and structures, excluding the value of land. While GFCF contributes directly to GDP, only a portion of FAI shows up in the GDP numbers.

For some time, the distinction between the two concepts did not matter in interpreting economic trends because the two measures moved in lockstep in the national accounts, reaching 35 percent of GDP by 2003. Since then, the two have diverged, and GFCF now stands at around 45 percent of GDP while the share of FAI has jumped to 80 percent (see Figure 5.7). According to Goldman Sachs, fully two-thirds of this divergence can be attributed to growing differences in asset prices, particularly the increasing value of land.[53]

Overall credit levels and especially shadow banking have increased in line with the rapid growth in FAI rather than the more modest growth in GFCF. Given that the major distinction between the two measures of investment is the inclusion of land-related transactions, including price increases, this suggests that such transactions accounted for an increasingly large share of credit. In light

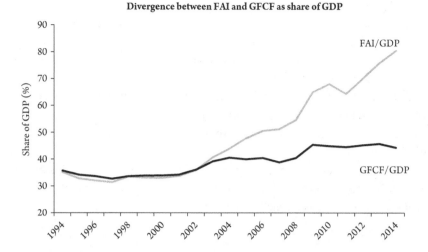

Figure 5.7 Investment and Growth Impact. Source: World Bank World Development Indicators; author's calculations

of the fivefold increase in the price of land over the past decade, it is not surprising that there has been a sharp decline in the impact of credit on GDP growth since it essentially has been facilitating the purchase and transfer of land-related assets whose prices have been soaring.

While some of this was wasted on speculative real estate projects, including the many examples of ghost towns, the bulk of it represents financial deepening and the unlocking of the hidden value of land. Once those values have been market validated, land price growth and the amount of credit being channeled to these uses will level off. That current property prices are broadly sustainable is supported by comparisons with property markets elsewhere. Few realize that property prices in Beijing and Shanghai in 2014, for example, were still only about half of the levels of New Delhi and Mumbai.[54] Moreover, affordability has been increasing as incomes rose faster than property prices. Eventually, China's property market needs to stabilize to facilitate a gradual shift in the allocation of credit back toward growth-enhancing investments.

Solving the Debt Problem through Productivity Gains

The prolonged slowdown in China's economy has generated a fierce debate about whether the country needs a new "growth model." All economies, however, are guided by the same growth models developed decades ago showing that growth depends on increasing investment and labor along with productivity or technological change. These principles have not changed.

The problem is that productivity of investment in China has fallen significantly since the GFC.[55] Declining returns on investment are inevitable as an economy matures, but China's decline has been more rapid than usual because of the distortive effects of its huge stimulus program. Addressing these distortions would lead to a significant rebound in productivity.

Some observers have argued that there is a trade-off between near-term growth objectives and implementing reforms. However, the trade-off is overstated. There are still significant gains to be realized from the more efficient use of labor and other resources. The challenge for Beijing is increasing productivity so the economy can grow at a more sustainable rate for the rest of this decade without relying on ever-increasing debt. China's proposed Third Plenum reforms provide the basis for moving forward.

China's Third Plenum Reforms Offer Solutions

Every ten years, after the new leadership is designated, a special session of the Communist Party, called the Third Plenum, is held to lay out policy initiatives. The Third Plenum for Xi Jinping and the other members of the current seven-person standing committee which forms the highest decision-making body in China was held in November 2013.

The summary decision document for that session highlighted fifteen key themes for reform covering sixty areas for action. The document rightly does not mention rebalancing between consumption and investment but does refer to relying more on domestic demand—which could be either consumption or investment—and increasing productivity.[56] This position is broadly on the mark. The Third Plenum proposed three major options for increasing productivity: a more efficient urbanization process, enterprise reform, and a more rational regional allocation of public investment.

URBANIZATION

The growth-enhancing part of the Third Plenum comes partly from setting out the broad objective of narrowing the rural–urban divide, which was detailed in the "New-style Urbanization Plan (2014–2020)" announced in March 2014. The new plan provides a framework for creating more equitable and environmentally sustainable cities. Objectives include increasing the urbanization rate to 60 percent by 2020 while providing more, but not all, migrant workers with full residency (hukou) rights.[57] Because most migrants do not have access to the social services and other opportunities for established residents, official urbanization numbers have overstated the "real" urbanization rates in China.

Smaller and medium-sized cities will now have more flexibility to absorb new migrants, but there is an unfortunate stipulation that the size of the largest cities would be "strictly controlled." A secondary objective is to improve the efficiency of the urbanization process by discouraging urban sprawl and unproductive investments. Domestic demand would be stimulated by the construction of better local transport networks and connecting some three hundred cities to high-speed rail. Weaknesses in the plan include lack of specificity on how these objectives would be met, including financing options and restricting labor flow to the largest cities. The latter is unlikely to succeed since migrants are attracted to where the best jobs are and these have been in the largest cities where the potential productivity gains from urbanization are higher.

The tendency in the past to treat rural and urban areas as separate economic entities has added to the inefficiencies and exacerbated inequalities. This illustrates the continued potential for securing productivity gains from a better-managed urbanization process and moderating spatially driven income differences. Thus the package of Third Plenum reforms, if implemented aggressively, dealing with rationalizing land markets, ensuring more equitable access to social services, and liberalizing labor migration through *hukou* reform has the potential to ratchet up productivity-driven growth and promote equity.[58] This would help capture the large differences between the productivity of workers in rural areas and their urban counterparts. Although China has been urbanizing rapidly, some 44 percent of people remain in rural areas, which suggests that potential productivity gains are still substantial.[59]

Ironically, if Beijing succeeds in these initiatives, continued rural to urban migration would make rebalancing less likely in the near term since these structural shifts tend to reduce labor's share of income and hence the consumption share of GDP. Yet by maintaining rapid economic growth, these shifts would help sustain China's unprecedentedly high rate of consumption growth, further improving the living standards of the average Chinese citizen.

SOE REFORM AND THE PRIVATE SECTOR

Allowing the private sector to play a more prominent role could also unlock massive gains in productivity. This has been a recurring theme over the past decade, but the case for empowering the private sector has never been as strong as it is now. Addressing productivity differences between private and state-owned firms did not matter as much when returns on assets were rising for both groups and differences were narrowing in the years before the GFC. Both cohorts took a hit during the crisis, but rates of return for private firms have since rebounded sharply, hitting 11 percent before falling to 9 percent, while the rates of return for state-owned firms have fallen to 4 percent (see Figure 5.8). This difference of

Figure 5.8 Private and SOE Profitability. Source: CEIC; author's calculations

around five percentage points illustrates the potential productivity and growth benefits that could be secured with reforms.

Reforms that simply call for leveling the playing field between state and private firms will not increase productivity significantly. Liberalizing interest rates and opening up credit allocations to more private firms can help, but bolder policy actions are needed. These include getting the state out of a range of commercial activities and opening up other areas, especially services, for private entry by both domestic and foreign firms.

The government's intentions to reform the enterprise sector were outlined in a September 2015 policy statement and subsequent actions. The statement drew a somewhat tepid public response given its lack of details and intentions to shield the largest and more strategic SOEs from privatization while allowing for minority private participation. It also indicated a reluctance to shed poorly performing firms. But the statement also provided opportunities for improving the performance of the commercially oriented SOEs and holding managers more accountable while also allowing personnel policies to reflect business practices.

The major ambiguities lie in how classification of firms will be handled and the way that newly created investment or holding companies will operate. The intention is to classify SOEs into public services and commercial subcategories that will be treated differently regarding the extent of state involvement and control. But the decision as to which category firms will belong to is largely determined by the firms themselves and by local officials with interest in protecting the status quo. The investment company referred to as State Capital Investment and Operating Companies could, in theory, play an active or passive role in how a firm operates but thus far there is little evidence that a strong push toward reforms will emerge in a system where insider control remains largely unchanged.

There remains an urgent need for a major restructuring of SOEs operating in areas with excess capacity, notably the heavy and commodity-intensive industries such as steel and power generation. The reason for the poor performance of these SOEs is the decline in their "turnover" rate for inventories, which indicates excess capacity and delays in cutting back production. Consolidation and some bankruptcies are necessary. This intention is part of the government's so-called supply initiative announced in early 2016, but the pace of implementation has been slow.

Reforms to curb the privileged position of SOEs would address many of the vulnerabilities in China's financial system. Most SOEs benefit from explicit or implicit government guarantees that give them and their creditors few incentives to limit their borrowings. This has made SOEs the primary bad actors driving the excessive accumulation of corporate debt. Curbing them will free up capital for more productive small and medium-sized private enterprises (SME). But for this to happen, opening up protected activities to private firms—both domestic and foreign—is critical. This is particularly important in services since China has one of the most restrictive investment regimes in the world (see Chapter 8).

DISTORTED REGIONAL INVESTMENT ALLOCATION

Finally, productivity could be enhanced by rationalizing the allocation of public investments across regions (see Chapter 4). Currently, investments in the interior provinces, especially the far west, have been given priority because of political as well as equity concerns. This strategy has encouraged overly elaborate infrastructure projects and excess property construction. Although these investments have had some success in reducing regional disparities, they are a costly remedy since economic returns on most projects in the far west are much lower than along the coast. There is more to be gained by facilitating migration of labor from isolated regions rather than by trying to channel more infrastructures to those areas.

Whether China will implement the necessary reforms to improve the efficiency of the urbanization process, allow the private sector to play a more prominent role, and rebalance its regional investment strategies remains to be seen. As a general principle, the Third Plenum policy statement called for the market to play a "decisive role" in the economy but also signaled the contradictory intention that SOEs would continue to play a "dominant" role. Should the allocation of resources be increasingly guided by market principles and the various productivity-enhancing reforms identified are rigorously implemented, together they could boost China's growth rate by up to one to two percentage points annually, making the March 2016 announced growth target for the Thirteenth Five Year Plan of 6.5 percent achievable in principle.

FISCALS REFORMS TO INCREASE DOMESTIC DEMAND

Many of the distortions in China's economy have come to be reflected in the current financial problems, but their origins lie in its broken fiscal system. The privileges of SOEs have encouraged irresponsible behavior that has generated excess capacity, encouraged overbuilding, and accounted for much of the growth in corporate debt. Though China will likely avoid a hard landing, it must enact more decisive fiscal reforms to prevent the country's current problems from recurring.

Without a revamped fiscal system, the government remains excessively dependent on bank credit for public spending. Many of the recent reforms, including eliminating controls on interest rates, have focused on financial liberalization. The general assumption for more than a decade has been that China's interest rates were too low, but with financial liberalization they have instead fallen since the GFC, suggesting that they actually may have been too high (see Box 4.1). Given China's fiscal and financial system, interest rate liberalization will do little to inhibit the unsustainable accumulation of local government debts. Instead, the budget must be strengthened and government revenues increased. Shifting the responsibility for funding public services from the banks back to the fiscal system would also foster greater transparency and accountability and thus help address corruption.

However, the short-term impact of curbing land sales of local governments on top of the economic slowdown is taking its toll on fiscal revenues. The consequences will require a delicate balancing act, coupling some monetary easing with larger than anticipated fiscal deficits if GDP growth is to be kept close to the official targets for 2017 and later. This means that even with the requisite reforms, the debt-to-GDP ratio will continue to rise for at least another year or two.

Fiscal reforms are also essential to solving the problem of inadequate domestic "demand." Unique to China, the demand problem is that households have less control over assets, notably land and key natural resources, which the state owns. Thus, compared to typical market-based economies, households in China derive less spendable income from nonwage sources in the form of dividends, rents, and transfers. Income from property amounts to around 5 percent of disposable income in China, whereas the average for other countries tends to be around 10–20 percent. Transfers from the government amount to less than 10 percent in China but average around 25 percent for other countries.[60] The burden for increasing consumer demand rests with altering the role of the state in providing services and transfers for households in ways that are market friendly but also respect China's state-dominated economy.

Surprisingly for a socialist economy, China's government expenditures as a share of GDP lag far behind OECD countries.[61] Consolidated government expenditures are less than 30 percent of GDP and, even after adding expenditures financed by off-budget revenues and land sales, total expenditures are about 35 percent of GDP compared with 45 percent for OECD economies. Further, the proportion of government spending that goes to social services and transfers is only about two-thirds the level of comparable middle-income economies.

These fiscal reforms would provide a stronger revenue base, realign social services responsibilities and allow increasing government expenditures to provide the necessary demand to utilize existing capacity. Together with productivity-enhancing reforms, this would offset the loss in demand caused by curbing wasteful investment spending. A China that better balances the supply and demand aspects of growth would be capable of growing in line with targets for the remainder of this decade and beyond.

LOOKING FORWARD

The increasing pessimism these days is the result of the continued decline in monthly economic indicators along with renewed concerns about China's rising debt-to-GDP ratio and reemergence of shadow banking. This should not have been a surprise given the time required to work off its excess property stock and reduce capacity in the heavy industries.[62]

China's slowdown is the result of a double whammy—a combination of a longer-term structural decline typical of a maturing economy on top of a shorter-term cyclical contraction in the aftermath of the GFC. While its debt problem is serious and needs to be addressed, it is highly unlikely to produce the crisis that many have been suggesting. For the moment, Beijing has little choice except to let the cyclical downturn play itself out while tightening up on financial management and strengthening accountability to reduce the risks of moral hazard. But it also needs to move forward on the necessary productivity-enhancing measures and fiscal reforms to increase demand if a moderately rapid growth path is to be sustained.

CHAPTER 6

Emerging Economic, Social, and Political Tensions

Three decades of economic revival have restored much of the vitality that China last displayed two centuries ago when it dominated the global economy. Yet concerns about the economic, social, and political sustainability of its growth path have intensified, and corruption is now seen as threatening the legitimacy of the Communist Party. The new leadership has reiterated a commitment to further economic reforms, but the political system, at least in its formal elements, appears to be stuck in a time warp even as societal behavior has become much less constrained when judged against historical benchmarks.[1]

China's impressive growth record has been facilitated by the unique relationship between the power vested at the center and its provinces. This has encouraged experimentation and incentivized regional officials to prioritize economic growth—and for the most part, this has helped maintain political stability. Rapid growth, however, has not spared China from increasing social unrest over widening disparities, environmental degradation, and economic disputes.

Those focused on the economic slowdown are asking whether a more innovative and services oriented growth process will require less state involvement, thus indirectly raising concerns about the prospects for systemic shifts in governance. More generally, the accountability and capacity of the administrative system are being questioned because of incidents like the 2015 equity market collapse and the deadly Tianjin warehouse explosion. Politically charged initiatives, including President Xi Jinping's tightening of civil liberties, have intensified discussions about the potential for governance reforms that would be acceptable to the Communist Party and yet responsive to the needs of a more sophisticated society.

Among former premier Wen Jiabao's parting thoughts as he left the scene in 2012 was that dealing with pressures for political reform would be a high priority for China's incoming leadership. Yet, President Xi has thus far come down firmly against any political liberalization that might weaken the dominance of the Communist Party. Elevating the rule of law and tightening controls on the media, along with the anti-corruption campaign, are seen as supporting this objective. Some interpret this as a consolidation of Xi's authority in preparation for future economic reforms, but others see similarities with the more rigid policies in the prereform era.

Discussions about China's political evolution are normally grounded in debates over democratization, military security, and human rights. The focus here is on the economic perspective, beginning with how China's economic transformation has affected social and economic outcomes and the likelihood of political liberalization.

Later, we will link this discussion to the views laid out by Daron Acemoglu and James Robinson that one cannot separate politics and economics in the determination of a country's development prospects.[2] In particular, they argue that successful countries are those with "inclusive" institutions and these are unlikely to exist within authoritarian regimes. But China is different in the sense that its unique decentralized system has led to more inclusive outcomes even if political expression has been tightly controlled. More generally, many observers have noted the contrasts between the U.S. and Chinese versions of market-led versus state-led capitalism. Yet there may be more similarities than differences in the problems both systems face.

Conflict between Economic and Political Liberalization

When Deng Xiaoping opened up the economy more than three decades ago, the premise was that economic liberalization would precede political liberalization. For a generation mired in poverty and coping with the excesses of the Cultural Revolution, hopes for a better material life far outweighed any urgency to channel energies into political expression.

With double-digit growth rates and surveys showing China topping other countries regarding citizens' satisfaction with their economic prospects, any nascent pressures for political reform seemed unlikely to gain traction.[3] But acts of social unrest have grown exponentially, and damaging events such as the Sichuan earthquake (shoddy construction, 2008), a national milk scandal (poor food safety standards, 2008), a high-speed rail crash (weak regulatory regime, 2011), and revelations about senior leaders such as Bo Xilai ("misconduct," 2013–2014) and Zhou Yongkang ("misconduct," 2014–2015) have shaken widely shared but previously largely dormant emotions about accountability, corruption, and justice.[4] With a rising middle class and greater awareness of what is unfolding globally, there is mounting speculation about when and what form political liberalization might take.

Some of these pressures stem from Deng Xiaoping's reforms, which fostered exceptionally rapid growth but also gave rise to disparities and frictions that the social and economic institutions were unprepared to handle (see Chapters 3 and 4). Nor were the local authorities in a position to deal with concerns that reflected more systemic weaknesses in governance without direct guidance from Beijing.

Incidents of social unrest have revealed vulnerabilities in China's decentralized form of government regarding the means employed by local bureaucrats and Party officials to deal with protests. On occasion, senior leaders have expressed concerns that clumsy handling of valid grievances could jeopardize the legitimacy of the Communist Party. China's unfinished reform agenda is now seen as exacerbating social and political tensions and increasing the risks emanating from the current economic slowdown. Thus it is not surprising that some noted China scholars such as David Shambaugh have called this a lethal combination and said that "it is hard not to conclude that we are witnessing its final phase."[5]

Decentralization Affects Economic and Political Liberalization

China is unique compared with other authoritarian regimes in that citizens have traditionally perceived the leadership as having the people's best interests in mind, while they blamed local authorities for what goes wrong in their daily lives. The instances of regime change in the Middle East and earlier cases such as Indonesia reflected the sense that the top was the problem. The situation is different in China, since any oppression of the masses was usually seen as coming from local officials, while the senior leadership residing in Beijing was there to help. This made it unlikely that random disturbances would trigger a fundamental change in the power vested at the center of the system.

China's unique center-local governance arrangements judged provincial leaders against two broad objectives: economic growth and social and political stability (see Figure 6.1). Most of the regional leaders—Party secretaries and governors and, in some cases, major city mayors—are appointed by Beijing, and routinely rotated under the auspices of the Party apparatus. Thus they are more responsive to signals set by the center than by their local constituents.

Beijing provided the regions with the flexibility to experiment with economic reforms in response to the centrally established goals.[6] Resource flows from the center supported the growth and financial targets for each province (see Chapter 3). This system encouraged initiatives to be piloted in the provinces

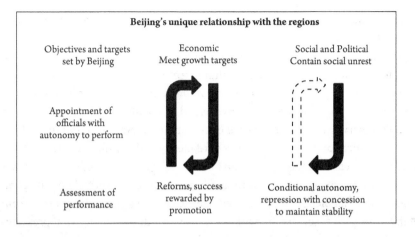

Figure 6.1 Center-Local Relations. Source: Author

before being disseminated nationally. This was the case with many of China's most heralded early reforms and, more recently, with Shanghai's Pilot Special Free Trade Zone, which is now being replicated in several other cities.[7]

Decentralization of responsibilities also allowed provincial leaders to take whatever measures they felt appropriate to maintain social and political stability as long as national economic objectives were not being jeopardized. Unlike economic objectives, where the relevant policy actions are easier to conceptualize and progress is measurable, social and political concerns are harder to assess and the feedback loop—as represented by the arrows between Beijing and the provinces in Figure 6.1—is more tenuous. In the absence of strong civic organizations and effective channels for popular expression, identifying a workable solution has become increasingly difficult under the existing governance arrangements.

Local authorities are often reluctant to use consultative processes to calibrate the preferences of their communities. In turn, affected groups often feel that they have limited options to express grievances except through public demonstrations. Incidents of social unrest are thus used to assess and deal with such grievances in ways that traditionally have helped preserve the legitimacy of the regime.

Such incidents can provide the cue to adjust policies to maintain stability, but compromises often come with reprisals to establish the limits of such protests. This process of "repression with concession" has reinforced the special role of the security apparatus to operate without the constraints that might result from bringing in other perspectives.[8] But using this sort of conditional autonomy to deal with social unrest is also fraught with risks; excessive force can lead to more violent collective actions, and concessions may encourage protestors to extract more from the system.[9]

These arrangements provided incentives for provincial leaders to perform but shielded Beijing from blame if something went wrong locally. The strategy has proven to be exceptionally effective in promoting growth through economic liberalization and has, for the most part, helped to maintain calm in society, even though this has come at the expense of any broad-based movement toward political liberalization.[10] But the increased frequency and significance of social protests have revealed vulnerabilities that can no longer be ignored. President Xi's current campaign against corruption and his elevation of the rule of law combined with a harsher position on civil liberties would seem to be another form of the principle of "concession with repression" for dealing with social pressures while keeping the focus on economic progress.

Disparities, Environmental Degradation, and Social Unrest

The number of incidents of mass social unrest has risen from an officially reported 50,000 annually a decade ago to an unofficial estimate of over 180,000 in recent years.[11] Among the prominent factors identified as reasons for these protests, four stand out. The first relates to a growing sense of injustice over widening income disparities. The second emanates from labor disputes, especially the discriminatory treatment of migrant factory workers. The third comes from conflicts over the use of land and other assets. And the fourth arises from more recent concerns about environmental degradation.

There are also signs that protests brought on by dissatisfaction with the political system have been increasing.[12] In the aftermath of the 2016 Party Congress meetings, such frustrations showed up in circulating letters and website postings about censorship of views that are not blessed by the Party. While economic concerns can be dealt with through concessions if the local authorities have the financial means to do so, protests that challenge the role of the Party or administrative system do not lend themselves as readily to compromises.

Could China's growth strategy have been implemented in ways that would have kept in check these pressures for change in governance? China's growth strategy was unusual for being spatially "unbalanced," in concentrating production along the coast. The competitive edge that this process provided put the country on a rapid growth trajectory, but it also fostered an unusually sharp increase in income disparities that only moderated in recent years as more funding was channeled to the interior provinces.

The Gini coefficient, an indicator of inequality, increased rapidly, approaching 0.5 before leveling off.[13] Unlike many other developing countries, China's worsening income inequality is largely spatial in nature (see Figure 6.2).[14] This is the result of widening income differentials between the coastal and inland provinces and between urban and rural areas (see section on income disparities in Appendix A). Some would call these disparities "good disparities" since they are not the result of stagnant growth in certain segments of society or regions but rather the consequence of unusually high and sustained growth in urban areas and along the coast.

Currently, the ratio of urban to rural per-capita income is about three, and per-capita GDP in the coastal region is more than twice that in the western region. Rural incomes have been increasing by 4–5 percent over the past twenty-five years—which is remarkable by international standards—but this is only about half of the rate of growth in urban incomes. As a result, the trend lines for disparity indicators either level off or reverse during periods of sharply rising rural incomes.

Scholars utilizing alternative approaches or sample surveys have come up with Gini numbers in the range of 0.6 due to recent growth in private activities and wealth effects.[15] Whether the bias in the official numbers is more serious in China than in other countries is unclear, but the pace of economic expansion in China and its nature would suggest that disparities are likely to be significantly worse than the official numbers indicate. Only in recent years have regional disparities begun to moderate, but differences within urban areas are now offsetting most of the gains so that the overall Gini has not declined significantly.

Some have argued that the escalating sense of injustice doesn't stem from realized income inequalities being so extreme since most individuals compare themselves with their neighbors rather than others far away.[16] Instead, it comes more from the feeling that equal access to opportunities has been compromised

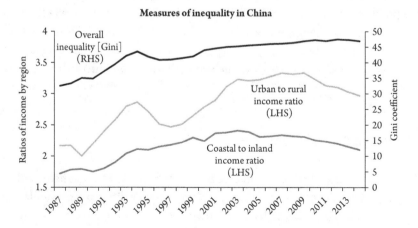

Figure 6.2 Inequality Measures. Source: CIA World Factbook; National Bureau of Statistics of China; author's calculations

despite the dramatically improved living standards in the post-Mao era. The struggle of increasingly larger cohorts of college graduates to find suitable jobs in a tightening market is feeding into these tensions.[17] Discontent has been exacerbated by the lack of rules, preferential treatment of well-connected groups, and a growing perception that personal relationships are now a must for advancement.[18] The many examples of extreme wealth creation from concentrated ownership and exploitation of assets and privileged access to income-generating opportunities is leading to widespread cynicism.

A shift in public opinion is also evident in the escalating public concerns surrounding environmental degradation. For decades, the public's preoccupation was with securing higher incomes, and pollution was a secondary issue. Local officials were motivated largely by investment and growth targets set by central and provincial leaders with little concern about the quality of life. With ambient concentrations of most pollutants exceeding recognized standards several times over, the world's image of Beijing became one of its smog rather than the Great Wall and Forbidden City.

Countless studies have keyed in on the sizable economic costs of pollution, including the hundreds of thousands of deaths that could be avoided if China's air quality was brought in line with acceptable norms. Most of China's major waterways are unfit not only for drinking but also for irrigation. The complexity of the causes and the cost of potential solutions are daunting, ranging from weaning China away from its excessive dependence on cheap coal to reversing industrial and farming practices that have contaminated the country's soil and major rivers.

Only in the last few years, with the growth of a more prosperous and urbanized middle class that is more concerned about quality of life, has there been a change in opinions about the environment. These concerns have now reached the point that China is now as likely as any developed nation to take the lead on global climate change issues. This contributed to the agreements reached between the United States and China on climate change in 2015 during President Xi's visit to the United States and the success of the subsequent Paris climate change accords.

Mitigating Social Concerns

A major weakness of the economic liberalization process was that fiscal and financial systems did not do enough to moderate income differences.[19] While any dynamic growth process will lead to inequalities in outcomes, in China's case its economic institutions did little to maintain what was historically seen as relatively equal access to opportunities.

China's difficulties in responding to emerging needs emanate from the unusually limited role that the budget plays in financing social and environmental expenditures in an economy where the state controls the bulk of resources. While responsibilities for public services have cascaded down to local levels over the years, this has not come with the necessary revenues from the center to fulfill these obligations.[20] Instead, local authorities have increasingly relied on divisive land sales to balance their books.

As indicated in the World Bank's *China 2030* report, even with a major tax reform in 1994, expenditures on social services that were needed to compensate for regional income disparities have been relatively low. Social expenditures amounted to little more than half the levels as a share of GDP of other middle-income countries and a third that of OECD economies (See Table 6.1).[21]

Such low levels have also exacerbated the sense that access to social services has become ever more differentiated by income class. Poorer regions have been provided with less funding on a per-capita basis than better-off coastal areas and have thus been unable to provide the same quality of education and health services. Over time their residents have become increasingly disadvantaged, with less chance of gaining access to the top national universities and better paying jobs. These differential opportunities eventually manifested themselves in increased regional income disparities even as incomes in backward areas increased substantially.[22]

This shortfall reflects limited efforts to develop more equitable cross-provincial revenue-sharing mechanisms commensurate with the needs of a decentralized system. The problem has been made worse because until recently Chinese SOEs did not pay significant dividends to the budget—which could have been used to balance social expenditures. As SOEs profits soared, so did their clout within the political system, which has forestalled moves to alter such policies.[23]

Table 6.1 **China's Budgeted Social Expenditures Are Too Small**
(Budget expenditures as a share of GDP, 2010)

	High Income OECD	Middle Income		China
		Upper	Lower	
Total Expenditures	41.6%	33.1%	36.1%	25.7%
Social Expenditures	26.9%	16.2%	15.4%	9.4%
Other	14.7%	16.9%	20.7%	16.3%

Source: Calculated from World Bank, *China 2030*, Table 1.2.

Rather than strengthening its fiscal system, China relied on its banks to fund the increased demand for infrastructure over the past several decades.[24] The resulting expansion in bank lending to local governments skewed credit lines in favor of better-off localities that were more creditworthy. Thus, the option for handling redistributive transfers through decentralized budgets was not available, while the "quasi-fiscal" expenditures done through the financial institutions reinforced, rather than offset, growing disparities.

These problems have also been compounded by the spatially differentiated delivery systems for providing social services in China. Historically many social programs, including medical and unemployment assistance, have been operated independently as either rural or urban.[25] This separated the better-off urban residents from rural, thus weakening the financial viability of such dual-track arrangements and leading to lower-quality services in poorer areas.

Migrant Workers Exacerbate Tensions

No segment of society feels these social pressures more than the 250 million migrant workers who account for nearly half of the urban labor force in many major cities.[26] In the early years of reform, migrants were eager to leave the hinterland for jobs that paid multiples of what they were formerly eking out. But without formal residency (hukou) rights, their children usually were not eligible to enroll in local schools, nor could they qualify for health insurance or apply for jobs restricted to established residents. Despite the emergence of a private property market, migrants were also more limited in their housing options.

Initially, these deprivations did not seem to matter since their work was seen as temporary and the savings provided security for dependents left behind. Over time, however, with the growing regional divergence in the quality of social services and wage differentials shaped by locality and residency status, what was viewed as temporary became de facto permanent.

Periodic campaigns to repatriate migrant workers only contributed to their sense of being second-class citizens. With the maturation of a younger generation without the pre-reform poverty experience, their inferior status no longer matched aspirations in a modernizing China. Thus, even with wages growing at double-digit rates in recent years, increasing numbers of migrants have become more active in their demands—contributing to acts of civil disobedience.

Policymakers continue to be reluctant to liberalize the residency system for fear that China's major cities would become unmanageable. Established urban residents also worry that increased labor inflows would depress their wages. And without more revenues, cities feel—mistakenly—that they would not have the resources to meet the service needs of such a large contingent.[27] Current policies promote labor flows to smaller cities but strictly limit flows to the largest cities. The consequence is that China's largest cities are less densely inhabited compared to large cities globally, and its smaller cities are more densely inhabited (see Figure 6.3).

Such policies impact negatively on productivity and future growth prospects. While most observers and the Chinese themselves believe that China's major cities are too large, they are actually too small because of their lower densities and the adverse impact this has on travel times, pollution, and costs of providing social services (see Box 6.1).

These restrictive migration policies have created distortions in population settlement patterns. Those who remained trapped in rural areas or smaller cities cannot easily leave to seek better positions elsewhere. Although China's urbanization rate has risen rapidly to 56 percent in 2016—compared to 20 percent over three decades ago—it should be much higher.

China's restrictive labor migration policy is a major reason for its relatively skewed income disparities compared with other countries.[28] Such restrictions have also held back demand for housing and thus made it more difficult to reduce the excess stock of new construction. Much of the excess is in the smaller cities, and despite their much lower housing prices many migrants prefer to move to the larger cities, where jobs are likely to be more abundant and higher paying. Some migrants are moving back to their original localities as employment opportunities are now available more widely, and the higher costs of living in major coastal cities coupled with the lack of residency rights make staying less attractive.

Liberalizing hukou policies would allow market forces to play more of a role in guiding such decisions. The social as well as economic consequences would be positive. Such reforms are being addressed under the new urbanization policy

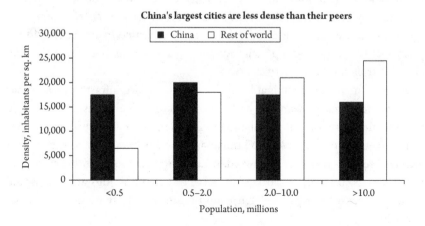

Figure 6.3 Density of Cities by Size. Source: World Bank, Urban China; Demographia.com

promulgated in 2014. But the time frame for full liberalization is too long and the bias against settling in the largest cities in favor of the smaller and medium-sized cities limits its growth-enhancing impact.[29]

Dealing with Social Tensions and Disparities

Dealing with these social tensions is complicated by the range of issues and related political risks. Migration pressures, for example, are often linked to the frequent disputes over land use. Because local authorities are starved of much-needed revenues and lack a system of property taxes that could serve as the fulcrum for their revenue base, they have been forced to sell off land rights to balance their budgets. Property rights are still not fully developed, and land ownership rests with the state. In many rural areas, land is collectively owned, with migrant families having a claim even when the head of household may be working elsewhere. Procedures for selling use rights vary by locality. By under-paying current rural owners and charging market premiums to developers, local officials can capture huge margins. This has encouraged overbuilding and exacerbated debt problems (see Chapter 5).

For migrant families to move, they need to be able to "capitalize" the full value of their rights to individual or collective holdings and relocate with enough assets to start afresh in other localities. Lacking such options reduces their incentives to relocate elsewhere on a permanent basis. Thus recent experiments in allowing such rights to be sold should be encouraged.

Many have argued that a more spatially balanced growth process would address some of the concerns over widening income disparities. As discussed earlier, this has been the rationale of government policies over the past decade to promote more investment in the interior provinces. While this has helped to moderate regional income differences, the tendency toward wasteful infrastructure expenditures in the interior regions has been carried to an extreme in the years after the GFC. This is a major reason why returns on investment have declined sharply for the country as a whole.

A more financially sustainable solution is not to use infrastructure investment as the primary means for addressing regional income disparities but to provide more support for social and environmental services through provincial budgets. In the process, the human and social capital base in the less advantaged regions would be improved. And, along with more flexible migration policies that would allow workers to move to where the jobs are, this would promote a settlement pattern that would more effectively moderate income disparities.

Box 6.1 **Are China's Largest Cities Actually Too Small?**

Many hope that urbanization can provide the productivity increases needed to sustain future growth. But others worry that China's major cities will only sink into a morass of social and environmental decay. A key question is whether China should continue its policies to discourage growth of its largest cities.

The pressure for cities to grow comes from the power of "agglomeration economies." These are the benefits from concentration of firms and workers. The resulting economies of scale and network effects drive down costs and lead to specialization. Unfortunately, there are often negative consequences as cities mushroom in size. For firms, rising costs of land and labor reduce the advantages of big cities and for workers; congestion and higher living expenses reduce their appeal. If China continues to handle its urbanization the wrong way, its citizens will remain mired in a net of pollution and clogged streets.

These risks, however, have less to do with city size than misguided urban management policies. Beijing's core, for example, is not being appropriately developed, with vast blocks of underutilized parcels while affordable housing is pushed too far out from where the jobs are. A fascination with ring roads impedes rather than facilitates traffic flow. The consequence is excessively long commutes with more traffic-related pollution than necessary and costlier provision of social services because of the higher capital costs of serving a dispersed population. Similarly, Shanghai's density of population declined by about 20 percent over the decade 2000–2010 because of the policy to push development to satellite towns. These are all costs which could be avoided by a more rational, density-oriented approach to urban planning.

Yet China's planners continue to see the solution as developing new cities and facilitating the flow of people into the smaller ones. Incentives for this to happen are reinforced by limited local-level financing options. Provincial governments have relied on the conversion of rural land for urban use to fund their obligations. Even in the megacities, incorporating suburban land is more appealing than making rational use of the core. The consequence is that urbanization has ended up dispersing people and activities rather than increasing density. Over the past several decades, the urban population has expanded 2.5 times, but urban land area has increased eightfold.

Instead of actively trying to disperse growth to small new cities, China's planners should embrace the agglomeration economies which militate for larger but more densely inhabited cities—smart people like to mix with other smart people, and globalization has increased financial returns for large firms. Megacities like Beijing and Shanghai have continued to grow because of buoyant higher-value services even as their manufacturing base has shrunk.

What China needs is a more efficient urbanization process—one where cities are allowed to evolve organically in response to changing conditions. This will require a financing system that provides the right incentives, social services and residency policies that facilitate rather than restrict labor mobility, land use guidelines that promote more concentrated rather than dispersed development, and transport systems that encourage a more efficient location of activity. This would likely lead to larger, denser, and more environmentally friendly cities while also generating the productivity needed for China to meet its growth objectives.

(This box draws on Yukon Huang, "China Needs Beijing to Be Even Bigger," *Bloomberg*, September 9, 2013 and World Bank, *Urban China*, 2014.)

Origins of the Current Corruption Campaign

Among the social concerns, corruption looms as the major vulnerability in perceptions about China's governance system. The new leadership is now widely seen as dealing more seriously with corruption than with economic reforms. The campaign has the strong support of the public, but its immediate economic implications are more mixed. Not only has conspicuous consumption declined but officials have become hesitant to make even routine operational decisions. This has accentuated the current economic slowdown. These concerns raise important questions about the role that corruption has played in shaping China's development over the past several decades.[30]

The public discourse in the media and among academics on corruption in China is wide-ranging and often confusing.[31] How does one define corruption? What is its impact on the economy? And what are the systemic remedies?

In discussing these issues, three points stand out. First, most studies based on cross-country experiences have shown that corruption retards economic growth. But China is an outlier. This raises an obvious question of whether China managed to grow so rapidly because of or in spite of rampant corruption. Second, the more a country develops, the more likely that corruption diminishes, but in China's case the opposite seems to be happening. And third, many studies conclude that by contributing to the economic decline, corruption leads to political instability. This has encouraged speculation about whether efforts. address corruption in China will eventually lead to political liberalization.

Corruption has featured prominently in China's dynastic history, but this current bout ironically stems from the well-regarded reforms launched by Deng Xiaoping. His opening up of the economy paved the way for a hybrid socialist market economy, which—similar to the situation in the republics of the former Soviet Union—is particularly prone to corruption.

The creation of a "dual-track economy" with a parallel market- and state-driven activity created the incentives for corruptive interactions among three key players. One is the private entrepreneur who saw the potential to prosper by providing a better product but lacked the resources to do so. Enter player two, a representative of a state enterprise who could provide the resources—typically property or financing provided by SOCBs. Both, however, needed the blessing of player three, the local official and Party member who had the authority to make the collaboration politically acceptable.

For this process to work there had to be the potential for considerable gain. The interactions among the various state and private agents were not strictly legal, and there were few existing rules or regulations to guide the process. This gave rise in the early stages of China's opening up to the development of TVEs— a marriage of private interests with resources controlled by local authorities to establish small-scale manufacturing activities. These TVEs are seen as pioneering examples of economic reform in China's initial phase of industrial development but in retrospect, they can also be seen as examples of budding corruption.

Corruption and growth thus went hand in hand. In other countries, corruption typically retards growth because it represses investment, which is the primary determinant of growth. But China is different since its investment rate has been increasing rapidly. Corruption in China helped entrepreneurs and the emerging private sector interests to get around the excessive regulations and controls in its overly centralized bureaucracy. In fact, one could argue that it has improved rather than impeded investment efficiency.

Moreover, as discussed earlier, China's unique regionally decentralized administration checked the growth-inhibiting aspects of corruption by setting investment and production targets that incentivized local officials. This fostered a unity of purpose so that even as corruption flourished, the collaborators worked to make growth the guiding principle for governance. This was reinforced by competition among the localities to meet these growth targets by supporting productivity-enhancing reforms.

Corruption in the transition phase was also exacerbated by the high tariffs and existence of dual prices for consumer and producer goods—one market determined and the other subsidized or controlled. This created the opportunity for illicit gains through price arbitrage. Huge illicit profits were realized by manipulating the official and unofficial prices for basic consumer items such as rice and textiles and by smuggling foreign goods. Unification of output prices and tariff reductions eliminated most of these rent-seeking opportunities more than a decade ago.

Today the problem lies in the distorted prices for key inputs such as land, energy, capital, and labor. Many of the most egregious cases in the headlines are about land seizures by local authorities for commercial development, diversion of subsidized lending to state firms for unintended purposes, and misuse of underpriced energy resources.

The corruptive nature of these transactions is most strikingly illustrated in the way that land transactions have been handled over the past decade. A private property market was only created in the late 1990s, and thus its underlying value could not be established until then. This all changed in 2003–2004, when official auctioning of state-owned land for development was initiated and prices surged over the past decade. As discussed earlier, this created the opportunity for local authorities to secure huge profits in working with private developers.

Preferential access to financing underpins another major source of corruptive activity. SOEs get funding at below-market rates, supposedly for investments that serve the interests of the state, but at times such funds are diverted to serve other purposes in exchange for illegal payments. In areas like energy, where the state controls its use with differential prices depending on the purpose, there are also significant opportunities for diversion.

Addressing Corruption

It is thus not surprising that President Xi Jinping's corruption campaign targeted energy companies and financial institutions initially and why land acquisition practices and interest-rate liberalization rank so high on the reform agenda. Going one step further, few realize that liberalizing labor migration and residency eligibility would also help moderate corruption since there is even a gray market for buying residency rights in major cities.

China's rapid growth has encouraged even more corruption since more wealth creation means more can be siphoned off. Corruption has also been nurtured by the increasing gap between salaries being paid to public officials compared with their private and foreign counterparts in a globalized world. The most vulnerable period in the transition from a centrally controlled to a market-driven economy is when the rules of the game are unclear. The danger is being stuck in the transition. Thus, the defining question is whether China will eventually fulfill its Third Plenum pledge that the market rather than the state will be the decisive force for allocating resources. Otherwise, corruption will continue to flourish. Taking this process one step further, Minxin Pei suggests that the nature of China's corruption (i.e. its collusive nature) coupled with unclear property rights may eventually bring down the regime.[32]

While corruption has not led to its characteristic economic stagnation, its negative consequence—in the form of the demoralizing effect on perceptions of equity and justice—is driving the current anti-corruption campaign. Campaigns tend to be run by "moralists" who argue that fundamental changes in values are needed to curb corruption, in this case to preserve the credibility of the Communist Party. It is this need to maintain legitimacy that drives President Xi's actions.

The more economically oriented leaders tend to focus on altering incentives by eliminating regulations that nurture corruption. Thus, simplifying investment procedures and lowering tax rates are the priorities, making even the negotiation of free trade or investment treaties instruments to reduce corruption (see Chapter 8).

The current corruption campaign is heavy on dealing with nonstructural factors and moral suasion by trying to reign in bribes and greed through enhanced penalties. The chance of going to jail for corruption used to be seen as very low—making corruption a low-risk, high-return gamble. The leadership's push to persecute both "tigers" and "flies" changes the risk-benefit calculation, and this is indicated by the sharp increase in recent cases (see Figure 6.4).

The scaling back of salaries in 2015 for senior executives in SOEs as part of the anti-corruption campaign was more of a symbolic gesture, and one that is unlikely to help. Since it widens the gap between what Chinese SOE managers are paid compared with their wealthier private counterparts, the incentive to be

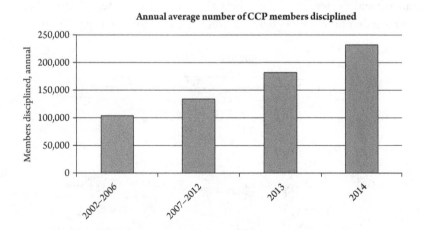

Figure 6.4 Party Members Disciplined. Source: Central Commission for Discipline Inspection China

corrupt increases. Ultimately President Xi will succeed only if more is done to address the structural factors driving corruption, including the excessive role of the state and Party in economic activities. In a practical sense, if the campaign is to reach some kind of closure, some form of a general amnesty for all but the most egregious cases may at some point be necessary given how pervasive corruption has become in the administrative system.

Breaking the corruptive relationship between the key players in a dual economy requires separating the roles and responsibilities of the four major agents driving China's economic system—the Party, the government, enterprises, and banks. China's growth model—until recently—can be depicted as a big round Chinese dining table with a central pillar representing these four agents driving the economy which is represented by a round table top (see Figure 6.5). All four agents are working closely together, which is why collective action is so effective in China, but a contributing factor is that corruption serves as the binding glue. This model has served China's growth objectives, but given the rising social tensions and the increasing complexity of the economy, such an arrangement may no longer be sustainable.

Ultimately, China needs to move to a "Western" dining table with four separate legs, creating a firewall between the government and the Party and their influence on enterprises and banks, both state owned and private. While on paper much of the economy has become more "private," the influence of the state still permeates much of the major decision making among economic agents, regardless of their formal ownership arrangements. Breaking these relationships would require some form of political liberalization to promote the much needed accountability and transparency to curb corruption.

Most of the corruptive behaviors lie in the state's control over resources and financing and the way that local officials can influence its use. Privatizing those SOEs that do not play a strategic role would be a tangible first step. But thus far,

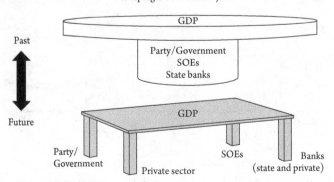

Figure 6.5 Reshaping the Economic System. Source: Author

the government's actions have been less dramatic in advocating more diverse ownership by allowing private interests to purchase minority shares. Without the power to influence decisions, the private sector has shown little interest in investing in these SOEs. Similarly, the SOCBs have an outsized influence on economic activity through their preferential access to the huge savings of Chinese households. The pressure that these banks feel to enter into transactions that are unduly influenced by Party and local officials is a major vulnerability in the current system.

Abusive land practices are being addressed as part of the current new urbanization program. This entails addressing sensitive issues including the rights of individual farmers to sell the "use rights" for land that historically was under collective ownership, and using more transparent processes for developing parcels in urban areas. Such actions would eliminate much of the illicit activity that has flourished in recent years.

For these issues, the problem is that accountability is diffuse and the line between regulatory and executive roles is blurred. Ironically, the corruption campaign was inspired by the desire to preserve the dominant role of the Communist Party in the "system." But clarifying these relationships is likely to require a redefined role for both the Party and the rule of law to build the necessary mechanisms for accountability. Many of these transgressions can only be revealed by allowing the public to play a watchdog role. Yet, in today's environment, for an individual or civic group to do so may not be acceptable.

Prospects for Political Liberalization

Turning to the work of Acemoglu and Robinson, we now have a better understanding about why China's type of authoritarian regime did not lead early on to the kind of "extractive" institutions that end up only channeling resources to a small group of vested interests.[33] Until recent years, China's unique decentralized competitive system fitted their typology of an "inclusive" institution that created the incentives for growth and shared benefits even though it was part of an authoritarian regime. In this environment, there are countless examples of individual entrepreneurs who rose from running a food stall or parlayed an idea into substantial wealth largely outside of the state-run system.

This structure has worked well for decades, but wealth creation has ironically given birth to vested interests that may now be distorting outcomes. It is plausible to argue that the interrelationships among the key state agents are now evolving into extractive institutions, operating in some cases more for their own benefits rather than for society as a whole.[34]

The system is no longer seen as generating the kind of productivity-enhancing benefits as in the past. As China moves from middle- to high-income status, some form of political liberalization may be needed if prosperity is to be realized. When it does come, the path in China's case is unlikely to follow Western democratic movements and is more likely to come from within the Party system and begin at local levels rather than the center. Local authorities are hard pressed to handle the social and political tensions that have emerged over the past decade, and they do not have the means or flexibility to address the underlying factors triggering such resentment. Thus, they are often left to their own discretion, and depending on the circumstances, their responses vary from mild to forceful acts of repression, concessions, or occasionally just neglect.

The highly publicized protests that took place in late 2011 between residents in Wukan, a small village in Guangdong province and local authorities over disputed land sales provide an example of how such conflicts have been handled across the country.[35] The details that triggered this incident were all too familiar—disputes over village land sales to developers, followed by protests, arrests, and the suspicious death of a jailed representative. These prompted appeals to higher provincial officials who, in meeting villagers' demands, allowed the election of locally supported officials and reinforced the perception that the senior leadership remained a potential savior. Such incidents, however, can have unpredictable longer-term implications. Another round of protests resurfaced in September of 2016 over the removal of the elected official allegedly on the grounds of corruption.

More generally, social dissatisfaction emanates from the lack of credible options for protestors to express their concerns without incurring the wrath of security officials. Venting one's frustrations in a way that one believes will be taken seriously by the authorities can be as important as actually resolving an issue. If such protests are seen as legitimate outlets for such complaints, then these incidents can help stabilize, rather than undermine, the political system.[36] However, growth in the numbers of such episodes, without evidence that this has led to less confrontational approaches, suggests otherwise.

Many protestors at the local level used to believe that China's senior leaders would be on their side if they only knew the reality. The center was also seen as more sympathetic because targeted social programs are typically publicized as initiatives coming from Beijing. That local authorities lacked adequate resources to carry out their responsibilities was overlooked. Thus, the impression was that the center cared, but local officials were rapacious.

This follows the dynastic tradition of "petitioning the emperor" and is reinforced by a tacit understanding that top leaders must live in a reasonably clean "fishbowl" environment and be subjected to behavioral constraints. The crosschecks that come with a turnover in the top leadership in Beijing every decade also mean that blame is less personalized. All this is consistent with the approach that successive generations of leadership have been taking. Yet this approach has been severely weakened by the recent revelations that those at the top may be as tainted as others. Thus, unlike past corruption campaigns, Xi's leadership has been emphasizing that leaders as well as followers are being targeted.

The proposition that economic liberalization will give birth to political liberalization is an old story—and it has happened elsewhere. A random act of social unrest could end up triggering more fundamental political change. That recent protests have been treated relatively more harshly suggests that the authorities recognize that they are standing near the edge.

How China handles this complex set of issues will have profound implications for the process of political liberalization. The sheer frequency of these protests is proving to be a drain on the energies and resources of local authorities. Spending for domestic security is now greater than the allocation for national defense—even though defense spending is the focus of global attention.

Moreover, there is greater risk today that such events may become a rallying cry nationally or even internationally. These risks have increased in part because of the rise of social media along with greater civic awareness among a more informed middle class. With Weibo (Chinese micro-blogging), information dissemination has become more transparent and immediate, with the effect of putting more pressure on local authorities before they can effectively contain such incidents. Something that begins as a relatively isolated incident can be transformed into a more widespread movement.

Despite China's impressive economic achievements, the challenge is to find a way to push ahead with political liberalization that meets popular aspirations but is also acceptable within the Party system. Back in 1998, the passage of a law that established more open village-level elections gave hope that change could grow out of this option when the political circumstances evolved. The nature of such elections—their true competitiveness and links with local Party relations—varies across localities, but they did offer a basis for broader participation in governance at the county level.[37]

If truly representative and empowered, such elections would put in place local officials who are more accountable to the needs of the people.[38] Issues such as land use rights, enforcement of labor laws, environmental protection, and even corruption would become part of a more serious dialogue between communities and their local representatives. The relative priorities to be given to growth and social objectives would become the subject of more participatory processes. It would also escalate pressures for a change up the system since many issues cannot be resolved at the most decentralized levels. Such reforms would reduce the need to protest to expose grievances and push the political system to take such concerns more seriously without having to appeal to senior leaders for ad hoc interventions.

A logical complement would be more independent judiciaries beginning at the lowest provincial levels. This would have to be supported by a more sympathetic approach to dealing with social unrest that would integrate security considerations into a broader view of how such grievances should be handled.[39] The embrace of the rule of law at the Fourth Central Committee Plenum in 2014—where it was named as a high priority—was initially greeted with widespread support. Subsequently, the issuance of instructions about "the comprehensive advancement of Socialist rule of law" revealed that the process of deepening legal reform was more likely to strengthen the role of the Party in carrying out its policies than to serve as a means for moderating abuses in the current governance system.

Many are still hoping that this initiative will eventually create pressures for accountability and further political reforms. But the process of political liberalization in China will not follow the norms of Western democratic movements. Many Chinese instinctively reject the idea that an American or European model is the only option and look askance at the idea of China's system being mocked by outsiders. To succeed in today's China, political reform needs to find support from within the Party structures and emanate from the sentiments of a rising middle class that is searching for something beyond material success.

When Will Political Liberalization Begin?

The Arab Spring movement years ago and halting experiences in many fragile states rekindled speculation about political change in China. But more appropriate are the experiences of the highly successful but formerly autocratic neighbors of China—South Korea and Taiwan.[40] Studies on the democratization process in those two economies have elaborated on the similarities and differences in what took place. Some have tried to apply these lessons in speculating about implications for China's future.[41]

Political liberalization in both economies was a gradual process that began around the same time in the second half of 1980s. A rising middle class influenced by the United States was instrumental in promoting democracy. It is worth emphasizing that both South Korea and Taiwan embarked on political liberalization at about the same purchasing-power adjusted per-capita income level of US$12–15,000 and at the same level of urbanization (65–70 percent). This was accompanied by a sharp rise in the share of high-value services in the economy. It is no coincidence that the emergence of a more knowledge-based economy, exemplified by the role that high-value services play in driving growth, can generate pressures for political liberalization.

China, however, is different in some key aspects. In particular, Korea and Taiwan are seen as having more ethnic and regional divisions that led to a more pluralistic sociopolitical attitude within the population. China is viewed as culturally more homogenous despite its many ethnic minorities with differences delineated more by economic factors.[42] As illustrated by the characters in Evan Osnos's book *Age of Ambition*, it becomes harder for an authoritarian state to control aspirations and placate popular concerns as a society become more sophisticated and connected via the internet and social media.[43] In contrast, the rationale for authoritarian control is much stronger during the manufacturing stage, when development is typically more dependent on access to land and financial resources largely controlled by the state, than when knowledge-based services become the source of income generation.

Comparing China with South Korea and Taiwan provides some clues on when political liberalization might occur. Although China has already reached their level regarding per-capita income, it is still far behind regarding the pace of urbanization, share of high-value services, and activism of its middle class. Other factors also suggest that political liberalization will occur later, motivated in part by a more adversarial relationship with the United States. While one can argue that Chinese society is not as diverse as that in Korea and Taiwan, its middle class is becoming more sophisticated and moving beyond purely economic aspirations.

Historical experiences tell us that authoritarian systems based on a strong one-party system are less likely to experience a sudden crisis-driven collapse compared with a military or one-man dictatorship.[44] If a regime change did suddenly occur, the consequences would be chaotic. There would be no obvious alternative to replace the current system, given China's historical lack of Western-based democratic traditions.

The pressure for change will only grow, however, as the economy becomes more dependent on globally connected services and the authorities find it increasingly difficult to control the dissemination of information.[45] Current efforts to curb corruption are unlikely to strengthen the role of the Party when the solution requires getting the Party out of many economic activities. All this will become part of the clamor for free expression in a system that lacks enough credible outlets for its citizens to vent their feelings.

Just as Deng Xiaoping foresaw that political liberalization had to be left to his successors pending progress on the economic front, the current consolidation of authority and need to restructure the economy likely means that significant political change should not be a near-term expectation. Taking this into consideration, China might reach the phase when political liberalization begins sometime around the second half of the next decade, or 2025–2030.[46]

China's State-Led versus Market-Led Capitalism

Underpinning the ongoing discussion about the need and likelihood of political liberalization in China is a more narrowly focused debate about the role of the state and market in guiding China's particular form of capitalism. This debate has been nurtured by a widespread sense that the US model of market-led capitalism represents one extreme and China's state-led version of capitalism represents the other. Most observers see the two systems as fundamentally different not only in the way they operate but also in the challenges they face. The reality, however, is that the two systems may actually have more commonalities than differences.

The two extremes have been depicted in the past as a choice between the Washington Consensus and the Beijing Consensus. But this differentiation is misleading.[47] Contrasting political systems have encouraged such a sharp distinction, but the challenges both countries face in dealing with their variations of capitalism are surprisingly similar (see Box 6.2).

In the aftermath of the US-triggered GFC and prolonged budgetary problems in the Eurozone, many began to question the virtues of the idealized Western version of market-led capitalism. The apparent success of China's state-led capitalism at that time in driving double-digit growth seemingly provided an alternative, although with China's current economic slowdown, the proponents for a more market-led approach are once again in the ascendancy.

China's impressive economic performance in the early 21st century reflects the positive interaction between effective planning and an incentivized system that has worked with the market rather than against it. It has avoided much of the inefficiency inherent in state-led approaches by embracing cross-provincial and external competition. However, as its economy becomes increasingly complex and globally more connected, Beijing is being pressed to allow the market to play an even greater role.

The debate between the role of the state and the market is often misguided. The challenge is to find the right balance. Both the state and the market are political as well as social institutions that depend on each other. Markets do not always behave sensibly—but neither do governments. Nor do free markets operate with the neutrality and benevolence that is depicted in textbooks.[48] When formal rules and adherence to moral principles are both weak, the public ends up bearing the consequences of self-interested players. Therefore markets are not always self-correcting, but government-devised solutions often merely delay the inevitable.

Box 6.2　**Both the United States and China Face Similar Challenges**

Moderating rising income disparities: America's version of capitalism has had no more success in curbing inequality than China's. Both have generated a Gini coefficient of inequality around 0.45, but different factors are at play. The dominance of China's SOEs and Party connections is seen as exacerbating disparities. But crony capitalism and dollar politics in the West can be just as pernicious. Both favor connected insiders over innovative outsiders. Globalization is also under attack for exacerbating disparities. The incomes for highly skilled workers have increased while returns to the average worker have stagnated across countries. This has contributed to stagnating wages for middle-class workers in the United States and widening disparities between China's trade-driven coastal areas compared to its interior. Trying to moderate such disparities with regulatory and fiscal policies runs the risk of stifling innovation in both countries. However, there is no escaping the need for the American economy to invest more to increase the productivity of its workers. For China, it is more about moving up the value chain to keep growth going.

Designing effective regulatory systems: State-run services can be as vulnerable regarding inadequate regulatory regimes as private provision. The allegations of China's lax food safety standards and poor safety of its high-speed railways illustrate the importance of separating regulatory and operating responsibilities. But the US model of encouraging private provision of utility services is seen as being prone to rising prices and limiting choices as monopolistic forces emerge. It is in the financial sector that both systems face the greatest risks of weak regulatory regimes. Mergers have only increased concentration in the United States and accentuated the risk of "too big to fail." Much has been done to strengthen regulations, but many still feel that incentives for risk taking have merely resurfaced elsewhere. But China's state-led approach in banking has its own problems in generating quasi-fiscal deficits hidden in excessive bank lending with the hidden costs of such practices fueling speculative property bubbles and risky shadow banking.

Reshaping fiscal and financial systems: Both systems are being challenged to use their financial and fiscal systems to support innovation and provide more public services. The share of government expenditures relative to GDP has increased across all countries, reflecting the increasing pressures on the state to meet growing social needs, but this has fostered concerns about affordability in the West. Meanwhile, China's budget plays a surprisingly limited role in an economy where the state controls the bulk of resources and has a broader range of responsibilities. The consequences are excessive reliance on its banks to fund activities that should be financed through the budget and shortchanging much-needed social and environmental services.

Managing risks associated with size: Large corporations can easily undermine regulatory strategies. "Too big to fail" in the West can be just as pernicious as "too big to manage" in China. Scale economies characterize many industries, and therefore frontrunners not only take the lead but can also stifle others and ultimately capture the interests of the state. This has been as true for big banks in the United States as for the large state monopolies in China, which are getting ever bigger due to plans to promote consolidation and mergers. Both systems fail if there is not strong competition and protection of investors, lenders, and smaller firms against monopolistic practices and fraud.

Promoting innovation: Traditionally, market-led capitalism was seen as being more effective in fostering innovation, but increasingly America is perceived as having lost much of its dynamism because the state has not played a supportive enough role. The GFC has shaken the basis of the market-led version of capitalism, mainly because of lack of appreciation of the risks associated with innovation. America's brand of innovation may be undiminished, but the challenge of defending its strengths has increased. For China, a much broader range of industries is needed as its economy becomes more sophisticated. And the state is seen as being unable to jumpstart such initiatives compared with the private sector. China's major state companies may have a prime position at home, but abroad they are not yet global champions of true innovative practices. If domestic returns are high, pressures to innovate or take risks may be reduced. Abroad, their managers may make wasteful investments because financial costs are undervalued and the state has seemingly unlimited resources.

(This box draws on Yukon Huang, "China and the U.S., Capitalism's Odd Couple," *Bloomberg*, December 5, 2012.)

Market-led capitalism draws its legitimacy in democracies from the belief that everyone has an equal chance of getting rich even if outcomes turn out to be unequal. It is the sense of fairness that matters. State-led capitalism is legitimized in authoritarian regimes because it is assumed to provide more equitable opportunities as well as outcomes. Yet the credibility of both systems is currently under attack because of what is seen as an unholy alliance between officials, vested interests, and financial institutions that have resulted in excessive payoffs for a select few.

Both the Washington and Beijing versions of capitalism have produced impressive results but fallen short in specific aspects. The American system may in principle seem preferable, but the Chinese system in practice appears to be doing a better job preparing for the future. China is putting its money in infrastructure, education, and renewable energy to become more competitive. At the same time, the United States is putting too much into consumption, wasteful health services, and the military—compromising future growth.

America's brand of capitalism has generated exceptional innovation, but its inability to forge a collective view because of the primacy accorded to individual rights and vested interests has prevented the country from addressing longer-term needs. Its political process is often mired in ideological debates and personalities rather than actions. In contrast, China has shown a knack for forging collective solutions that have enhanced the welfare of hundreds of millions, but often at the cost of individual rights.

China's approach is often seen as being more pragmatic, but whether it can provide the flexibility to spur innovation and satisfy personal aspirations is uncertain. It still falls far short compared with the United States largely because of the latter's far more advanced institutional and human capital base. China uses capitalism primarily as a means to achieve its objectives, not because it truly embraces its underlying beliefs.

As many have noted, both America and China need to find the right mix between the "invisible hand of markets" and "the visible hand of the state." Excessive dependence on either can create excessive returns for a few by giving them unfair advantages and shortchanging the needs of society.

The argument for capitalism lies in its potential for increasing the welfare of society and satisfying personal needs in generally respected ways. America's form of democracy may have an intrinsic legitimacy that the Chinese system lacks, but the concern today is over the problems that emerge when the system is so internally divided that it cannot function effectively. But China's version is also increasingly seen as being excessively overbearing and losing the trust of its people.

Both systems are now under pressure to deal with their perceived weaknesses. It is the rule of law which ensures legitimacy and effectiveness in both systems. China needs a more effective legal system for governing the actions of *the state*, while for America it is about governing the role of *markets*. The success or failure of each country in dealing with these challenges will determine whether it will continue to prosper.

CHAPTER 7

China's Trade and Capital Flows

China's global influence emanates from its economic rise and impact on trade and foreign investment. When Deng Xiaoping launched his reforms in 1980, the economies of the United States and Europe were both about five times that of China's in size. After three decades of double-digit growth, China has achieved parity in purchasing-power terms (see Figure 7.1).

While size matters in judging global significance, China's direct impact on other countries comes primarily through its emergence as the world's largest trading nation, a premier destination for foreign investment, and a source of surging outward capital flows. These shifts have fundamentally altered China's external economic relations with its neighbors, with the West, and with other emerging market economies. All this has been part of a global-ization process which until recently was seen as generally having benefited both developing and developed countries. But rising protectionist senti-ments have led to pushback against globalization in the United States as well as in Europe.

As with the other topics addressed in this book, views on the nature of these shifts differ significantly, making it difficult to forge constructive solutions. This chapter revisits the roles that trade and foreign investment have played in shaping China's development. From being largely a regional player, the country is now, in 2016, the primary export destination for some forty countries—compared with ten a decade ago, with key relationships extending to all the continents.

With success came concern. In the mid-2000s, the international financial community was preoccupied with China's huge trade surpluses and its impact on global macro-imbalances. China's soaring levels of foreign reserves raised largely misplaced outcries that America would be held hostage to Beijing's com-mands and would allow it to broaden its external economic influence.[1]

Despite China's recent economic slowdown and lower trade deficits, public sentiments on the nature of United States–China economic relations have not evolved as quickly. President Trump's anti-China trade comments echo long-standing complaints of Congressional leaders and segments of the business

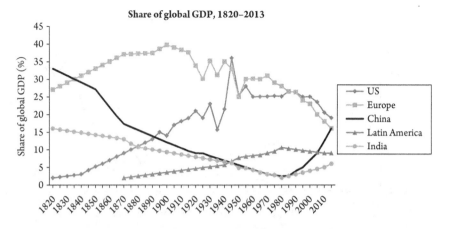

Figure 7.1 Global GDP Shares. Source: Angus Maddison, Statistics on World Population, GDP and Per Capita GDP; author's calculations

community that China's exchange rate is undervalued, even though years of appreciation have led most analysts to conclude otherwise.[2] Its persistent bilateral trade surpluses with the United States are seen as harming America's labor market. China also has its share of critics in the European Union, with many voices accusing China of mercantilism and unfair trade practices and calling for a "fortress Europe." Moreover, there has been a noticeable shift in the sentiments of Western investors regarding the difficulties that they now have in accessing China's domestic market.[3] This is occurring despite China being ranked consistently as a highly attractive foreign investment destination—second only to the United States.[4]

FDI's Role in Developing China's Industrial Base

When China initiated its reform process, it was desperately short of foreign exchange but reluctant to borrow from the West. Instead, its industrial capacity was developed mainly through FDI in the SEZs along its coastal borders (see Chapter 3). By 1985, China's eastern region had captured 92 percent of FDI compared to 8 percent for the central and western regions. Following these initial successes, a further wave of policies to encourage FDI was rolled out in the early 1990s, leading to a surge in foreign investment from $4 billion in 1991 to $50 billion by 1997. This was followed by another surge from 2004 onward to levels in excess of $300 billion today (see Figure 7.2).

Utilized FDI in China for the two decades prior to 2000 totaled $308 billion, of which Asia accounted for nearly 80 percent of the accumulated total, compared with 16 percent between the European Union and the United States.[5]

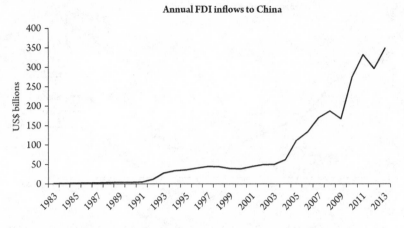

Figure 7.2 Inward FDI. Source: World Bank World Development Indicators

Overseas Chinese were able to operate more comfortably than Westerners within a system where the rules were opaque and personal relationships were essential to deal making. For the largely Asian foreign investors, China provided an ideal base to relocate production to achieve the scale, specialization, and cost advantages necessary to compete globally.

Western multilaterals were more comfortable with contracting Asian-run firms to handle the production process while focusing more on design and distribution to consumers at home. This pattern has continued since most of the profits come from marketing rather than from production, which is vulnerable to cost pressures and low profit margins.

The results have been astonishing. In 1978, China accounted for less than 1 percent of global trade, ranking thirty-second among all nations with total imports and exports of $20 billion. By 2010, China was the world's largest exporter, with total merchandise trade exceeding $3 trillion, 150 times the 1978 level. Since the early 2000s, foreign-invested entities have accounted for over 50 percent of China's total industrial exports. While cheap labor and currency are often cited as China's competitive advantages, in reality, Chinese policies created an attractive climate for foreign investors, and they were the driving force behind China's industrial development.

Evolving Regional and Global Trade Relations

By 2010, China had replaced the United States as the primary export destination for most Asian economies and is now also rapidly becoming their major source of investment financing. This shift was especially significant for ASEAN, given its centrality as a political grouping that both the United States and China have been catering to for decades. Initially a minor player, China overtook the United States, European Union, and Japan as the largest trading partner for ASEAN around the time of the GFC (see Figure 7.3).

This shift came primarily from the rise of the East Asian production network of which China is the regional hub importing components from other East Asian economies for re-export to the West. The emergence of the network changed the nature of China's trade relations with the world. China's trade surplus was modest until 2004 and then increased rapidly. Most of this increase was due to its surplus from processing trade, while the balance from "ordinary" trade (trade based entirely on domestic materials or components) was minimal or negative.[6]

China's increasing economic presence also raised concerns about its political influence. A decade and a half ago, there was widespread concern about whether China represented a threat or an opportunity for its neighbors. Most had assumed that exporting via China rather than directly to the West would result in a lower share of global trade for their respective economies. But from 2000 to 2010, China's surging imports of parts and raw materials from its East Asian partners more than compensated for any declines in their direct exports to the West.

Even as China's share of global trade in parts and components soared from around 2 to 11 percent from 1993 to 2006, ASEAN's share increased from 8 to 11 percent. The share of the more developed Asian economies (South Korea, Taiwan, and Japan) remained constant but shifted to higher-value components from less profitable assembly activities.[7]

Overall, the efficiency gains from specialization and economies of scale from using China as the central hub benefited everyone in the region, leading to an increase in East Asia's share of global manufacturing exports from 28 to 35 percent. As a measure of the extent of its increased competitiveness, the foreign reserves of the East Asian economies (ASEAN, China, South Korea, Taiwan,

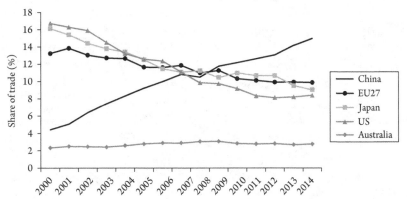

Share of total ASEAN trade by country/region

Figure 7.3 ASEAN Trade Partners. Source: UN Comtrade

and Japan) quadrupled from around $1 trillion in 2000 to $4 trillion by the eve of the GFC in 2008.

Post-Global Financial Crisis Regional Trade Patterns

In the aftermath of the GFC, some subtle changes have emerged in China's trade relationship with its Asian neighbors. Although China's non-processing-related imports increased rapidly up to 2012 in response to its stimulus and massive construction programs, they then began to fall steadily, with China's economic slowdown contributing to the collapse in global commodity prices.

Reduced demand in the West has also meant a decline in China's imported components from its East Asian partners. This decline in imports has been sharper than the fall-off in China's exports to the West since China is now producing more of the needed components itself rather than importing them.[8] This has occurred despite China's rapidly rising wages because production has been moving inland to lower-cost centers.

There are significant variations among ASEAN countries in the composition and size of their trade balances with China reflecting their differing economic structures (see Figure 7.4). Singapore and Vietnam have been running deficits with China for around a decade, with the former's coming from imported consumer products and the latter's from imports of capital goods to support expanding investment levels. Malaysia has been running substantial surpluses with China given its rich natural resource base and strength in exporting electronic components. More generally, China's imports from ASEAN have stagnated in recent years while its exports to them have continued to increase. The net effect

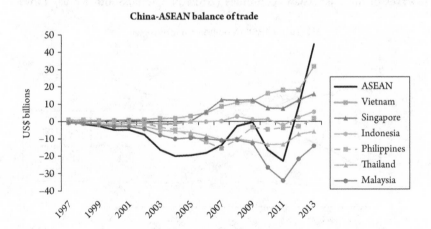

Figure 7.4 China ASEAN Trade. Source: UN Comtrade

of shifting from a trade deficit to a trade surplus with ASEAN is that trading with China is no longer such a growth driver for those countries as it was a decade ago.

This shift has begun to feed into renewed concerns among many Asian countries about their economic prospects, and stagnating employment trends and wages have aggravated these sentiments. Excluding Japan, most East Asian economies have performed relatively well compared to other regions over the past decade, with GDP growth averaging 3–6 percent annually. But growth in real wages has been tepid or even negative—unlike the pattern in 1990s when wages were increasing in line with GDP growth. The unsuccessful efforts of policymakers throughout the region to stimulate growth in wages have had political repercussions.

Largely unrecognized is China's impact on labor markets in the other countries in the regional production network. From 2005 to 2014, China's wages rose by 300 percent, pushing them higher than wages in Malaysia, Thailand, and the Philippines.[9] This generated concerns that cost pressures would lead to outsourcing of production from China to less costly countries like Vietnam or Bangladesh.

While some outsourcing has occurred, it has been less than initially predicted. Despite China's surging wages, its labor productivity has been increasing even faster so that "adjusted" labor costs have been contained. To remain competitive in producing components that feed into the network, other Asian countries have had to maintain productivity-adjusted costs that are on par with China. Since productivity increases in most other East Asian economies have not kept pace with China's, their wage increases in real terms have been minimal or even negative compared with increases of around 10 percent annually in China. The largely unrecognized fact is that China has steadily been gaining a larger share of global exports, and the composition of its share has also changed. For example, China now exports relatively less shoes but has become the dominant exporter of drones.

Although China's exports fell slightly in 2015, global exports declined much more. UNCTAD data show that China's share of global exports rose to nearly 14 percent from 12 percent in 2014, the highest share any country has achieved since the United States in the late 1960s.

US and China Trade Imbalances and Exchange Rate Controversies

China's foreign investment-led industrialization process created the capacity for it to become globally competitive, and membership in WTO provided access

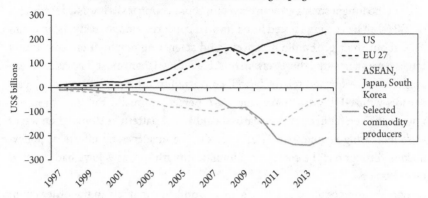

Figure 7.5 Global Trade Balances. Source: UN Comtrade; Global Balance of Trade

to Western markets. This led to a dramatic increase in its trade surpluses to over $250 billion by the time of the GFC in 2008. These surpluses were offset in part with trade deficits with its production network partners and commodity producers elsewhere (see Figure 7.5). The size of these imbalances has led to China being blamed for lost jobs, unfair competition, and low wage growth in the United States and Europe, although much of it represents an "accounting" shift among countries in the region.

Complaints about unfair competition are politically very popular in the United States. Ask the average person in Washington or manufacturing centers such as Detroit and he will likely say that China's huge trade surpluses are driving America's trade deficits. But, as a former chairman of the Council of Economic Advisors Martin Feldstein wrote, "every student of economics knows, or should know, that the current account balance of each country is determined within its own borders and not by its trading partners."[10] Popular sentiments are flawed in two key aspects. First, the longstanding worry about America's huge trade deficits actually has little to do with the emergence of China's large trade surpluses. Second, trade balances are the result of multilateral rather than bilateral relationships.

The confusion is driven by the fact that US-China bilateral trade imbalances come partly from China being the point of final assembly and shipping to the United States of parts and components produced by other Asian countries. This makes it difficult to determine which country is really responsible for the bulk of the value of finished products that end up in America.

On the first point, it is easy to show that US and China trade balances are not directly linked. US trade deficits became significant around the late 1990s and peaked around 2005 (see Figure 7.6). But China's trade surpluses did not become globally significant until around 2005. Moreover, when China's trade

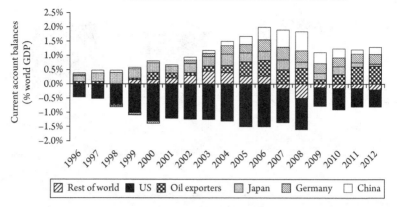

Figure 7.6 Global Current Account Balances. Source: IMF World Economic Outlook; IMF staff calculations

surpluses were surging during 2005 to 2008, America's deficits began to diminish. How could China be responsible for America's trade problems, when in fact, America's trade problems existed long before China even became an export power and their balances moved in opposite directions?

Answering this question requires an understanding of national accounting principles. A trade deficit is the result of a country spending more than it produces or investing more than it saves. This typically comes from excessive government deficits, households going into debt from consuming beyond their means, or both—such aspects have characterized the American economy over the past several decades. Moreover, inflows of capital into the United States during periods of global financial uncertainties exacerbate such deficits. In such circumstances, a country will generate a large trade deficit, but which countries show up as being sources of the offsetting trade surpluses is incidental.

America's bilateral trade deficits were concentrated among the more developed East Asian economies in the late 1990s, notably Japan, South Korea, Taiwan, and Singapore. But this then shifted to China after it became the center of the regional production sharing network after obtaining WTO membership in 2001. Figure 7.7 indicates that US manufactured imports from Pacific-Rim countries have remained at about 45 percent of total US manufactured imports from 1990 to 2014, but China gradually captured an increasing share of Asia's exports to the United States as the last stop in the global assembly chain during this period.[11] Thus the appearance that US trade deficits are linked with China's surpluses is misleading; it is really about deficits with East Asia more generally, with much of the higher-value components being produced by countries other than China.

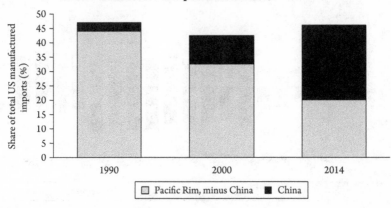

Figure 7.7 US Manufactured Imports by Source. Source: US International Trade Commission DataWeb; Congressional Research Service

Apple products are a good example: they are generally assembled in China but their key parts are produced elsewhere. China captures very little of the value added of an iPhone through assembly, while most of the value added (and profits) originate from the components produced in Korea, Japan, and Taiwan. Some studies suggest that of the $750 for a typical iPhone imported and sold in the United States, China gets only $8. The rest goes to other Asian manufacturers and the largest share goes to Apple in the form of profits.[12]

The Apple example is particularly significant given the composition of American imports from China. The top two categories of US imports from China are computers and communications equipment, indicative of a significant amount of value that China is not actually responsible for, since the relevant components are made outside of China.[13]

The other major source of tension is the perception that China's export strengths are largely due to its exchange rate being deliberately undervalued, giving it an unfair production advantage. Exchange rates do influence trade flows, but other factors matter more. If the exchange rate is fixed, then shifts in other prices—notably of labor and land, and eventually overall producer and consumer prices—bring exports and imports into balance over time. Even if a country runs huge trade surpluses and keeps its exchange rate constant, inflation will restore balance over time by making exports less competitive and imports more attractive. Thus economists focus less on nominal exchange rates and more on the real effective exchange rate which incorporates a country's price changes relative to its major trading partners.

How important was a fixed exchange rate in driving China's trade surpluses? China's trade surpluses fluctuated with the economic cycles and did not become significant globally until 2004/2005. Until the early 1990s, when China was still developing its industrial base, its economy operated under a multiple exchange system designed to ration its limited foreign exchange. After it established a unified exchange rate in 1994, the rate was generally seen as over- rather than undervalued—especially in the period before and after the AFC. Ironically, China was widely praised then for not devaluing its currency to remain competitive when many other Asian currencies had collapsed.

After joining the WTO in 2001, many analysts thought that the renminbi would be under additional pressure to depreciate, since China had to liberalize its import regime as a condition of membership and new exports would take time to develop. But the reality was far different. China gained a significant share of the global export market from becoming the center of the regional assembly network and from productivity-enhancing investments that led to a surge in labor productivity. Structural shifts and policy changes—not the exchange rate—were the major factors driving China's export success.

But appreciating the exchange rate can help moderate trade imbalances once they emerge. When China's trade surpluses increased to 5 percent of GDP, it moved away from a fixed peg to the US dollar and began to appreciate the renminbi in 2005. The combination of a steady appreciation of its nominal exchange rate and increasing consumer prices triggered by surging wages and property prices contributed to China's real effective exchange rate appreciating by about 50 percent by the end of 2015 compared with a nominal increase of 35 percent since 2005.[14] The modest depreciation that occurred in 2016 was in response to global market pressures as higher interest rates in the United States led to a stronger US dollar and substantial capital flows from China and other emerging market economies. As most analysts noted, China used its reserves to keep the renminbi stronger than it would have been without government intervention. The widespread view that Beijing has not allowed the renminbi to appreciate significantly over the past decade is simply wrong.

While this rapid appreciation eventually helped moderate China's trade surplus, its impact was much less than expected. Much more important was the surge in China's investment rates and rising imports related to its construction boom coupled with slackening import demand from the United States and Europe as their economies went into recessions. China's current account surplus fell from a high of 10 percent of GDP in 2008 to around 2–3 percent by 2012, where it has remained as of 2016. While changes in the real exchange rate contributed to the declining trade surpluses, the major factors were shifting investment and savings trends in the West and China.

More generally, studies have shown that adjustments in exchange rates have a much smaller impact on trade balances today than they did decades ago.[15] Manufacturers are increasingly relying on imported inputs rather than trying to produce all the parts themselves. As a consequence, if exchange rates fall, the boost to exports is not that great because increases in the price of imported components will partially offset the benefits from higher export receipts. Similarly, if the exchange rate appreciates, exports do not fall that much because the cost of imported inputs will decline. This factor is especially relevant for China's trade given the very high share of imported inputs in its exports of finished products to the West.

Capital Flight and Exchange Rate Management

More recently, exchange rate issues have resurfaced in the context of a sharp decline in China's reserves. This took place as Beijing was shifting to a new mechanism for establishing the value of the renminbi. China's foreign reserves soared from 2000 onward, driven by large trade surpluses and capital inflows, reaching nearly 4 trillion US dollars by mid-2014 (see Figure 7.8). This occurred as the renminbi appreciated rapidly. However, from 2015 to early 2017 there were periodic bursts of net capital outflows, despite positive, although lower, trade surpluses. Altered expectations about the value of the renminbi triggered these outflows.

Until 2015, the renminbi was essentially pegged to the US dollar. However, with the current economic slowdown and a large decline in the values of most other Asian currencies in the range of 20–40 percent, the renminbi was increasingly seen as being overvalued. Since the US dollar has been appreciating in recent years, tying the renminbi to the US dollar was seen as pushing its value in the wrong direction. Thus in mid-2015, China moved to peg its currency to a basket of currencies, and in the process allowed the renminbi to fall in value. This

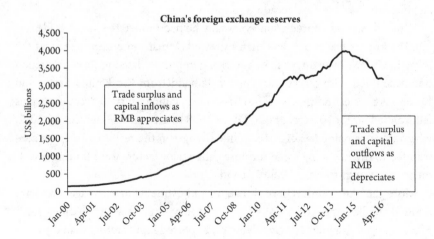

Figure 7.8 China's Foreign Exchange Reserve. Data Source: People's Bank of China

caused some short-lived turmoil in global markets with traders concerned that Beijing might be moving toward a strategy of depreciating to gain trade competitiveness. However, while China's intentions were poorly communicated, it had no such intention.

Market reactions were overdone. Most of the capital outflows were due to firms paying off their external borrowings to protect themselves from future renminbi depreciations, and the rest can be seen as portfolio diversification as firms and households invest an increasing share of their liquid assets abroad. The latter has been facilitated by more liberal capital controls until they were tightened up in 2016. As of end 2016, China reserves have hovered at around 3 trillion US dollars. Most analysts expect a continued but modest decline in the value of the renminbi because of the global currency realignments driven by the impact of Brexit and likely rising interest rates in the United States. Under these conditions, the level of China's reserves will likely continue to fall.

Globalization and US Job Losses to China

Even if China's exchange rate becomes less of a concern, emotions in the United States and Europe are likely to remain strong regarding the perception that manufacturing jobs have been lost to developing countries like China and that the incomes of the middle class have suffered from globalization. Such sentiments have been aggravated by concerns over cross-border flows of workers and refugees and real or imagined job losses from trade agreements such as NAFTA (North American Free Trade Agreement). This has derailed ratification of the TPP and jeopardized negotiations between the United States and Europe on a trade agreement, and was also seen as a factor underpinning the United Kingdom's referendum to leave the European Union.

The decline in manufacturing jobs in the United States is not the China issue that many have made it to be. The share of manufacturing workers in the United States has been declining continuously since the end of World War II, and the total number of manufacturing jobs peaked in 1979.[16] China's trade with the United States didn't take off until the early 2000s, well after the US job decline began. But the decline in jobs accelerated given the size of China's surging trade surpluses a decade ago, according to Massachusetts Institute of Technology professor David Autor and his collaborators, who have studied the relationship between trade and employment.[17]

The loss of American manufacturing jobs, however, has been driven by forces largely beyond the control of any leader or country. Technological advances, shifting industrial expertise around the world, and the availability of low-cost labor if not in China then elsewhere (India, Mexico, and Vietnam) would have made the decline in manufacturing jobs inevitable in the United States as well as Europe. Nor would tariffs or reneging on trade deals bring many of these jobs back. As noted by the Financial Times's Martin Wolf, from 1990 to 2016, US manufacturing output rose 63 percent while employment fell by 31 percent due to rising productivity.[18]

Globalization inevitably links product and labor markets across countries, either from the increased flow of goods across borders through trade and investment, or via labor in the form of migration. The process can be moderated but trying to stop it with trade barriers or restrictions on migration will ultimately prove ineffective and the costs will show up in reduced growth and welfare for all countries.

Theory, as well as comparative experience, tells us that there is a natural shift from manufacturing to services as a country develops and reaches high-income status. With this "success," workers shift into more knowledge-intensive jobs in services. The more routine industrial assembly-type jobs are nearly guaranteed to be lost either to robotics or to plants overseas that can utilize lower paid workers. Within East Asia, Singapore is perhaps the best example. As it rose quickly to become one of the richest countries in the world, its labor force shifted increasingly away from manufacturing to high-value services which warranted the higher salaries of a more sophisticated, developed economy.

Thus the preservation of manufacturing jobs per se should not be the objective, but generating the demand for more skilled workers should be. This process is not smooth, and it often takes many years—even in the United States and Europe—for those without the necessary skills to find alternatives to the assembly-type jobs that have relocated to developing countries overseas.

What made the process seem like a China issue was the speed and size of the loss in jobs that began with the surge in East Asian trade surpluses as China became the center of the regional production network a decade and a half ago. Much of the perceived job loss was, in reality, more of a loss in American and European firms' competitiveness to their counterparts in Japan, South Korea, and Taiwan rather than to China's low-skilled assembly-type activities.[19]

With the decline in East Asian's trade surpluses, the pattern of job losses has changed. Contrary to popular perceptions, manufacturing jobs have actually been increasing in the United States since 2010. America's exports to China are also becoming a major source of job generation. The Department of Commerce estimates that some 350,000 new jobs were created for this purpose in the United States during between 2009 and 2014. In contrast, the manufacturing labor force in China has been declining, as their salaries are now twice that of Vietnam's and four times that of Bangladesh's. But China is not really "losing jobs" to the United States as some are now claiming. Rather, Chinese workers are shifting into services and away from manufacturing—as was the case with the other successful economies moving from middle- to high-income status.[20]

Yet the reality is that the "hollowing out" of the middle class in the United States and Europe has given rise to frustrations that can no longer be placated by simply appealing to the supposed virtues of globalization. In theory, globalization leads to net welfare gains for the world by uplifting the poor in developing countries and encouraging more innovation in the advanced economies. But there are uncompensated losers in the process.

As many commentators have noted given the rise of populist pressures in the West for protectionism, political systems need to find ways to address local interests without giving up the benefits that globalization can bring. This will involve more programs to cushion the structural changes, such as training programs, improved education, and targeted social welfare services. Countries like China need to play a role in the process by being more sensitive to the external consequences that their own structural shifts have created in the West and among other developing economies.

China's Outward Capital Flows

While FDI was the primary means by which foreign capital flowed into China during its development, China's outward capital flows are more varied and a recent phenomenon. The distinction between China's ODI—defined as having at least a 10 percent managerial stake in a foreign subsidiary—and China's aid and project-related loans is blurred (see Box 7.1).

Box 7.1 **FDI Data Distortions**

In today's globalized world where money is even more mobile than goods, FDI is hard to track and often gets routed through other countries before arriving at its final destination. China's inward FDI follows its trading supply chain, with most of China's FDI coming from neighboring Asian countries. However, these numbers are distorted by investment from Hong Kong, which typically makes up the majority of total inward flows to China. FDI numbers from Hong Kong are notoriously distorted by Chinese "round tripping" of investment that gets looped through Hong Kong to take advantage of preferential tax policies and the role of subsidiaries. Aside from Hong Kong, China's second largest "investor" is the British Virgin Islands, a tax shelter for corporate profits which had more FDI to China than either Europe or North America.

Direct investments account for less than half of the outward capital outflows, while the rest are in the form of aid and semi-concessional loans often linked to infrastructure projects. Multiple objectives guide China's outward flow. Much of it has been directed to secure resources in Africa and South America for domestic investment needs. More recent foreign investment activities have been driven by geopolitical objectives and the desire for higher returns from China's reserves, which are parked largely in low-yield government securities in the United States and Europe.

Chinese state-owned banks that provide the money for overseas investment—the China Export-Import Bank and the China Development Bank (CDB)—also handle China's official aid programs and commercial lending (see Box 7.2). The interest rates that these two banks provide to developing countries are often much lower than market conditions would warrant. This makes it difficult to distinguish between FDI and investment projects supported by loans, and those projects that are financed by grants to build stronger bilateral relationships.

FOREIGN AID

Like China's ODI, its foreign grants and concessional loans have increased dramatically in recent years. A 2013 Rand study looking into China's foreign aid and government investment activities found that China's total aid and related financing commitments went from $1.7 billion in 2001 to $124 billion in 2009 and $189.3 billion in 2011.[21]

Box 7.2 Role of Key Agencies, CDB and Export-Import Bank, and Private Outward FDI

In the past, China's outward investment has been shaped by large SOEs that were able to secure favorable terms from China's Export-Import Bank and CDB. These included trade, construction, and energy companies. The China Export-Import Bank and CDB are also the primary administrators of China's concessional loans. Also worth highlighting is the role played by the China Investment Corporation, China's sovereign wealth fund, which tends to be a passive investor looking for steady returns. Though in the past, state-owned firms dominated outward investment, particularly in pursuit of natural resources, China's investors are increasingly led by private entrepreneurs who see opportunity in Western brands and technology. A 2013 government report on China's outward investment showed that private FDI accounted for 45 percent of total outflow compared to 55 percent for SOEs.

Over the past decade and a half, China has become a major source of financing for developing countries globally. This has generated concerns about whether China's lending policies are undercutting the practices of traditional Western donors and their respective export credit agencies and not just multilateral development banks. Geostrategic implications have also heightened sensitivities.

At first glance, the notion of China as a major source of financial assistance defies logic. The world has never seen a case where a developing country was providing so much concessional financing, sometimes to countries whose citizens are richer than its own. No wonder that Beijing has been reluctant to broadcast the details of its assistance programs for fear that its citizens would question why they are being asked to give to others when there are still so many unmet social needs at home.

China's aid began in the 1960s when the country was much poorer, but back then the motivation was to gain support for its claim as the sole representative of the Chinese nation. Relatively less well-off and small African and Latin American nations with votes in the United Nations were the targeted recipients. Today, as a rapidly growing middle-income country with outsized amounts of foreign reserves, the objective has evolved to securing resources, accessing technology, and building goodwill as a rising great power. Particularly noteworthy have been China's infrastructure projects, which draw on its experienced and vast labor force.

The amounts that have been offered have been the subject of much speculation, since hard numbers are difficult to come by and definitions vary. Reports that China's aid flows exceed the total provided by everybody else often mix concessional with commercial lending and even FDI. Announced amounts often reflect vague intentions and bear little resemblance to actual utilization.[22] Aid levels began to surge about a decade ago when China's trade surpluses became significant. While natural resources were the main draw for Chinese aid to Latin America and Africa, strategic objectives have driven aid to Southeast Asia and more recently to Central Asia.

A Rand study using a broad concept of China's "foreign aid and government invested activities" found that over 80 percent of the investment projects from 2001 to 2011 were in natural resources and infrastructure.[23] Ninety-five percent of China's aid to Latin America during this period was pledged after 2008, growing to approximately $80 billion. According to a study by the Inter-American Dialogue, China's $37 billion in commitments in 2010 alone already exceeded lending by the World Bank, the Inter-American Development Bank, and the US Export-Import Bank combined for that year.[24] China's loans to Latin America are larger and growing faster than their counterparts, with most of the money (largely from CDB) flowing to Venezuela, Brazil, Argentina, and Ecuador. Two-thirds of all of China's loans were categorized as loans for oil.

China's aid money to Africa tells a similar story. Infrastructure and natural resource development programs were the two largest categories of aid.[25] Cheap loans from the Export-Import Bank have also been extended to African governments to purchase telecommunications equipment, installation services from Chinese firms, and agricultural machinery. The Infrastructure Consortium for Africa estimates that $13 billion in commitments for infrastructure have been extended in recent years.[26] While it is hard to distinguish whether this is aid, commercial loans, or direct investment, it's not hard to imagine why China is now Africa's number one trading partner.

Within Southeast Asia, China is considered the "primary supplier of economic and military assistance" to Burma, Cambodia, and Laos, while also providing them with an "implicit security guarantee, solicited or unsolicited."[27] Most of its assistance flows to Indonesia, Malaysia, and Thailand are for infrastructure rather than natural resource extraction, which is why project sizes are not as large as in Latin America and Africa.

China's aid gives it a substantial economic presence, but it can also impact negatively on foreign relations, as with recent projects in Burma and Sri Lanka that were halted as new leaders responded to criticisms of their potentially negative consequences and allegations of corruption. Capital flows, along with trade links, have promoted the process of regional integration with ASEAN nations even as these countries have sought to hedge against China's rising influence, particularly with the tensions emanating from the South China Sea island disputes.[28] A decade ago Japan was by far the primary aid donor to Southeast Asia, but China is rapidly achieving parity using a variety of financing approaches which are likely to be augmented by its "One Belt, One Road" (OBOR) initiative (see Chapter 9).

China's state-sponsored aid and investment activities in South Asia and the Middle East have been more modest. Lending to South Asia from 2001 to 2011 was primarily shaped by infrastructure and financing needs rather than natural resource development. Middle East countries have received aid for oil and gas projects, railway construction, and debt forgiveness.

In many ways, China's investment in the developing south fills the niche for a lender that purports to understand these countries' needs better and comes with more flexible financing terms. More recent trends suggest a wider range of target countries and more varied diplomatic objectives. China's funding provides an alternative to Western export credit agencies, which can require substantial upfront fees to protect financing costs.[29] World Bank loans are also seen as having many conditions. In contrast, Chinese loans come with fewer strings attached, though they often require borrowers to spend a share of the loan on Chinese goods and labor.[30]

OUTWARD DIRECT INVESTMENT

The rise of China's ODI is a relatively recent phenomenon and has drawn considerable attention because of its geopolitical implications. Insignificant in the

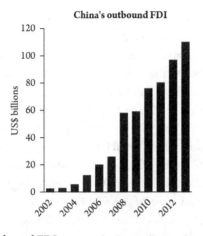

Figure 7.9 China's Outbound FDI. Source: Rhodium; Ministry of Commerce China; author's calculations

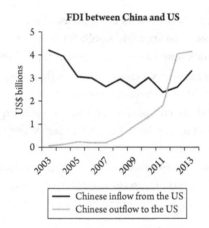

Figure 7.10 US-China FDI Flows. Source: Rhodium; Ministry of Commerce China; author's calculations

early 2000s, it surged in 2008, more than doubling from the previous year (see Figure 7.9). Since 2012, China's FDI flows to the United States have been rising rapidly and now exceed US investment flows to China (see Figure 7.10). China's outward flows of over $100 billion in 2013 placed China as the third largest outward investor in the world for the second year in a row. While the sharp decline in China's reserves in 2016 has led Beijing to cut back on some highly publicized foreign investments, some predict that China will become the world's largest investor by 2020, with its overseas assets tripling from its current $6.4 trillion to nearly $20 trillion.[31]

Similar to tracking inward FDI, tracking China's ODI presents statistical challenges.[32] When FDI transit zones like Hong Kong, the British Virgin Islands, and the Cayman Islands are discounted, the UN Commission on Trade and

Development FDI statistics shows that the United States has typically been the top destination for Chinese outward investment.[33]

The Heritage Foundation has created its own dataset (China Global Investment Tracker) to monitor China's outbound investment using a broader definition that includes both FDI and state-supported lending of over $100 million. It also shows the United States to be China's number one investment destination as of July 2015. This gives a somewhat misleading picture about the significance of the United States. Total flows to Europe, which is about the same size measured by GDP as the United States, are much larger. Chinese government statistics show about twice as much FDI going to the European Union as to the United States, and most of the FDI flows to the United States are fairly recent. When China's ODI, portfolio investment flows, and infrastructure contracts are summed up, North America (United States and Canada as a region) becomes less significant compared with East Asia—including Australia—and Africa (see Figure 7.11).

China's outward investment flows are a focus of increasing attention given their size as well as potential strategic significance. Much of the anxiety stems from the role that China's state-owned companies play and the nature of their investments, which raise security concerns. Also worth noting is that the quality of some of these investments have become a source of skepticism. Many observers wonder how some of these companies can finance such acquisitions given that they are highly indebted themselves. The answer is that they are often backed by the financial resources of the state.

If the objective is to lock up resources or to acquire technology that might be helpful to China's longer-term interests, and the cost of capital is seen to be low, then the likelihood that Chinese companies will overpay or get themselves into

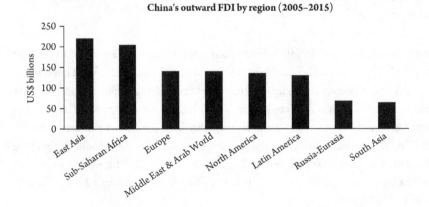

Figure 7.11 Outward FDI by Region. Source: Heritage China Investment Tracker; author's calculations

unfavorable arrangements is significant. Many such examples have been cited.[34] Nevertheless, the reality may be less alarming since the acquired firms may be of greater value to China than other countries in terms of technological importance or access to resources and market shares that would otherwise have been hard to secure.

The rise of China's outward foreign investment comes at a time when US and EU companies are increasing their complaints about being discriminated against in gaining access to China's growing domestic market. Accusations that Chinese firms use cybertheft to steal technology further exacerbate emotions. By late 2016, these factors have led many countries to take a more cautious position toward Chinese investors, especially if the firms are state owned. Moreover, China's diminishing external reserve position has put a brake on the financing that its companies have available to invest abroad. Together these factors are likely to moderate the pace of expansion in China's ODI in the coming years.

CHAPTER 8

China's Foreign Investment in the United States and European Union

Until recently and contrary to popular perceptions, foreign investment flows between China and the United States have been almost negligible in comparison with the much larger flows between China and the EU. Few realize that the differences between the United States and the European Union in their respective investment relations with China are due largely to the nature of their trade relations and the differing impact of China's restrictions—not political sensitivities.

Ongoing negotiations of BITs will serve as the primary means for China to engage the United States and European Union on economic policies in the coming years. Both the United States and the European Union are likely to be confronting China with concerns about its restrictive investment practices, pressures for technology transfer, market access, and intellectual property rights (IPR) protection at a time when China seeks to move up the technology ladder.[1]

China will continue to complain that it is being discriminated against by being classified as a "nonmarket economy"—and thus subject to special WTO restrictions and greater scrutiny. These frictions are also aggravated by China's complaints about the opaqueness of America's security review process and America's accusations that China resorts to cybertheft to acquire commercial advantages.

Investment Relations between China and the United States and European Union

The prevailing perception is that US firms invest a lot in China. The logic is reinforced by the fact that the United States and China are the two largest economies and trading nations. It is thus surprising that over the past decade, only about 1–2 percent of America's investment has been going to China and only about 2–3 percent of China's outward investment has been going to the United States.

In contrast, countries like South Korea and Japan have historically invested around 20 percent of their FDI in China.

For comparison, consider the European Union, which in its economic size ($18 trillion) and trade with China ($500 billion) is comparable to the United States. Over the past decade, annual flows of EU's FDI to China have been roughly double that of the United States, although they began at around the same level a decade ago. Similarly, until 2015, much more of China's outward FDI had been going to the European Union than to the United States (see Figures 8.1 and 8.2). So why have the United States and China not been investing in each other?[2]

Statistics can be deceiving. Because much of the FDI goes through tax shelters, it is hard to determine precisely the origin or destination of these flows. However, the EU's FDI numbers are subject to the same distortions yet show a

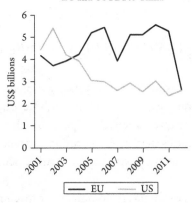

Figure 8.1 EU and US FDI to China. Source: United Nations Conference on Trade and Development; author's calculations

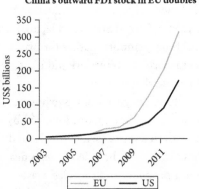

Figure 8.2 Chinese FDI Stocks in US and EU. Source: United Nations Conference on Trade and Development; author's calculations

comparatively stronger FDI relationship. Furthermore, the European Union has significantly greater inflows and outflows of FDI to Hong Kong than the United States, suggesting that it may be responsible for even more of the FDI flows to and from China that are routed indirectly through Hong Kong.

The European Union is known globally for its manufacturing prowess and a comparison done by Rhodium covering 2008–2011 shows that it has almost double the investment of the United States in both manufacturing and services in China.[3] Though China presents a large and potentially attractive market, its relative lack of natural resources compared to its population, its significant investment restrictions (particularly in areas of US strengths), and its weak property rights enforcement are seen as reasons for the low flow of FDI from the United States.[4] However, the question remains: Given similar barriers to entry in China and related concerns, why did EU investment flows with China grow more rapidly?

Trade Patterns Explain US and EU FDI Differences

From 2004 to 2013, US exports to China nearly tripled to $120 billion, yet it still ranks as the fifth largest exporter, behind South Korea, Japan, and the EU—which is ranked number one.[5] The EU's exports to China totaled 164 billion euros in 2014.[6] This suggests that the EU's economic strengths in manufacturing have been more complementary with China's market needs than has been the case for the United States.

The EU's top exports to China are dominated by machinery and transport as well as items targeted to both high-end consumers and industrial firms, making up 59 percent and 17 percent of total trade, respectively (see Figure 8.3). These sectors logically lead to FDI flows to support market penetration and servicing as well as the establishment of localized production capacity when conditions warrant. Compared to the United States and Japan, Europe has dominated China's transport and machinery import market for over a decade, accounting for about half of China's imports for transport and a quarter for machinery—twice as high as US or Japanese shares.

In comparison, the top three categories of US exports to China over the past decade and half have been oilseeds and grains, followed by aerospace products and then, surprisingly, by recycled waste (scrap metal and discarded paper) (see Figure 8.4). None of these categories have led to significant FDI. The reasons are obvious regarding food products and recycled waste. For aerospace products, Boeing has refrained from opening production plants in China, while its European competitor, Airbus, has had manufacturing centers in China since

EU exports to China

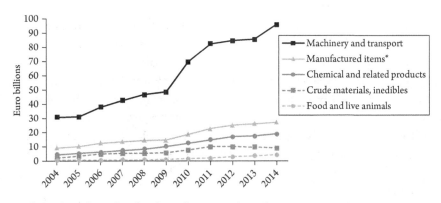

*Sum of manufactured goods and miscellaneus manufactured items

Figure 8.3   EU Exports to China. Source: Eurostat

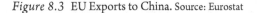

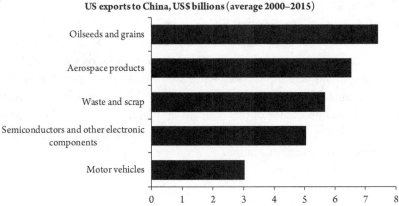

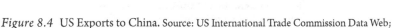

Figure 8.4   US Exports to China. Source: US International Trade Commission Data Web; author's calculations

2008 and has continued to expand its operations as China expanded flight services to its interior.

    Motor vehicle exports only became significant in recent years, and its emergence is somewhat surprising. The United States has been successful in creating a local market for American cars and recent announcements from General Motors indicate that this will be supported by substantially higher FDI flows. But the European presence in the auto sector has a much longer history, and the recent surge in exports of cars from the United States to China surprisingly is accounted for largely by European luxury SUVs such as Audi and Mercedes. These are made in the United States but given China's tax policies can be imported at a price that is lower than those made in China. The related FDI then turns out to be European rather than American.

EU and US trade relations with China illustrate how composition matters in shaping FDI flows. Manufacturing exports and investments are largely welcomed in China's domestic market and cater more to EU strengths, while China's closed services sector has a disproportionately more negative effect on the United States, whose strengths lie in higher-value services, notably information technology (IT) and finance. Of total US services exports in 2014, 19 percent came from the use of intellectual property (IP), compared to the EU's 6.4 percent of total service exports from royalties and licensing fees. Financial services also made up 12 percent of US services exports compared to the EU's 8.6 percent.[7]

China's economy has one of the most restrictive FDI services sectors in the world. According to the Organization for Economic Cooperation and Development FDI Restrictiveness Index, on a scale from 0 = completely open, to 1 = completely closed, the United States is less than 0.1, and China stands at over 0.4—well above the other BRICs—while the average for the European Union is around 0.05 (see Figure 8.5). China's most restricted industries are in high-value services such as communications, mobile telecoms, legal, insurance, finance, and banking services—precisely the areas of special interest to American firms. Given the recent decline in FDI, Beijing seems to have finally recognized the importance of this issue. In mid-January, 2017, a directive was issued liberalizing investment in several sectors, including financial services, telecommunications and education.

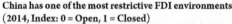

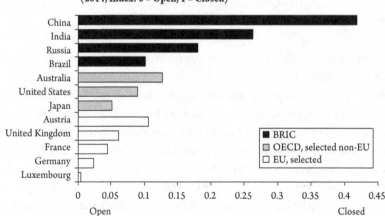

Figure 8.5 Investment Environment Comparison. Source: OECD FDI Restrictiveness Index

Another reason for lower US investment in China compared to the EU is that EU trade provides about twice as much value added in the manufacturing process within China than does such trade with the United States (see Figure 8.6).[8] American firms like Apple also operate in a way that tends to involve little direct FDI coming from the United States. Although Apple products are manufactured in China, the company actually responsible for production is a Taiwanese firm—Foxconn—which accounts for the bulk of the FDI required. Thus, while most Americans think that Apple must be heavily invested financially in China, the reality is that most of the investment comes from other sources.

Furthermore, major US companies with a visible presence in China, such as fast food restaurants and hotel chains, operate as franchises. These US companies do not own their local affiliates but rather license and receive franchise fees, although they may be involved in providing some of the products needed by their franchisees. Thus the presence of these US multinational icons in China does not necessarily show up as FDI in the official tallies.

Overall, the structure of trade relations between the United States and China does not lend itself as naturally to foreign investment as it does with the EU. But if China liberalizes its investment regime in favor of more high-value services, this could alter prospects.

Whether China will be given market economy status, as defined by WTO rules, is among the more contentious trade-related issues that still need to be addressed regarding China's relations with both the United States and Europe. When China joined the WTO, it was declared a nonmarket economy and thus subject to harsher treatment regarding the adjudication of anti-dumping cases and levying of countervailing tariffs. Securing market economy status would require comparing the price of Chinese exports to its domestic market—instead of higher-priced third countries—in anti-dumping cases and thus reduce the

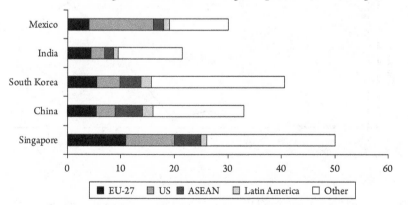

Foreign value-added embedded in gross exports 2014, % of total exports

Legend: ■ EU-27 ▨ US ■ ASEAN ▢ Latin America ☐ Other

Figure 8.6 Foreign Value-Added in Exports. Source: Deutsche Bank; OECD

likelihood of imposing tariffs. A decision was due in late 2016, with the United States seen taking a negative position and Europe having more mixed views.[9] With the lapse of time, a decision is now likely to require WTO adjudication.

Political and Security Sensitivities Affect China's Outward FDI

The United States and the European Union have reacted quite differently to China's rising outward investment. In addition to reciprocity and more complementary trade sectors, not to be overlooked is the fact that despite some recent setbacks, the European Union is more willing to let the Chinese come in. China's outward FDI stock in the European Union ($31.5 billion in 2012) is about double that in the United States ($17.1 billion). The divergence is largely due to the post-GFC years when annual flows were typically multiples higher for the EU (see Figure 8.7). The rise in China's investment in the European Union was significantly impacted by the opportunities for Chinese investors during the euro-zone crisis. However, no similarly large spike in investment was seen when the United States suffered its own financial crisis.

There are significant differences between the sectors targeted by China's FDI in the European Union and in the United States (see Figure 8.8). The Rhodium Group, which tracks China's outward FDI, finds that China invests significantly more in the EU's utilities and energy sectors. This is likely a consequence of the European Union being more open to such investments than the United States. The much higher amounts going to automobile, transportation,

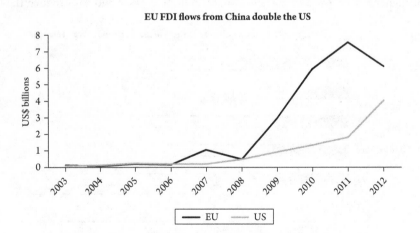

Figure 8.7 China FDI in US and EU. Source: United Nations Conference on Trade and Development

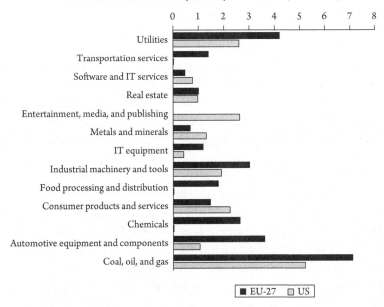

Figure 8.8 China's FDI in US and EU. Source: Rhodium; author's calculations

and machinery-related activities reflect the dominance of such products in the EU's trade with China. American strengths are clear from the attractiveness of its entertainment and metals and minerals sectors, while China's investment in US consumer products logically supports its huge exports of such goods.

For Chinese companies, the European Union also represents a much easier market to penetrate because it offers a greater choice of partners. This could be seen as a form of a "divide-and-conquer" strategy. If one EU member country restricted access to its market, a Chinese company could still enter through a different member country and gain access to the greater EU market in that way.[10] Though partnerships with individual US states are possible, the more agglomerated nature of US companies and overarching federal policies present a greater challenge. However, if an EU-wide BIT is negotiated that sets regional standards, this might actually make the European Union less accessible from China's perspective.

In this context, Britain's exit from the European Union (Brexit) would likely render it less attractive as a destination for FDI if it loses access to the broader EU market in the process. Moreover, the European Union itself becomes less attractive if it no longer includes the United Kingdom. Thus, Brexit is generally seen as a negative economic outcome for everyone in a global context but clearly economically more damaging for the European Union and United Kingdom than for countries like China and the United States.

The Committee on Foreign Investment in the United States (CFIUS), a multi-agency federal panel that determines whether deals with foreign corporations raise antitrust or national-security issues is one special cause for Chinese concern. CFIUS was a relatively quiet organization before the September 11 terrorist attacks, but the ensuing Patriot Act called for more stringent foreign investment controls to protect infrastructure systems and assets whose breakdown "would have a debilitating impact on security, national economic security, national public health, or safety."[11] While the United States considers itself a relatively open economy, CFIUS's category of "critical infrastructure" includes eleven sectors including basic areas such as agriculture and transport, as well as more sensitive areas such as finance and defense industrial bases (see Box 8.1).

In 2012, though China accounted for only a few percent of FDI into the United States, it comprised 20 percent of CFIUS cases and topped the list of countries whose proposed transactions were reviewed by CFIUS.[12] China's investments within the United States attract particular scrutiny due to US wariness over China's SOEs and security concerns. A few high-profile negative cases include US government interventions that prevented the state-owned China National Offshore Oil Corporation from purchasing California-based energy company Unocal; Sany Group's purchase of four small wind farms located close to US

Box 8.1 **Committee on Foreign Investment in the United States**

CFIUS is an inter-agency group chaired by the Treasury Department which screens foreign investment for national-security purposes. Its other members include the Departments of State, Defense, Commerce, Justice, Homeland Security, and Energy, as well as the Office of the US Trade Representative. It is responsible for evaluating mergers and acquisitions rather than green-field investments where foreign "control" over a domestic company may be a concern. CFIUS's responsibilities to investigate and review foreign investment of US businesses stem from a 1934 statutory authorization to block transactions which threaten US national security. The process typically starts with a voluntary filing by the foreign company, though CFIUS is also able to initiate a review. After CFIUS has collected sufficient information to begin the process, it follows a congressionally mandated timetable for reviews, leading to a formal report to the president if action is recommended. The president then decides whether he will act on the recommendation. Unlike other countries which also review inward investment based on economic interests, CFIUS's mandate is strictly concerned with national security. The vast majority of foreign investment in the United States, around 90 percent, is not subject to CFIUS review.

military facilities; and Huawei's acquisition of 3Leaf, a high-technology firm. Even Chinese company Shuanghui's purchase of US pork producer Smithfield Foods had to overcome political opposition in the form of Congressional petitions opposing the acquisition on the grounds of "critical infrastructure." It eventually passed the CFIUS review.[13] More recently, attention has shifted to China's interest in acquiring the capacity to make its own microchips as evidenced in the CFIUS blocking the proposed purchase by Chinese investors of a controlling stake in a unit of the Dutch firm Philips that manufactures a compound needed for production.[14]

Often, Chinese investment interests in energy, natural resources, and technology sectors in the United States do not fall into the more contentious investment categories. Still, the Chinese have cause to think that CFIUS is an opaque process and are confused over what investments are welcome. A Peterson Institute report on the prospect of a US-China BIT reported that even the possibility of going through a review was sometimes enough to prevent a Chinese firm from trying.[15] Congressional disapproval, intense media scrutiny, and negative public sentiment resulting from the few high-profile CFIUS cases can dissuade investors, especially those from a country that believes in "saving face." Chinese bidders are increasingly being saddled with an unofficial "CFIUS premium" to make up for the extra costs involved in their bids. In one cited case, it amounted to an extra $400 million in the transaction, or nearly 7 percent of the purchase price.[16]

Contrary to the high-profile negative sentiments over SOE investments in the United States, a majority of Chinese investment to the United States may actually be private. Nevertheless, the negative sentiments around CFIUS cases may be counterproductive to attracting smaller private Chinese investors.[17] According to the 2015 report to Congress by CFIUS, China ranks number one in terms of CIFIUS reviews, although it ranks fourteenth regarding the amount of foreign investment that is coming into the United States.[18]

National-security concerns are especially relevant in US high-tech sectors. Huawei, a Chinese telecommunications company, is one example of how US national-security concerns prevented the company's expansion while the European Union was much more open. In late 2012, the House Intelligence Committee released a report recommending that US companies reconsider doing business with Huawei and that CFIUS should block acquisitions, takeovers, or mergers involving Huawei and another Chinese telecom company, ZTE, citing both as a "threat to U.S. national security interests." The report went on to state that "China is known to be the major perpetrator of cyber espionage, and Huawei and ZTE failed to alleviate serious concerns throughout this important investigation."[19]

While being virtually shut out of the United States, Huawei has had better luck in Europe. Canada and Australia followed the US lead in blocking Huawei over cyber espionage concerns, but the United Kingdom took another approach. It set up a special center to examine Huawei's technology in 2010 that enabled UK experts to work with Huawei to gain the necessary assurance that the company's products met security standards.[20] In 2013, the UK prime minister met with Huawei's chairman after the group pledged to invest 1.3 billion pounds and expand the UK workforce to 1500. Huawei now comprises nearly 22 percent of mobile-network infrastructure spending in Europe, the Middle East, and Africa. By contrast, Huawei has less than 3 percent share of the telecom market in North America as of 2013, and it continues to pull out of planned investments on the continent.[21]

Nevertheless, such successes may turn out to be short-lived. Britain's new prime minister, selected in the aftermath of the 2016 Brexit referendum, has signaled a more cautious approach to China's investment ambitions by putting on hold Chinese-French financing of a nuclear plan on security grounds (the hold was later reversed). This was followed by concerns in Germany about a Chinese appliance maker taking over high-tech German engineering firm Kuka. Further away, security concerns caused Australia to ban a joint proposal by a Chinese SOE and a Hong Kong firm to take over its main electricity grid.

There are differences in how politicization affects US and EU attitudes toward FDI from China, as reflected in the statements issued at the conclusion of the US-China Strategic and Economic Dialogue and the EU-China Summit. At the end of the 2015 Strategic and Economic Dialogue, the US Treasury secretary's statement included issues like cybersecurity, China's foreign exchange rate, and the potentially unfair impacts of China's new national-security review process for foreign investments. The joint statement that came out of the EU-China summit did not touch on these topics, focusing instead on collaborative research and development, and mentioning security only in terms of how both parties might better work with each other.

From Trade to Foreign Investment Concerns

China's trade surpluses and exchange rate may become less contentious issues in the coming years as attention shifts to foreign investment concerns. Surveys of American and European firms operating in China suggest that their primary worries relate to recent actions taken by Beijing to promote "indigenous innovation" by excluding foreign companies from various sectors. Language in highly publicized development plans—such as "Made in China 2025"—also appear to promote domestic companies over foreign. China is seen as keen to develop its own technology as a means of offsetting rising wages and a shrinking labor force and has launched many initiatives to support this objective. Western governments and business associations have warned that any discriminatory policies will adversely impact future foreign investments in China.

At first glance, China's actions to restrict foreign investment would seem odd given the historically important role that foreign investment has played in developing its industrial capacity. The literature suggests that the key to escaping the so-called middle-income trap is for a country to become more innovative. This has been interpreted by China, however, as demonstrating the need to develop its own capacity to move up the value chain in production.

Technology Transfers Exacerbate Tensions with the West

China's leadership is moving forward aggressively in promoting innovation, decreasing barriers to entry in strategic sectors, more so for Chinese rather than foreign firms, while providing preferential tax policies. At least officially, Beijing says that it will encourage foreign investment in high-end manufacturing and modern services, with added emphasis on cooperative investment structures in the field of research and development.[22] The reality of the difficulties posed by developing innovative industries, however, makes this more complicated.

Promoting innovation resonates for both advanced economies like the United States and Singapore or developing countries like India and China. Many governments are struggling to put in place policies and special programs to become more innovative, but whether such efforts actually lead to the production of higher valued goods and more rapid growth beyond what would happen anyway is unclear.

What is striking is how closely measures of innovation correlate with how wealthy a country is. Figure 8.9 indicates that China is no more innovative in its high-tech production than would have been predicted by its per-capita income

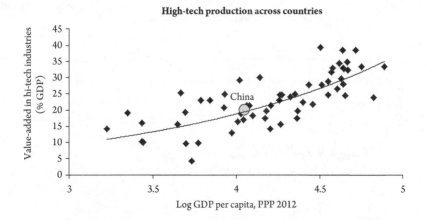

High-tech production across countries

Figure 8.9 Hi-Tech Production across Countries. Source: National Science Foundation Science and Engineering Indicators; World Bank World Development Indicators

level. Correlation, however, does not explain causality. It is natural to think that the more innovative a country is, the faster it will grow and become rich. But the relationship might also work the other way, that is, the richer a country, the more innovative it is. The point is that innovation comes from a range of factors, including the strength of institutions, a human capital base, and an environment that supports creativity—all of which only comes with becoming wealthier and more developed. This line of reasoning would suggest that it is very difficult for a country to "leap frog" and become more innovative than its per-capita income would indicate, or that trying to do so may be a waste of resources regarding achievable outcomes.

China, however, is unique in its capacity to "adopt technology" from others and to incorporate it into its own production processes. A World Bank study examined how fast and to what extent a sample of countries adopted more advanced technology using standards in the United States as the bench-mark.[23] The time frame involved looking at current production processes in these countries and tracing their origins to practices years or even decades ago in the United States and elsewhere. As indicated in Figure 8.10, starting from the early 1980s and into the 1990s, China was in a class by itself in the speed and depth of its adoption of technologies and practices from abroad. Most adaptation comes from importing higher-value equipment, FDI, leasing arrangements, and the purchase and reengineering of designs that originated elsewhere. Controversies come from what the media and businesses in the West refer to as outright theft.

As Chinese companies become more sophisticated, transferring technologies from more advanced economies becomes more difficult and competition with the West more intense. A China that was successful in producing shoes or assembling a laptop or iPhone presents a far different competitive challenge

Figure 8.10 Technology Adoption Intensity. Source: World Bank

than a China that is now able to construct a high-speed rail system or develop solar energy cells.

Much of China's future success, or lack thereof, will depend on developing its capacity to move up the value chain using technologies appropriate to the country's resource and institutional endowments. This is the rationale of Beijing's drive to develop indigenous technology. To outsiders, this intention gives rise to a sense of protectionism, unreasonable demands for technology transfer as a condition for market access, and—at the extreme—a license for IPR theft. This has created an emotional and politicized environment surrounding negotiations of the individual BITs between the United States and the European Union with China. Adding to these tensions have been the accusations that Beijing has been providing state support for cyber-related IPR theft.

Technically, the United States and Europe could be beneficiaries of China's continued economic development, with their comparative strengths in technology and high-value services industries. However, there are fears that this will only mean losing advantages rather than sharing in the potential gains, turning what could be an area of cooperation into a potential source of friction.

China feels that it needs to become more self-reliant and cannot continue to depend on foreign multinationals in the more strategic sectors. The examples of Japan and South Korea, countries that managed eventually to develop their own innovative capacities rather than rely on foreign firms, have convinced Beijing that this is the strategy to emulate. And as discussed later, IPR theft also featured in their historical experiences.

Thus, high-tech companies like CISCO and Qualcomm find themselves negotiating technology-sharing arrangements to make it easier to expand operations in China.[24] Hewlett-Packard and Intel appear willing to work with the Chinese government on joint ventures involving technology transfer— given the importance of China to their business prospects—but other firms, like Microsoft, face some difficult choices when attempting to operate freely in China.

China's poor record of protecting IP has made it a frequent target in the West. Cybersecurity was one of the top American priorities during President Xi Jinping's visit in September 2015. IP theft has become a central sticking point in Sino-American relations for obvious reasons. At present, China is estimated to be behind 50 to 80 percent of stolen IP globally. Valuation of the problem is difficult given that IP is an intangible asset, but annual losses from stolen IP are estimated to total $300 billion for the United States alone, a country with a stockpile of $5 trillion dollars in IP.[25] Further, as IP makes up 70 percent of the value of publically traded American companies, and protected IP supports 19 percent of the American workforce, China has frequently been deemed an IP thief unlike any other in the American media.[26]

Temptations to Steal Technology Are Hard to Contain

Consideration of the record of other countries that followed a development path like China's shows similarities between their developments and China's own. However, competition at the cutting edge of technology is so fierce and the required investments so costly that it makes little sense for a poor country to attempt to "go it alone" in developing so-called indigenous technology. That is, developing countries are almost irresistibly incentivized to acquire foreign technology legally as well as illegally.

While China draws a lot of attention, China's theft of IP is not so different from what other countries have done historically. Centuries ago, the United States was once a thorn in Britain's side, snatching up valuable technology that was protected by British law. The United States did the same in the post-World War II period, using Germany's technology to develop industries that could compete with European companies. The mechanisms through which China manages to acquire foreign IP are also nothing new—weaknesses in China's IP protection today are similar to those of Korea and Japan in the 1980s and early 1990s.

The US trade representative's *Special 301 Report* designates countries that do not provide adequate IP protection. China has been "watch-listed"—in other words, deemed a "violator"—in each of the last twenty-five years. Countries that began their development earlier, like Japan, Korea, and Taiwan, were all flagged in the early years of the report and eventually fell off the list as their domestic industries developed and regulatory performance improved. Japan was cited yearly until 2000.

Plotting the trends of both GDP growth and overall GDP per capita of these economies and highlighting the designation of these countries in the *Special 301 Report* in a given year shows us that, for the period over which we have data, these countries tended to be listed as violators when they were growing rapidly and also poor. And they generally fell off the list as they reached a higher level of development. Figures 8.11 and 8.12 show these relationships.

China is in a phase of development where countries are frequently listed as violators—China, India, and Indonesia are listed in every year, and Brazil in twenty-three years. Malaysia and South Korea are cited in thirteen and nineteen years, respectively. Japan was often cited in the early years of the report as well.

The acquisition of IP from developed countries will always look attractive to developing nations. The internet has further lowered the costs of acquiring useful material and allows for instant transmission. Of course, just as not all of Asia's success can be chalked up to IP piracy, not all of China's efforts to acquire IP are state sponsored, and not all of it is dependent on the theft of foreign IP.[27] China's lax IPR protection is not exceptional in a historical context and it is not

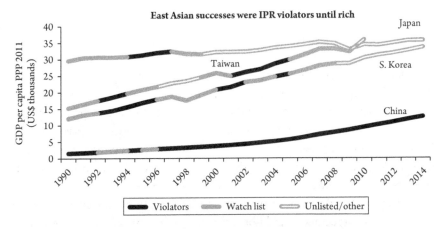

Figure 8.11 IPR Violators, East Asia. Source: World Bank World Development Indicators; Federal Reserve economic data; US Trade Representative Special 301 Report

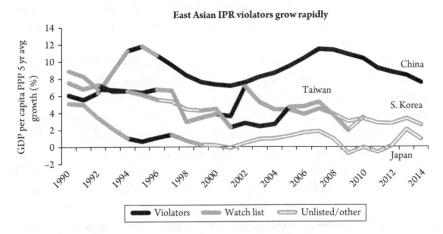

Figure 8.12 IPR Violators and Growth. Source: World Bank World Development Indicators; Federal Reserve economic data; US Trade Representative Special 301 Report

making more use of technology than we would expect for a country of its level of development, but its size sets it apart from the others.

What is happening in China is similar to what has happened elsewhere— China is attempting to develop internationally competitive companies in an environment where the entry costs are so substantial that the appropriation of foreign IP is incentivized. It is likely that as China develops and its domestic industries grow, its practice and protection of IPR will come more in line with international norms. Until then, the "transfer of wealth" that IP theft represents will likely continue.

China's Bilateral Investment Treaties with the United States and European Union

Security concerns and market access are issues that feature prominently in the discussions with China on foreign investment policies. Both the United States and European Union are now looking to write rules to govern their relations with China and are negotiating separate BITs that will invariably have a global impact (see Box 8.2). Given the relative differences between the United States and the European Union regarding their competitiveness in manufacturing and services, these agreements would have a differing impact.

Brexit has introduced uncertainty into these negotiations making it likely that any China-EU agreement would be delayed, pending resolution of the future of the European Union with or without the United Kingdom. China was not involved in either the TPP or Transatlantic Trade and Investment Partnership (TTIP), but the former has now been dropped by Trump administration and the latter is becoming less likely given rising anti-trade sentiments in the United States and Europe.

The BIT discussions represent an opportunity to discuss the further opening of China's services sector, create investor-state protections, and establish a fair mechanism for dispute resolution, especially for the inevitable frictions that will arise over technology transfer. Thus it would be unfortunate if this treaty was no longer on the table. If and when negotiations resume, the United States and the European Union need to be clearer about where investment is welcome, such as in clean energy and infrastructure, and where it is not by providing industry-specific promotion and assistance that might better match each other's strengths and needs. As noted earlier, EU-wide guidelines might actually result in fewer deals than has been the case with country-to-country agreements—thus some flexibility may need to be built in.

Both the West and China have much to gain from BITs. Investments in the United States and European Union would present far fewer risks than some of China's other infrastructure spending gambles in developing countries. Chinese investment would also help expand local tax bases in destination countries.[28] Studies show that Chinese enterprises on average pay their employees higher wages than domestic firms.[29] By helping Chinese investors to navigate the investment rules, the United States and European Union would be helping their own workers while aiding China on its own path to reform.

All parties realize that they have much to gain by opening up investment opportunities to the other, but the issue tends to be who is willing to do more to make this a reality. Thus the special free trade zones that China has been experimenting with recently is an attempt to open up previously closed sectors by

Box 8.2 **United States versus European Union BIT Comparisons**

A BIT establishes rules covering the treatment of foreign investment between governments. It includes legal provisions granting foreign investors nondiscriminatory access to the domestic market on par with other foreign investors. A BIT also provides firms with legal protections against expropriation without compensation, requirements to include local content or transfer technology, and access to a neutral investor-state dispute settlement.

US and EU Similarities: The main issues facing United States and EU businesses operating in China are market access, equal treatment, and IPR protection. Compared to China, the United States and European Union have relatively open markets and are looking to gain access to China's services sector and to shorten China's negative list of restricted sectors. US and EU firms also suffer from an uneven playing field with domestic Chinese firms in terms of additional licensing requirements. Both face mandates in several industries, including automotive, to form joint ventures with local Chinese companies and to transfer technology in exchange for access to the market (although this is prohibited under the WTO). Creating a legal framework is especially important for foreign business in China, where the legal system is less transparent and enforcement is inconsistent. Though a BIT would not be an immediate IP fix, it could remove ownership restrictions that force US companies in some sectors to partner with Chinese firms in order to invest, giving them a better position to protect their IP. BITs aim to draw a balance between protecting investors and maintaining government authority for discretionary actions.

US and EU Differences: US-China discussion of a BIT began in 2008, but only formally took off in 2013. As of mid-2016, the two sides were reported to have completed much of the framework for a treaty, though negotiated particulars are not publically disclosed. The main text of the treaty will be based on the 2012 Model BIT, the Obama administration update from the 2004 Model BIT. In addition to emphasizing investment protection and open, nondiscriminating market provisions, the United States particularly focuses on the development of "international legal standards." New provisions included higher transparency requirements for investor-state dispute settlements, though the actual mechanism for resolving arbitration remained largely unchanged. As both China and the United States feel they have been unfairly blocked from the domestic market, and US-China investment includes some of the most contentious bilateral economic issues, a more established neutral investor-state dispute settlement system is necessary.

All EU member states except for Ireland already hold individual BITs with China, which has been able to take advantage of a generally open investment climate in the European Union and gain considerable access to the whole market by entering less restricted countries. However, the Lisbon Treaty (2009) gave the European Commission authority to negotiate all future BITs. The first such EU-wide investment agreement is the EU-Canada Comprehensive Trade and Economic Agreement. The main breakthroughs include clearer protection standards and clarifications on when arbitration tribunals will apply, as well as clearer rules on the conduct of procedure in arbitration tribunals. Currently, the European Commission is in the midst of preparing new legislation dealing with the potential financial consequences flowing from dispute settlements with new rules for managing disputes under investment agreements with trading partners. How a possible Brexit might affect negotiations has become source of uncertainty.

moving to a negative list of activities that will be allowed to operate and enabling movement of capital into and out of these zones.

With the most contentious economic issues being IP protection, China's closed services sector, the role of SOEs, and national-security concerns, it is important to establish which sectors are open, which are not, and which (like clean energy) should be actively promoted for the global public good. A BIT could create a more streamlined process to manage disputes, provide protection for companies looking to make partnerships overseas, and designate the areas in which the strategic goals of the United States, the EU, and China align.

Uncertainties, however, have increased because President Trump's negative views on American firms investing abroad works against the logic of liberalizing investment regimes. Moreover, while in principle the new US administration should be welcoming more foreign investment for its growth-enhancing effects, concerns about security in allowing Chinese SOEs greater access to the US market are likely to result in a less welcoming position. This is reflected in the discussions initiated by the Trump administration to take a tougher line on China's investments in the United States and to broaden the scope of CFIUS reviews. Thus prospects for a US-China BIT have diminished.

CHAPTER 9

China's Impact on the Global Balance of Power

President Xi's strategy to elevate China's global presence is underpinned by the country's expanding trade and outward investment flows. Making the renminbi an international currency is designed to support this effort. While many countries welcome opportunities for financial collaboration with China, Beijing's increasingly assertive foreign policy, backed by its growing economic clout, has exacerbated regional and global tensions. This is reflected in the worsening public sentiments toward China in both the West and among many of China's neighbors.

Meanwhile, America's rebalancing toward Asia and related maritime maneuvers are seen by China as a strategy to contain its rise. This is further inflaming already strong nationalist emotions there and elsewhere in the region, most notably in Japan, Vietnam, and the Philippines.

China's strategy has been to launch a more ambitious version of the charm offensive that it undertook more than a decade ago. In the fall of 2013, President Xi unveiled his OBOR initiative, which aims to support infrastructure development along historic land and maritime routes to improve interconnectivity across Southeast, Central, and South Asia and through the Middle East to Europe. Beijing's plans have been substantiated by large amounts of lending, both bilaterally and through new multilateral institutions.

All this is to give credence to a vision of a more prosperous and connected region that President Xi has encapsulated in his "China Dream." This approach fits in conveniently with China's objective to extend its sphere of influence as a counter to America's initiatives in Asia and reinforces a long-standing objective to defend its "core interests" beyond Taiwan and Tibet, to include sovereignty claims in the South China Sea.[1] Some would argue that China's behavior is no different from the actions taken by other great powers in the past, but many aspects differ from the usual norms.

Asia's achievements over the past several decades were based on a remarkable period of regional stability and economic integration. The United States as the dominant global and regional power provided the comfort blanket for this to happen, and most countries would be pleased if this could just continue. But China is no longer willing to accept the United States as the dominant regional power and, given its own increased economic weight, now seeks an adjustment.

Many Asian nations recognize that China is destined to take a greater leadership role but still want the United States to stay engaged as a balancing power. For this to happen, China needs to be recognized as on par with the United States regarding its regional influence—an outcome that has not yet been accepted by the United States but underpins China's aim for what they call a new kind of great-power relations.

China's neighbors may not favor any change, but they also do not want to be pushed into choosing sides. Any enhanced role that the European Union might have been able to play to foster better relations would seem to have been lessened by Brexit, making it more likely that Europe will be preoccupied for years to come with its own internal issues. Thus, whether heightened tensions, intensified by President's Trump election, eventually lead to military conflicts or a more conciliatory process that will allow the region to remain stable and prosper is still to be determined.[2]

External Financial Initiatives and Internationalizing the Renminbi

Trade linkages and investment relationships have evolved in tandem with China's awakening, and both are reshaping the geopolitical environment as a rising power begins to challenge the established power. China is rapidly increasing its presence as a global investor and is now the world's third-largest foreign investor behind the United States and Japan.[3] Since implementing a "go global" investment strategy in 2009, China's ODI has grown at nearly 20 percent annually and is forecasted to overtake the United States as the world's largest by 2020.[4]

China's role as the world's leading trading nation and a major source of external financing paves the way for internationalizing its currency, a goal that is probably driven as much by strategic objectives as by any economic rationale.[5] China is employing a strategy that the United States knows well, drawing from one of the cornerstones of US foreign policy, the Marshall Plan, which helped cement America's post-World War II leadership role. From 1947 to 1951, the United States provided $13 billion in financial aid—an enormous sum at that time—to rebuild a war-torn Europe. The widespread use and accessibility of its currency, initially through aid and open capital markets and, in recent decades, through the willingness of trade-surplus countries to accept US dollars against America's trade deficits made it possible for the dollar to assume its presiding role. Similarly, through its loans, foreign investment, and currency swap programs, China's objective is to make the renminbi increasingly available as a global currency.

China successfully lobbied the IMF to include the renminbi in the SDR basket of reserve currencies in December 2015. At that time, the renminbi was the fifth most used currency for trade and could be converted in more than a dozen places outside China. It is used to pay for nearly 25 percent of China's merchandise trade, while foreign investors can own up to $1 billion of Chinese stocks and bonds. The People's Bank of China is positioning Shanghai and Hong Kong as major financial centers to support this process.[6]

But Beijing's capital controls were tightened in 2016 due to declining reserves. This will prevent the renminbi from being easily available everywhere, a significant obstacle to its becoming a truly global currency. Allowing the free convertibility of the renminbi would mean that China would have to give up much of its control over the value of its currency. If China followed the US experience, it would have to run large trade deficits or give renminbi away through foreign aid to make its currency readily available abroad.

An internationalized renminbi actually offers little distinct advantages, as China has shown no inclination of wanting to run trade deficits or to borrow abroad with impunity, which is the great advantage that America gets from having the dollar as the global currency. Nor is it plausible that a relatively poor country like China would be inclined to give its money away rather than lend it or use it to make acquisitions abroad. Thus, the renminbi is many years, if not decades, away from being a significant alternative to the US dollar. It currently accounts for only about 10 percent of global trade finance compared with America's 80 percent.

Moreover, trying to internationalize its currency in the midst of an economic slowdown and when Chinese investors are shifting capital overseas to diversify their investments leads to increased volatility. This is making it more difficult for China to deal with its immediate stabilization and growth objectives. Why then is the leadership so keen on promoting the status of the renminbi?

For the technocrats, internationalizing China's currency is actually a Trojan House to encourage the much-needed reforms in the financial sector for the renminbi to become eventually a major global currency. For the political leadership, the objective is to reduce China's vulnerability to a global financial system that America has used before as a weapon to complement its diplomatic objectives. Thus, security concerns more than economic gains may be driving the political support for promoting the renminbi as a global currency.

In 2012, the United States threatened to blacklist any bank that helped Iran's central bank sell the country's oil as part of penalties levied on Iran to discontinue its nuclear activities and has applied similar pressures on banks that have been doing unsanctioned business with North Korea and earlier with Cuba. With a US-China relationship described by a Chinese scholar as "shaking hands above the table and kicking each other underneath," it is no wonder that China is keen on internationalizing the renminbi, promoting it as a trade currency, and potentially using it in overseas investment mergers and expansions.[7]

Aside from efforts to internationalize the renminbi, negotiations on two contrasting regional trade agreements have major geopolitical implications. The United States promoted the now discarded TPP as a "high-standards" trade agreement with twelve participating countries rimming the Pacific Ocean, including several ASEAN countries and Japan, but excluding China. The TPP was intended to be more services oriented and addressed a broader set of non-tariff-related issues such as IP rights and environmental concerns.

Its prospects, however, were doomed by the criticisms emanating from both major political parties in the heat of the presidential campaigns. The TPP could have given participating countries more direct access to the United States and other markets, without routing regional trade through China. This would have come, however, at a higher cost to US consumers.

Some American policymakers had been selling the TPP domestically as a means of containing China, making it also an instrument to serve security objectives. Yet the logic of using the TPP to establish high standards for international transactions only made sense if used to steer Beijing's policies in this direction. Thus paradoxically, the ultimate success of the TPP depended on China eventually becoming a member.

Meanwhile, ASEAN nations are exploring a Regional Comprehensive Economic Partnership (RCEP), a more traditional free trade agreement proposed in 2012 that would enhance integration between the ten ASEAN members and China, Australia, India, Japan, South Korea, and New Zealand. With the TPP's demise, then RCEP becomes more important as a regional economic initiative. Courted by both the United States and China as potential partners, Asian nations stand to benefit more from not being forced to choose sides but by being opportunistic in their relationships.

There had been much speculation about the consequences for China of not being part of the TPP and whether RCEP would offset any of the lost benefits. For some of the smaller countries in the TPP, the benefits could have been substantial, but the disadvantages for China were likely to be small given that there was little overlap in the range of goods exported to Asian members of the TPP. Compared to the TPP, RCEP has a more goods-centric agenda and is less ambitious in setting standards. It also recognizes ASEAN centrality and offers access to India. If a reformulated TPP and RCEP eventually become realities, the major beneficiaries are likely to be those who are in both schemes. Otherwise, some would argue that member countries are more likely to benefit from the RCEP arrangements in the short term but from the TPP's approach over the longer term.[8]

Increasing Economic Clout and Foreign Policy Assertiveness

The increased scale of China's outward investment has been accompanied by new foreign policy initiatives which many have characterized as being encapsulated in President Xi's OBOR initiative. At the opening of the Asia Pacific Economic Cooperation (APEC) summit in November 2014, President Xi promised $70 billion in loans and infrastructure in the Asia Pacific region. Days later at the East Asia Summit, he offered $20 billion in preferential and special loans to develop infrastructure in ASEAN countries. These sums sit atop an earlier commitment to capitalize the China-initiated AIIB in addition to the new BRICS Development Bank backed by China, Brazil, Russia, India, and South Africa. President Xi has also promised at least $40 billion toward a Silk Road Fund, a more private-sector oriented initiative.

These activities, along with other external assistance and investment programs, make up OBOR, which some estimate could provide several trillions of US dollars in financing mostly for infrastructure projects over time.[9] These initiatives serve China's multiple objectives of diversifying away from foreign exchange reserves held in low-yielding US- and European-backed securities while utilizing China's infrastructure expertise and surplus industrial capacity to help its regional neighbors.

China's new foreign policy initiatives channel its huge foreign exchange reserves to fill a regional need for infrastructure development. The AIIB has drawn special attention given its political significance in giving China a leadership role in running a multilateral institution. A 2009 study by the ADB highlighted the critical need for further regional infrastructure investment in Asia and suggested that approximately $8 trillion was needed over the coming decade.[10]

That Asia's needs far exceed the lending capacity of the World Bank and ADB provided the rationale for creating the AIIB. The AIIB became fully functional in 2016 with a capital stock of $100 billion and the support of fifty-seven founding members, including all ten ASEAN nations.[11] China holds a nearly 30 percent voting share, while the United States and Japan have not signaled any intention to join, marking a significant break from the World Bank and ADB governance models—traditionally led by an American and a Japanese president respectively.

So far, public attention on the AIIB has been on the geopolitical implications of China having successfully created a new international institution despite resistance from the United States. The next stage will be even more challeng-ing as the new bank is now operational. Ultimately, its success will depend on whether it turns out to be a more efficient and responsive multilateral lending agency in line with President Jin Liqun's announced objective for the bank to be "lean, green and clean."[12] If successful, this will put pressure on the World Bank and ADB to reform their modus of operation, thus improving the international financial system and validating the creation of the AIIB.

In addition to advancing its diplomacy in East and Southeast Asia and main-taining its strong Pacific links to North and South America, China is now ex-panding its economic reach westward into Central Asia and beyond through OBOR. China's trade linkages with Central Asia, estimated by the IMF to be about $1 billion in 2000, skyrocketed to $50 billion by 2013, surpassing Russia in 2010.[13] China's imports from Central Asia mostly consist of commodities like crude petroleum and iron ore, while its new infrastructure investments include key energy pipelines, highways, and rail networks.

The current economic turmoil and international pressure on Russia have further spotlighted China's role as a regional economic stabilizer. More than just a commercial partner, China has emerged as the region's leading source of developmental finance and economic mediation. Like Southeast Asia, Central Asia remains a region that is investment starved and in need of upgrades to its crumbling Soviet-era infrastructure. Meanwhile, Russia, isolated economically by Europe and the United States because of its interventions in Ukraine and Syria, needs to maintain its relationship with China as an economic lifeline to the international community.

Xi Jinping's "China Dream"

At the outset of his term in 2012, President Xi spoke of "the great renaissance of the Chinese people" and put forth a new ambitious vision: "The goal of building China into a modern socialist country that is prosperous, strong, democratic, culturally advanced, and harmonious . . . by 2049, when the People's Republic of China marks its centenary; and the dream of the rejuvenation of the Chinese nation will then be realized."[14] His ambitious domestic agenda has been trans-lated by OBOR into a more proactive foreign policy and the aforementioned financing activities abroad. The success of this vision depends on forging a "new type of great-power relationship with the United States" which is a concept that has not resonated well with US policymakers.

The strategy behind his diplomacy is no secret. It involves strengthening rela-tions with China's neighbors and through the Asian continent and Middle East to Europe. By creating a network of mutual interests, the objective is to integrate

China's interests with the neighboring countries, so that they can benefit from China's development and China can benefit and gain support from theirs. Whether it is China's plans to build rail infrastructure through Greece to Eastern Europe or a $46 billion infrastructure spending plan in Pakistan to open new trade and transport corridors across Asia, the new linkages have the potential to connect Europe to China through routes that may become more important than its current links to the West through the Pacific.

Yet this approach is not being received with unbridled enthusiasm by China's neighbors. Many are worried about the middle kingdom's objectives and their own potential loss of independence. Some have expressed concern about the economic viability and social consequences of the proposed projects, and uncertainties about the governance principles being applied which could eventually reverberate negatively on China both financially and politically. Others note that China's inclination to deal exclusively with the political elites in authoritarian regimes is prone to failure when the wishes of the broader civil society are not engaged.[15]

Changing Global Perceptions: Tale of Two Crises

The 2008 GFC marked a landmark shift in the world economy, with repercussions on geopolitics that will be felt for years to come. Its impact on China's relations with the world and its neighbors will be even more important than the shifts that occurred after the AFC a decade and a half ago. Largely unmarred by the AFC, China helped buoy Asian economies and in doing so, China was seen as a friend to the region (see Chapter 3). Its huge stimulus program after the GFC similarly helped to keep Asian economies going in the midst of a collapse in the West. The similarities and contrasts between the aftermath of the two crisis episodes offer insights into how regional economic linkages have changed and their impact on perceptions and geopolitics.

Compared to America's absence during the AFC, the IMF's seemingly punitive corrective measures, and Japan's inability to act independently of the United States, China played a key role in preventing the situation from further deteriorating. It gained considerable credibility for not devaluing its currency and seemingly putting the goal of maintaining stability and development in the region above its own interests. Beijing dramatically increased the frequency of high-level visits to Southeast Asian countries and signed a flurry of new bilateral trade agreements, in addition to proposing CAFTA in 2000.[16]

While CAFTA was not formally institutionalized until 2010, China's trade with ASEAN increased nearly fivefold between 2000 and 2007 during the process of negotiation. The rapid increase in trade which aided Southeast Asia's

smooth financial recovery was largely credited to China, seen as playing a constructive role in the region, though it was strong demand in the United States
and Europe for East Asia's manufactured products that made the export boom
possible.

In addition to China's work with ASEAN to build a cooperative trade network, long since forgotten is that a decade ago China looked to diffuse tensions
over territorial disputes in the South China Sea. In 2002, China and ASEAN
signed onto the Declaration on the Conduct of Parties in the South China Sea,
pledging to resolve disputes peacefully, exercise self-restraint, and engage in
cooperative activities. China's approach to regional economic and security relations gave substance to its "win-win" foreign policy doctrine touting China's
"peaceful development," and professing that China's growth would benefit the
region. Amid double-digit economic growth, China was largely successful in creating, in the words of the then premier Wen Jiabao, the perception of China as
"the friendly elephant."[17]

During this period, dubbed "China's Charm Offensive," the concept of soft
power, as defined by Joseph Nye, took hold of China's foreign policy.[18] The idea
of soft power centered on the ability to get others to do what you want based
on attraction rather than through coercion or financial inducements. During
the decade 1993–2003, China's leaders, President Jiang Zemin and Premier
Zhu Rongji, showed themselves to be deft hands at cultivating the sentiments
of its neighbors amid China's rapid economic growth, as did their successors Hu
Jintao and Wen Jiabao up to the onset of the GFC.

The GFC severely damaged the credibility of Western financial institutions
and, coupled with the praise China received for helping to support the world
economy at a critical time by maintaining high growth rates, further strengthened China's image. Yet soon afterward, perceptions began to shift, indicating
that the reaction to China would be different this time because of China's economic rise—clearly displaying the practical limitations of China's soft power.

Tensions Escalate from the Island Disputes

Between the two financial crises, China's economy more than doubled in size
and with this came an increasing sense of self-confidence that influenced its position on regional security issues. In the aftermath of the AFC, many observers
felt that China had become less strident in asserting its claims to sovereignty
over islands in the South China Sea and preferred to play down territorial disputes and stress the need for joint efforts to exploit the submerged oilfields.[19]
But later things changed. In 2009, for a UN Commission deadline on territorial
claims for extended continental shelves, China submitted a map containing the

highly contentious "nine-dash line" claiming most of the South China Sea (see Map 9.1), including the maritime rights within the line.

In the East China Sea, a Chinese fishing boat collided with a Japanese Coast Guard patrol boat off the coast of the disputed Senkaku/Diaoyu Islands in September 2010, which ended in the seizure of the Chinese fishing crew and captain. Since the normalization of Sino-Japanese relations in 1972, the two countries had relegated territorial settlement over the islands to the distant future for

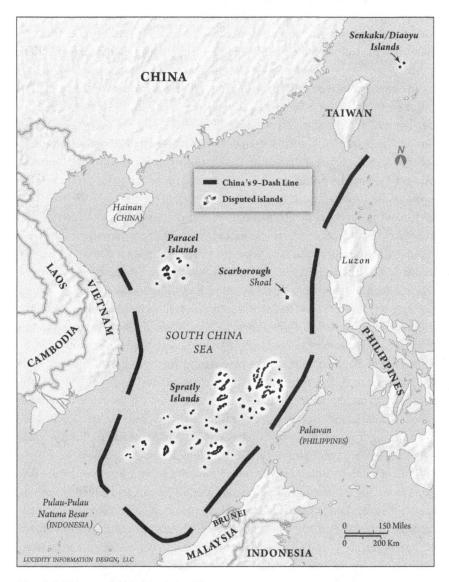

Map 9.1 Territorial Claims in Asian Waters. Source: Attribution in image

the sake of maintaining a stable present, and never before had detainees been held in maritime flares. The incident triggered memories of China's lingering resentment of a past full of humiliation, and anti-Japan riots in China escalated the conflict to a new emotional level. This event shook the status quo—which was tilted in Japan's favor as the sole administer of the islands—and called off previous gentlemen's agreements.[20]

Growing concern over a more assertive China and increased maritime conflicts affecting Japan and ASEAN countries set the stage for US re-engagement in the region. The United States, then optimistic that it had extracted itself from fighting in the Middle East, looked to strategically rebalance its focus to Asia, pledging to "play a larger and long-term role in shaping this region and its future."[21]

The consequence of this chain of events has been a sharp increase in US-China tensions and increasingly negative American public perceptions of China (see Figure 2.2), with some 55 percent of Americans now having an unfavorable view of China compared with 36 percent five years ago and 29 percent a decade ago. European sentiments are only slightly less negative. Negative opinions of China are especially pronounced in Asia among those countries most involved in the island disputes, with unfavorable ratings of 76 percent in Vietnam and 90 percent in Japan, although feelings are still quite positive in countries like Malaysia (17 percent unfavorable) and Indonesia (24 percent unfavorable).

America's dominant military presence in Asia following World War II was credited with maintaining peace, stability, and an environment supportive of regional economic growth. This time, America's engagement and China's more assertive actions have escalated tensions. A standoff between a Filipino warship and a Chinese surveillance vessel near the Scarborough Shoal occurred in the spring of 2012, prompting economic retaliation and heightened conflict. [22] In September of 2012, Japan moved to reassert control in the East China Sea, with the governor of Tokyo formally purchasing the islands from a private owner. According to an International Crisis Group report, the Chinese interpreted this action as "final proof that Japan had disrespected the tacit understanding and . . . freed Beijing from adhering to the status quo."[23] On September 10, Beijing announced territorial sea baselines around the islands, shocking Tokyo.[24]

The implications were not fully understood at the time, but even before formally assuming Party leadership in November, Xi Jinping had already been put in charge of the Leading Small Group on the Protection of Maritime Interest. From 2013 to 2015, many events illustrated China's changing position. These included creating a unified coast guard with more concentrated capabilities, setting up an air defense identification zone (ADIZ) in the East China Sea in November 2013 and subjecting all noncommercial air traffic to submit flight plans over most of the East China Sea, moving an oil rig into waters contested with Vietnam, and embarking on unprecedented land reclamation activities in disputed waters. Thus far, President Xi has walked a fine line in his foreign diplomacy between hard-power assertiveness over maritime disputes and calls for cooperative regional development.

The affected countries have repeatedly called on China to resolve disputes through multilateral forums rather than through bilateral negotiations. Such demands intensified after China seized control of the Scarborough Shoal from the Philippines. Much attention had been focused on the case brought by the Philippines based on the United Nations Convention Law of the Sea (UNCLOS) at the Permanent Court of Arbitration.

The July 2016 ruling provided a clear victory for the Philippines and went beyond what was expected. The court ruled that there is no legal basis for China's historical claims based on the nine-dash line that would give China the EEZ rights normally accorded to the ownership of islands. It also clarified what constitutes an island—as opposed to rocks, which are not capable of generating their own EEZ. Thus China's claim that it had such rights because of alleged sovereignty over various rocks was invalid. The ruling also went further in criticizing some of China's reclamation works as infringing on the rights of the Philippines and causing environmental damage.

Beijing reacted with a predicted refusal to recognize the validity of the ruling and threatened to introduce an ADIZ zone in the South China Sea as it had done in the East China Sea. China pointed out, as have others, that the United States has never ratified the UNCLOS and has at times ignored similar international rulings. If China continues with reclamation activities on disputed land formations, increased tensions would seem to be inevitable. In particular, moving forward with any construction activities on the Scarborough Shoal, which is seen as the red line, would likely trigger a round of counter actions on the part of the United States, the Philippines, and other affected parties.

Some observers have suggested that the ruling could help clarify the situation and nudge China and the other contestants to initiating serious discussions. Soon after the ruling, China did come out with a "white paper" and announcements that downplayed the role of the nine-dash line and differentiated between sovereignty and maritime rights. This distinction is important since it is the enforcement of the maritime claims rather than sovereignty per se—which the rule did not address—that has generated the tensions. Meanwhile Philippines President Duterte has signaled a greater willingness to negotiate with China and act more independently of the United States. This has introduced a new and possibly game-changing factor into the dynamics of the conflict.

The more pessimistic, however, see risks of a hardening of attitudes if nationalistic sentiments spin out of control and great-power politics complicate matters. Having won such a favorable judgment from the Tribunal, the leadership in the Philippines or even Vietnam may find it difficult to support a compromise especially if US-China actions become more aggressive in the region.

Prisoner's Dilemma and the Island Disputes

As the disputed territorial claims overlap among countries, with each adhering to a firm position that is unacceptable to the other, a cooperative solution is hard to envisage. The predicament is a good example of what economists and mathematicians have described in the field of game theory as the "prisoner's dilemma."[25] This celebrated puzzle explains why two completely "rational" parties might not cooperate, even if it appears to be in their best interests to do so. In the prisoner's dilemma, both sides think that by taking a hard position they will gain more, but in doing so, both are actually worse off. Both sides would have much to gain by striking a compromise.

Both the United States—as the surrogate for affected countries such as Vietnam and the Philippines—and China have the choice to ratchet up their aggressive acts in the South China Sea or to moderate them. Each side has reasonable claims to specific islands (or rocks) which result in overlapping maritime zones of control. The United States sees this issue as a challenge to its position as the dominant regional power. China sees itself as having broader sphere-of-influence claims based on historical factors and seeks to establish itself as a regional great power on par with the United States. In contrast, Vietnam and the Philippines are driven primarily by the potential energy and marine resources in the South China Sea, which are significant relative to the size of their economies and financial needs.

From each side's point of view, any sign of moderating while the other continues to become more aggressive would be evidence of weakness that would encourage the other side to be even more aggressive. Conversely, more forceful behavior if the other side moderates would lead to superiority. If both choose to become more aggressive, however, they would still want to avoid pushing the other into a military conflict—an untenable outcome for everyone.

The pattern that has emerged in recent years has one side taking what is perceived as a provocative act with the other responding in kind. The chain effects of such actions then continue. Yet both sides are wary of crossing the line and pushing the other to the point where military conflict might become a reality.

If both sides choose to moderate the situation, conflict could be avoided, and everyone would be better off. For this to happen, a neutral outsider is needed to mediate a mutually acceptable solution. Finding such a mediator with the credibility and stature to put forward a proposal acceptable to the two great powers and regional claimants would appear to be an insurmountable challenge, yet the outlines of such an agreement are out there.

Any acceptable solution would have to address the broader concerns of China and the more specific claims of the various affected parties. Each would have to feel that it was getting something of significant value, thus making it worthwhile to compromise. This might mean giving each party clear ownership rights to particular land formations that they already control or have "developed," along with the associated resource rights in limited surrounding waters. This would likely need to be supplemented by an agreement for joint development of maritime resources in areas with conflicting claims, such that everyone would agree to leave issues regarding sovereignty uncontested. Ensuring freedom of navigation and providing for security arrangements with the backing of both the United States and China would have to be part of the agreement.

For China to align its rhetoric for peaceful regional development with such an understanding would require recognizing that some of the broader issues entail a multilateral resolution process and toning down provocative activities. Acknowledging China's ownership of specific "island-like formations" and giving it a recognized role in regional security arrangements on par with the United States might provide the necessary incentives. America's credibility would be enhanced if it signed on to the UNCLOS and gave up rights that it has claimed by treating certain land formations in the Pacific as islands when they are in fact rocks if judged against the Tribunal's recent ruling.[26]

Should China act more aggressively in the South China Sea, Southeast Asian countries will turn to the United States, while if the United States exacerbates tensions by acting overly militaristic, these countries will bear much of the consequences and argue that they should not be forced to choose. Most of the neutral Asian players realize that having both the United States and China in the region can be a positive force, contributing to a balance that provides options rather than domination by any one power.

Rising Tensions as Two Great Powers Adjust to Each Other

Graham Allison Jr. of the Harvard Kennedy School applied the concept of a "Thucydides Trap" to the Sino-American relationship. Looking back to Ancient Greece, Thucydides, an Athenian general who chronicled the Peloponnesian War, noted that "it was the rise of Athens and the fear that this inspired in Sparta that made war inevitable." Allison noted that twelve of the sixteen cases since 1500 in which a rising power rivaled a ruling power resulted in war.[27]

Whether or not Xi's ambitions for realizing the China Dream will lead to an escalation of conflicts or new opportunities for cooperation depends on how

China is perceived and the reaction of the United States and others. Professor Allison, however, did not imply that conflict is inevitable and, if one looks closely at the cases, a key factor in these historical conflicts was proximity and the strong possibility of domination and occupation—factors that do not exist in the Sino-American relationship.

Since rapprochement and normalization of relations in 1979, China and the United States have walked a fine balance between economic integration and security concerns. However, the current strained relations are a far cry from what the then deputy secretary of state Robert Zoellick had in mind in 2005 when he encouraged China's integration into the global system as a "responsible stake holder."[28] At that time, the "Group of Two" (G2) also became a popular characterization of US-China relations. While acknowledging that the international system had accommodated its rise, China then resisted the "G2" terminology, preferring to focus on continued domestic development and recognizing that its economic rise had benefited from the existing system.

China, the "Abnormal" Great Power

But Beijing is not a normal emerging great power by the usual standards.[29] The nature of its economic rise has been atypical. Domestic vulnerabilities constrain its capacity to maneuver, and the Chinese leadership has yet to craft a nimble and effective international role. And as its economy becomes more market oriented, its growing pains are laid bare. All this has had the effect of elevating tensions and aggravating insecurities with China's neighbors and beyond.

China is the first great power to be a developing country. It is fixated on trying to escape the middle-income trap since it can no longer prosper just as a producer of low-cost goods and wants to move up the technology ladder to compete with more advanced economies. China also faces a peculiar challenge in that it is getting old before getting rich. Even by 2030, only about 10 percent of China's population will be relatively well off (defined as within the top decile of global incomes), compared with about 90 percent of the population in the United States and Europe.

China's economic rise has pushed it into the unique position of becoming a superpower earlier than expected. Some see Beijing as being able to exercise considerable influence, but in reality, its ability to do so is limited. In transitioning from the passive approaches characterizing the Deng era, China's institutional base and experience in dealing with sensitive global issues lag well behind its impressive economic achievements, placing it at a disadvantage in working with other major powers.

Moreover, in shifting to a slower but more normal growth trajectory, instability and risks are amplified by the task of coping with the threats coming from a potential debt crisis and destabilizing capital outflows. Thus, its economic successes do not translate necessarily into greater self-confidence at this stage in its development. This prospect has exacerbated anxieties within the Chinese leadership, with those concerns spilling over into foreign policy decisions aimed partly at diverting attention away from domestic problems to real or imagined threats abroad.

Adding to the pressure on the leadership to bring stability and success is the country's long history. Unlike the other great powers, whose rise represented a steady and continuous and process, China is a returning great power—one that accounted for 30 percent of the global economy two centuries ago but saw its share fall to less than 5 percent by 1950. Even after three decades of double-digit growth, it accounts for only about half of what it once did.

China does not see itself as the unstoppable economic powerhouse that some Western observers have suggested. Its vulnerabilities will continue to constrain its behavior on the international stage. The leadership recognizes that if it ever succumbs to a major economic crisis, adequate financial support from the global community is unlikely to materialize not only because of the sheer size of its needs but also because of differences in shared values with other major powers.

Over much of the last decade, friction with China has been most often reflected in trade and investment disputes that revolve around perceptions that China does not compete on a level playing field (see Chapters 7 and 8). Recent accusations about cybersecurity transgressions only exacerbate tensions, accentuating the image of a China that cannot be trusted. Further complicating matters is that China's overseas search for new energy sources and natural resources has led it to be portrayed as favoring "rogue" regimes and undercutting OECD guidelines. These concerns are unlikely to change in the near future, which means that the negative perceptions of China's approach will persist or even intensify.

This is not the path that Deng Xiaoping laid out decades ago. As far back as April 1974, in a special address to the UN General Assembly, he declared that "China is not a superpower, nor will she ever seek to be one. If one day China should change her color and turn into a superpower, if she too should play the tyrant in the world, and everywhere subject others to her bullying, aggression and exploitation, the people of the world should identify her as social-imperialism, expose it, oppose it and work together with the Chinese people to overthrow it."[30] In 2003, Zheng Bijian, a Party theorist, echoed this opinion, explaining that China's economic ascendancy should be seen as a "peaceful rise" that posed little threat to its neighbors but offered many benefits to the world at large.[31]

But circumstances have changed. As explained by the Asia watcher, Douglas Paal, Xi Jinping's statements in 2013 "represented an end to the previously prevailing dictum of former paramount leader Deng Xiaoping's ... variously translated as keeping a low profile in foreign affairs. Xi argued instead for an activist, focused, strategic foreign policy, deploying China's considerably enhanced assets to achieve China's dream of a return to greatness."[32] Asia Society's Orville Schell observes: "We remain nostalgic for those quaint days when Chinese leaders still followed Deng's admonition to his people ... Now that it is stronger, however, its leaders ... (are) no longer willing even to press the comforting notion of 'peaceful rise.'"[33] The discussion is now about how China's increasing nationalism and related security interests have hardened its foreign policy positions. This has created the impression—fair or unfair—that Beijing is more inclined to use its economic clout to advance core interests than to strengthen political relationships.

Dealing with Differing Perceptions and Rising Tensions

China is convinced that the United States will never peacefully accommodate the rise of China and will seek to contain it. This belief was summarized in a five-point consensus circulated among the Chinese leadership in 2014 summarizing internal conclusions about US strategic intentions to (1) isolate China, (2) contain China, (3) diminish China, (4) internally divide China, and (5) sabotage China's leadership.[34]

On the part of the United States, perceiving China's economic revival as a threat to the established order has actually made it more likely that China will become one. American actions or inactions give China cause to promote alternatives to the status quo, such as when America delayed the proposal to allow China a larger voting share within the IMF and World Bank. This encouraged China to pursue its own type of institution, with the AIIB being the outcome.[35]

Still, the view that "Chinese leaders have decided that their success depends on being networked with the modern world" holds merit.[36] While China may not be a rule breaker, it is likely to be a rule challenger. In creating the AIIB, China looked to abide by international norms, taking advice from recognized US experts and other international agencies while crafting new institutional rules for a leaner regional financing institution.[37] China is also likely to be operating in the gray areas on many issues and looking to push the boundaries where it feels justified in doing so. Thus far, China has succeeded in raising maritime territorial claims well beyond its own coastal borders as an issue of international dispute.

Cybersecurity is another area where China will push the limits in the absence of clear and accepted frameworks. In response, the United States has been emphasizing the difference between using such means for economic gains versus security objectives, with the former being unacceptable.

Many observers have noted that it is in the interests of the West for China to become even more integrated into the global system, not just economically but also politically. The key issues are the terms of China's integration into the system, and in this regard, both sides are choosing to use a combination of soft and hard power when it suits them. In this contentious relationship, success comes from being able to strategically command both.

Though China cannot catch up to US military capabilities in the foreseeable future, US hard-power capabilities are constrained by concerns about how far it is willing to go in engaging militarily with China over the island disputes. While China has growing military and naval capacities in the region, it is in China's best interests to maintain stable regional commerce. At the same time that it has engaged in unprecedented reclamation activities in disputed waters, China has maintained a commitment to protect maritime trade. Beijing also released more details of its construction activity, listing the structures for civilian and emergency use. It further indicated that the construction on the islands will help with maritime search and rescue, disaster relief, environmental protection, and offer navigational assistance, as well as have undefined military purposes.[38] While it accuses the United States of provoking unnecessary military tensions in the region, its own actions nevertheless have been seen as overdone, aggressive, and insensitive in the court of public opinion.[39]

A Renewed and Warily Regarded Charm Offensive

Economically speaking, China now has a lot more money to give than it did during its previous charm offensive in the aftermath of the AFC. Beijing's current strategy of ramping up ODI is no secret. "China's basic policy of diplomacy with neighboring countries is to treat them as friends and partners, to make them feel secure and support their development. China should create a closer network of common interests, and better integrate China's interests with theirs," said President Xi at a seminar on neighborhood diplomacy in October 2013.[40]

With a strategy of building enhanced economic integration, China is strategically attempting to link its rise with the rise of the rest. To assuage concerns of its growing economic power among its neighbors, China is looking to trade and investment as a way of creating win-win relationships and maintaining the regional peace it needs for continued development.

Still, money and friendly rhetoric will not buy love. Though enhanced trade during China's previous charm offensive helped to garner goodwill, much of the media's coverage of its OBOR initiative has questioned its intentions and highlighted the apprehensions of the targeted participants.[41] Commentators have noted the possible harmful side effects to local industries in countries that cannot compete with cheaper and better-quality Chinese manufactured goods; historical animosities and mistrust as in Vietnam; and heightened security concerns in Turkey and India.[42] In Central Asia, China's intentions are viewed warily by potential beneficiaries such as Kazakhstan—who worries about becoming dependent on China—and even by Russia—who worries about losing long-standing influence.

Similarly, though investment in infrastructure plays into the hands of what China's surrounding developing nations want, it is not hard to see how a debtor and creditor relationship can turn sour, as they have many times.[43] In these and other countries, China's close association in the past with authoritarian regimes and reluctance to engage with other segments of society ultimately leads to reversals when these regimes evolve.

Contrary to China's insecurities around containment, the most limiting factor in China's soft power is itself. If the conduct of a country's leaders and people do not appeal to others, then that country's actions will reap little respect. With its increasing crackdowns on public discourse, a new rule limiting foreign nongovernment organizations, suppressed ethnic tensions, and tightening control over the internet, it is no wonder that China is struggling to charm the global community.

Thus, many wonder why its leadership does not pursue a more conciliatory approach that would provide more comfort to outsiders. The answer comes in this case from China's fixation on protecting its core interests, including its sovereignty claims over disputed islands. If this is the sacrosanct goal, then no amount of soft power can be effective in winning the sympathies of either its neighbors or already suspicious parties in the United States and Europe.

But these foreign policy and security concerns will not necessarily prevent China from advancing its interests, both economic and strategic. The fact that US allies like the United Kingdom, Australia, South Korea, and most recently Canada broke ranks to join the China-initiated AIIB despite US calls for caution suggests that most countries believe that working with China is desirable in areas where there is an economic rationale and engagement serves longer-term political objectives. China is thus likely to make progress in strengthening its regional economic links, with newly passed free trade agreements with South Korea and Australia, future agreements like the Free Trade Area for the Asia Pacific (FTAAP), and proposed BITs with the United States and EU.

The United States is struggling to balance its military presence in Asia with a stronger economic one, and finding that the game has changed. Moreover, the persistence of conflicts in the Middle East and acts of global terrorism will inevitably divert its attention away from security concerns in Asia. While

China might see its own strategy as ultimately a win-win, to the United States it is perceived as win-lose because of the relative decline in its power in the region.

Differing Perspectives on Geopolitical Issues

The most visceral global reactions to China's perceived assertiveness come from interactions that impact America's security interests, interests that are shared to varying degrees by other Asian countries. China's real intentions in supporting the six-party talks on North Korea, for example, are questioned. Taiwan is a continuing point of contention with the United States, and Beijing's positions on Tibet and, increasingly, Xinjiang attract emotionally tinged criticism from many quarters.

On these geopolitical issues, China has been firm in supporting its long-standing principle of noninterference, which was shaped by concerns of how the West might one day target China. The interactions are also influenced by differing strategies and timelines. In such disputes, China has preferred to put off addressing the issues. This approach reflects its belief that many sensitive issues will resolve themselves eventually without the need for confrontation, and that waiting will promote better outcomes.

Political differences between China and Western powers only heighten this divergence, as democracies like the United States tend to deal with policy implications according to election cycles, while China's leaders are more able to formulate long-term policy plans. But events have often forced China to react before it really wanted to. The result is that China's response is often reactive and not well considered.

Deng's admonition that China should avoid getting involved in external issues is no longer the guiding principle for Beijing. In this context, defending its core interests is not seen by China as being more assertive but rather as ensuring that the country can move forward on its "rightful path." This is clear in the context of ongoing territorial disputes. China may or may not be the aggressor in all of these incidents. But it can be seen as being guilty of not staking out more clearly in advance what it would tolerate and its long-term intentions regarding the ambiguities surrounding its intentions in the South China Sea.[44]

Engaging an "Abnormal" Great Power

President Xi views Deng's passive foreign policy as an anachronism, no longer a workable option for China now that the actions of others are forcing China to react sooner rather than later. Beijing believes that responding aggressively will forestall future disputes, but such behavior has only increased tensions with regional partners and drawn the United States into establishing a greater presence in the region—both unanticipated results of a potentially self-defeating strategy.

Historically, all great powers—including the United States, Germany, or Japan— have at times pushed aggressively to support their national interests at the expense of others. In this sense, China is not an exception. In an ideal world, China would not be seen as a threat to be contained but as a strategic competitor that can be brought in when needed to help reduce tensions and ensure more constructive outcomes on sensitive global issues. The choices for the West seem to be either providing China with more say in dealing with these issues to encourage a more cooperative relationship or taking a harsher position to illustrate the costs to China of taking more aggressive positions.

A more collaborative approach requires greater openness on the part of both China and the United States. And the two powers should concentrate on promoting stronger commercial relations, which will help avoid fueling tensions over hot-button issues like sovereignty. Beijing can start by taking the lead in supporting open markets and fighting protectionism as President Xi did in his 2017 Davos speech. This would help China counter criticisms of its trade practices and put pressure on the United States and other developed countries that are moving toward more inward-looking policies as evidenced in the 2016 US presidential elections and Brexit debates.

As it seeks to increase its outbound investment, China also needs to support a more level playing field. More open capital markets and bilateral and multilateral investment agreements can help ensure equitable treatment and provide more flexibility to address security concerns. China needs to be sensitive to international norms about its use of aid money, but the West can also learn from China's more efficient use of assistance for infrastructure investments. Thus, everyone should hope that the creation of the AIIB can help bridge such differences if both the United States and Japan eventually join and China and the United States and Europe begin working toward broader regional trade and investment agreements.

Given the charged nature of sovereignty disputes, China and other Asian claimants might be well served by setting aside sovereignty issues and focusing on narrow confidence-building measures or negotiating less contentious resource rights. The United States should avoid making commitments and carrying out provocative acts that destabilize the situation and appear to favor one claimant over others. And because the disputes are complex, with multiple claims and overlapping interests, China should recognize that multilateral approaches involving concerned regional parties as well as other neutral interests or advisory groups can help achieve fairer and more inclusive solutions—the type of solutions that China has historically favored.

Rather than taking actions that intentionally or unintentionally give rise to perceptions that the United States is trying to contain China, the United States—along with other major powers—should take pains to stress the benefits of more active participation in shaping the international agenda as China enters a riskier period of economic transition. The key is convincing Beijing that its interests are best served by forging solutions now and showing that compromise and cooperation will help China in the long run. For this to work, the United States needs to assure Beijing that its concerns will be heard in the context of a "new kind of great-power relations."

CHAPTER 10

Conclusion—Cracking the China Conundrum

Headlines in recent years have become increasingly pessimistic about China's economic and social problems. Yet the country's growth slowdown and missteps along the way should have been expected for a maturing economy that is still transitioning to more market-based institutions.

This discussion has implications for the often-heated debate about the role of the state in influencing China's development path, a role that many link to broader concerns about prospects for political liberalization. Currently, much attention is focused on President Xi's corruption campaign and the tensions created internally at a time when China's expanding external presence is exacerbating tensions with its neighbors and the United States. On all these issues, opinions vary widely and are often misguided—illustrating why it has been so hard to forge constructive solutions.

Diverging Views on China's Economy

CLASH BETWEEN PESSIMISTS AND OPTIMISTS

The years 2015–2016 are likely to go down as when public opinions about China's economic prospects soured. During the March 2016 meetings of the National People's Congress, sentiments were reported to be as gloomy as the seasonal smog because of the declining economic indicators and fears of capital flight. One major rating service (Moody's) downgraded its assessment of China at that time, and Standard and Poor's soon followed.

Breaking a decade-long trend, Pew's 2016 survey indicates that Americans for the first time see the United States—not China—as the world's leading economic power, even as China's GDP (adjusted for living costs) recently surpassed America's. Typical of the many headlines were the media reports from the 2016 World Economic Forum quoting various luminaries on China's economic prospects, such as George Soros saying that "a hard landing is practically unavoidable."[1] Nearly every article reporting on China's growth rate for 2016 coming in at 6.7 percent began with the observation that this was a twenty-five-year low.

But no country can grow at double-digit rates forever—the issue is not whether growth will moderate but by how much. For the growing number of pessimists, China's GDP growth is projected to decline precipitously to around 3 percent before the end of this decade (see Figure 10.1). Such sentiments are being expressed not just by perennial doomsday forecasters but also by highly regarded experts. Former US Treasury secretary Lawrence Summers and Lance Pritchett, his colleague at Harvard, have predicted a sharp drop-off in China's growth rates within a few years based on comparing China with patterns deemed more "normal" for a country at its income level.[2] But China's track record has been anything but normal in the past, and there is no obvious reason why it should now become normal.

In contrast to the many bearish predictors, optimists see the potential for 7 percent growth well into the next decade. Justin Lin, a former chief economist of the World Bank and now at Peking University, remains confident about China's ability to prosper over the coming decade,[3] and Peterson Institute's Nicholas Lardy argues that "the popular narrative is not well supported by the facts. There is little evidence that China's economy is slowing significantly from

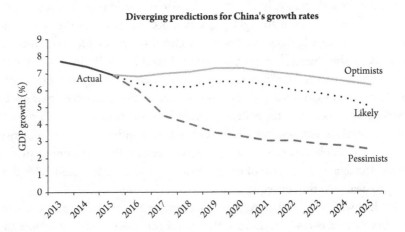

Diverging predictions for China's growth rates

Figure 10.1 Views on China's Growth Prospects. Source: World Bank World Development Indicators; author's estimate

the 7 percent pace reported by the government . . . It is not the picture of an economy heading for a hard landing."[4] In Europe, long-standing French observer Francois Godement has noted that China is in the midst of a cyclical slowdown and while many were too optimistic in the past, many are too pessimistic today.[5]

With the right policies, Beijing can establish the foundations of a "new normal" to grow at a more sustainable rate of around 6 percent into the next decade before an inevitable decline materializes as the economy matures (see Figure 10.1). In comparison with other upper-middle-income countries, past and present, growth around 6 percent would still represent exceptional performance. China's recent growth rates are still multiples higher than the 1.7 percent average for high-income countries and the 2.0 percent average for the other upper-middle-income countries.[6]

DEALING WITH DEBT AND PROPERTY BUBBLES

The more hardened pessimists see a country trying to cope with multiple financial challenges from surging debt levels to a runaway property market and capital flight. Even one such problem can overwhelm policy making; dealing with several would seem to be an impossible undertaking.

While China's debt problem is serious, the potential near-term destabilizing implications are exaggerated (see Chapter 5). Much of the attention has focused on China's debt-to-GDP ratio which having surged over the past decade still puts China in the middle of the pack—higher than most developing countries but lower than most developed ones and about the same as the United States. This would seem about right—China is not really a typical developing economy, but neither is it fully developed.

The concern, therefore, has been on the size of the *increase* in China's debt ratio over the past seven to eight years as more indicative of the risks. And indeed, the increase has been very rapid by global standards and is still increasing. Most of the change, however, can be explained by credit financing that facilitated an unusually large increase in property prices, given the emergence of a private property market a decade ago. The increase in debt, therefore, may not be as serious a problem as many believe, provided that the current level of property prices is sustainable. Moreover, China's debt problem differs from previous crisis cases in that its debt is concentrated in the state sector rather than among private agents. The financial strength of the government also gives it considerable flexibility to deal with the consequences.

While it will take a few more years for China to absorb the surplus property and eliminate excess industrial capacity, a major collapse in real estate prices and widespread bankruptcies are unlikely. However, persistent credit easing for so many years has encouraged excessive speculation in selected property and commodity markets and unnecessarily propped up what many have called "zombie" firms, mainly large SOEs in the heavy industries and construction. Vulnerabilities have also been compounded by the weak financial regulatory system, making it harder to assess the risks of a plethora of shadow-banking products that have recently remerged.

More generally, soaring debt levels reflect an excessive reliance of local governments and SOEs on bank loans rather than funding from the public budget or bonds for infrastructure investments. It also reflects the tendency in a state-dominated system to over-invest since implicit state guarantees shield local governments and SOEs from bad financing decisions. As such, the solution to China's debt problems ultimately lies in reforming its fiscal system to reduce reliance on commercial banks to fund state-driven mandates and ensuring that the costs of misallocation are borne by the responsible entities, for example, by making greater use of penalties and bankruptcies.

A strong turnaround in growth is not in the cards these days, but neither is a hard landing if policy makers take a more disciplined approach to financial and fiscal management. The uncertainty lies in what will happen after the bottom is reached. Unlike most other economies that have been mired in a prolonged slowdown, China still has options for establishing a moderately rapid growth path. Those holding this more benevolent view see a country that has consistently defied expectations in the past thanks to its willingness to reform as circumstances evolved. But whether it will do so in the future is being seriously questioned by many observers.

PROJECTING CHINA'S FUTURE GROWTH PATH

The growth path that China has been following is similar to the one taken decades earlier by other East Asian success stories like Japan, South Korea, Singapore, and Taiwan. This was based on high levels of investment supported by incentives to promote industrial production and trade, along with a shift of workers from rural to urban-based activities which ratcheted up productivity. After decades of rapid growth, all these economies glided into a slowdown phase, but there were significant variations in the growth rates during the transition.

Japan's growth rate fell off sharply after the Plaza Accord in the mid-1980s when it agreed to a huge appreciation of the yen. This triggered what many call the lost decade(s), marked by a collapse in property and asset prices. The other economies managed to maintain reasonably strong growth for a decade or more before slowing down after reaching high-income levels. Figure 10.2 plots the comparative growth paths for these four economies from the beginning of their strong growth phase, the early 1950s for Japan and Taiwan and the 1960s for South Korea and Singapore, against China's beginning in 1985. In this comparison, China seemingly has the potential to grow at rates in the 5–7 percent range for the next five to ten years.

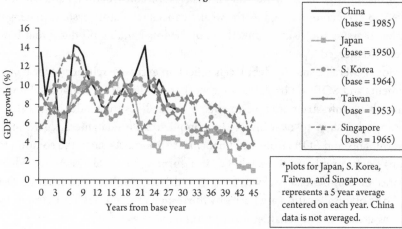

Figure 10.2 China and East Asia Growth Trends. Source: World Bank World Development Indicators, Penn World Tables.

Some of the more pessimistic analysts have argued that having grown above the norm in the past, China's future growth will be below the norm in the future because its debt-fueled investment driven process cannot be sustained.[7] But depending on the policies it adopts, China still can perform as well or even better than others since its remaining untapped growth potential remains considerable.

The others reached a major slowdown phase defined as growth in the 5–7 percent range at a per-capita GDP of around $20,000, which—given China's current GDP per capita of around $13,000—would take China another five years or more to reach. A 6 percent growth rate would thus seem to be a reasonable medium-term objective. This compares with the 13th Five-Year Plan (2016–2020) target of 6.5 percent. China still has abundant opportunities to increase productivity at this stage in its development compared with the other East Asian economies (see Chapter 5).

Many have argued that a more sustainable growth path depends on moving away from the old investment and export-led growth model to a more consumption and services-driven one. This argument is misleading since achieving China's growth objectives is possible without significant rebalancing in favor of consumption at this juncture (see Chapter 4).

Economic growth ultimately depends on the quality and quantity of investment and human capital along with productivity or technological improvements. Consumption does not drive but is the consequence of long-term growth. How the share of personal consumption to GDP evolves depends on the stage that a country is at in its development process. The objective should be to maximize the growth of consumption over time, not, as some have suggested, its share relative to GDP. China's goal should be to increase the efficiency in its use of resources. Paradoxically, this is likely to prolong the unbalanced phase of its growth process rather than cut it short.

That the consumption share has increased slightly in recent years is seen by many observers as evidence that "rebalancing" is already underway. This impression is misleading. The growth rate of consumption has remained robust and steady in real terms at 8–8.5 percent for more than a decade. With GDP growth slowing to less than 7 percent, the share of personal consumption has increased since wages (household incomes) have not declined as rapidly as GDP. But there is nothing reassuring about this; it is merely the consequence of the economic slowdown.

Nor will the shift to a more services-oriented economy automatically solve China's problems. The recent surge in 2015–2016 of the share of services to GDP to 50 percent and the commensurate decline of the share of industry to 40 percent overstate the extent that the structure of production has evolved. As recently as 2012, the respective shares were the same at 45 percent. The subsequent divergence is due to the role that price deflators play in estimating value added.[8] With the growth of wages remaining relatively high but commodity and producer prices collapsing, real growth in the more labor-intensive services has been exaggerated.

Moreover, the rise of services does not necessarily translate into more rapid economic growth. In general, productivity growth in services is more difficult to realize than in manufacturing. This is a major factor explaining why GDP growth in high-income countries is lower than in developing economies, since services tend to be a larger share of the economy in high-income countries.

BALANCING SUPPLY AND DEMAND

In the jargon of economists, many countries currently are suffering from a problem of excess capacity and the need to bring the demand for goods and services in line with the excess supply. This is a consequence of slower economic growth, which is reflected in depressed consumption and investment at home and diminished global trade externally. In this environment, the debate typically has been about the diminishing effectiveness of monetary versus fiscal policies to encourage more economic activity not only in China but also globally.

For China, the supply problem shows up primarily in the excess capacity in heavy industries and an overbuilt property market. The solution means reducing capacity and developing markets for new and more sophisticated products. The demand problem is exemplified in the sharp decline in the investment intentions of firms. Stimulating demand involves moving forward with structural reforms to increase productivity so that more investment will be undertaken because it is profitable to do so and not because the government says so.

China's ICOR, a measure of the returns on investment, was improving up to the GFC but then began to deteriorate. Some decline is inevitable as an economy matures. As such, China's GDP growth rate was destined to fall eventually, as did the growth rates of the Asian tigers decades ago. But the inefficiencies built into China's massive stimulus program in response to the GFC and the delays in implementing the reform agenda exacerbated the decline. Even so, investment productivity in China has not been significantly worse than other emerging market economies in the postcrisis years. Nevertheless, if China is to escape the so-called middle-income trap, it needs to focus more on increasing productivity and less on simply investing more in infrastructure.

In dealing with both demand and supply issues, China can draw on the principles laid out in its own 2013 Third Plenum reform policy statement, specifically that the market should play a "decisive" role in allocating resources. Major productivity gains would be realized by narrowing the gap in rates of return between private firms and SOEs. More game-changing approaches, including privatization and bankruptcies, are needed beyond the current emphasis on diversifying ownership. In addition, there are quick gains to be realized by opening up entry to private competition in higher value services—such as education, health, and finance—and in protected activities that have been the exclusive domain of SOEs—such as telecommunications and energy. Thus the January 2017 directive to liberalize foreign investment in these activities is encouraging. In contrast, the current centralized support for promoting innovation and more technologically sophisticated industries runs the risk of overspending in areas where returns are likely to be low in relation to other needs.

Potential reforms also include a more efficient urbanization process with a less restrictive labor migration and residency system. This would increase demand for urban services and related investment returns. In addition, moderating the excessive investments in the far western region is warranted since such expenditures have been generating much lower returns relative to the coastal and central regions over the past decade.

In dealing with the demand problem, the low share of consumption to GDP that most observers focus on cannot be solved by simply trying to encourage households to consume more since they have already been consuming at record rates. Instead, attention needs to turn to restructuring the budget. Unlike a typical market-based economy, the state controls almost all of the major assets—such as land and energy resources—and the returns on such assets in the form of rents and profits accrue largely to the state rather than directly to households. Short of privatizing ownership of such assets, buoying up overall consumption demand depends on increasing the share of services and transfers provided to households through the government's fiscal system.

For a socialist economy, China's formal government spending as a share of GDP lags far behind those of OECD countries. A stronger revenue base and realigned social programs would allow consumption-related expenditures provided by the government to increase significantly. Thus, fiscal reforms are the key to resolving the demand problem, and such measures would also complement the productivity measures needed to solve the supply problem.

China has reached an inflection point in its development path. What needs to be done was laid out in its Third Plenum Policy statement. China does not need a "new growth model," but it does need the next generation of "policy entrepreneurs" to wring out the inefficiencies in the current one. This combination has served China well in the past and if it continues, more sustainable but still relatively rapid growth for the medium term is achievable.

Evolving Role of the State

China's economic slowdown is reviving the debate about the role of the state in promoting growth. This has drawn more attention than usual because of the importance that President Xi has placed on curbing corruption, which is putting stress on the political system and dragging down economic activity.

CHINA'S STATE-DRIVEN GROWTH

What distinguishes China's state-driven approach from other countries is its capacity to *mobilize for collective action versus concern for individual rights*. This reflects the strong role of the state in building support among the broad masses as well as elites for growth-enhancing policies which has occasionally come at the expense of civil liberties. This raises uncomfortable issues for both sides of the debate on the relative weight to be given to political liberalization versus economic progress—a debate which is usually settled by personal biases rather than technical arguments, thereby widening the gulf between China and its critics.

A generally accepted view among OECD countries is that well-functioning institutions and a less interventionist government are conducive to promoting efficiency and growth. If so, how does one explain why China—with its seemingly weak institutions and dominant state presence—was able to grow so rapidly for so long before its current economic slowdown? Part of the answer is the unique role the state played in shaping growth-enhancing incentives and fostering competition (see Chapters 3 and 4). However, the way the system has evolved in recent years has introduced some unresolved risks.

The standard framework for understanding the workings of a market-driven economy is based on the concept of the firm operating in competitive markets, unencumbered by government-driven distortions. Growth depends on a country's resource endowments, the quality of its institutions, and supportive but not over-bearing government policies.

That the state has played a major role in driving China's economy is well recognized thanks to its five-year plans and the prominence of its SOEs in production. Unique to China is the role that centralized Party directives and personnel processes have played in incentivizing the administrative system. By encouraging competition, this has helped China to contain the worst aspects of the distorted signals and "soft budget constraints" that afflicted the other centrally planned economies in the former Soviet Union. In China's system, local authorities are motivated to promote growth. Efficiency comes from having different jurisdictions and their affiliated enterprises compete against each other for their relative positions. They also compete to build the new institutions that China needs as it moves toward becoming a more market-oriented economy.[9]

When the state and the market complement each other, the results can have a dramatic impact on productivity and living standards, as has been the case during most of the post-Mao era. Since the onset of the GFC in 2008, however, a confluence of events has altered these relationships. The creation of LGFVs put local governments into direct competition with existing firms in property-related commercial activities and also enlarged the opportunities for corruption by local authorities. The government's stimulus program channeled loans through the financial system to SOEs and local authorities, which made such opportunities even more attractive.

Initially, these relationships helped redirect resources that were monopolized by the state, such as land, into more productive use in partnership with private agents. Over time, however, this process has become distorted, resulting in wasteful expenditures that the leadership is currently trying to address.

As illustrated in a case study done by the Asia Global Institute, China's governance structures do not fit the usual analytical frameworks.[10] The state is neither an all-encompassing, uniform entity nor a collection of diffuse and chaotic agents. The economic system consists of a hierarchy of interwoven, multi-tiered regional governments and firms—state owned and private—operating under the aegis of centrally administered directives as well as market forces. When it functions well, the results can be striking, as evidenced by the rapid transformation of the economy. But when incentives are misaligned, the outcomes can include financial instability, environmental degradation, and surging corruption, which then provide fodder for those who see an imminent collapse.

President Xi's consolidation of power has been interpreted by the more optimistic observers as a precursor for bolder economic reforms in the coming years. For them, China will eventually allow the private sector to play a "decisive" role in guiding the economy as stated in the Third Plenum policy statement. But the many pessimists see in recent actions only hesitancy in addressing much needed productivity enhancing measures. Consolidation of authority means more centralized control over economic activities, continued protection of major SOEs and less competitive pressures in the market space. Thus China's move from its former collective leadership to relying on a single powerful leader might lead to a less dynamic economy and eventually political instability. Only time will tell if either of these two scenarios becomes the reality.

CORRUPTION AND ROLE OF THE STATE

A generation from now, historians may look back at Xi Jinping's tenure as marking a break with the past—when curbing corruption was taken seriously even at the expense of focusing on China's economy. The current anti-corruption campaign has the strong support of the public, but its near-term growth implications are worrisome. Along with the clampdown on public expression, the broader political implications are unclear given the reported tensions that have emerged.

Some observers see these efforts as restoring the sense of fairness needed to preserve the legitimacy of the Communist Party, while others see them as necessary for establishing a more efficient growth path. These observations raise questions about the role that corruption has played in shaping China's development in the post-Mao era.

Unlike other countries, corruption in China has broadly supported rather than retarded economic growth (see Chapter 6). Further, rapid growth has not led to the expected decline in corruption but its deeper entrenchment in the political and economic system. In China as elsewhere, corruption has a corrosive effect on society's sense of fairness and encourages social unrest.

In other countries, corruption typically retards growth because it represses investment. But China has been different. Its decentralized system has encouraged more rather than less investment and fostered a unity of purpose, so that even as corruption became widespread, the collaborators worked to make growth the guiding principle for their actions. Thus, the defining question for the success of the anti-corruption campaign is whether the leadership will allow the market to be the primary force for allocating resources and not the state—otherwise corruption will continue to flourish.

Many seeking a precedent for political liberalization in China point to the many examples of regime collapse, but the more relevant experiences relate to the very few successful outward-oriented developing economies that transitioned from autocratic to more liberal political systems, such as South Korea and Taiwan. Worth noting is that political liberalization in both economies began around the same time, at the same level of per-capita income, and at the same level of urbanization, triggering a sharp rise in the share of high-value services in the economy and creating an environment for systemic change.

In terms of these indicators, China is likely to reach the same stage of development when political liberalization is likely to emerge around the second half of the next decade. By then the natural forces driving the aspirations of the Chinese people, combined with the ease with which they can be expressed through social media, are likely to override the state's capacity to control all major economic and social decisions.

The process in China, however, is unlikely to follow the path of Western democratic movements or even the other East Asian experiences given its differing political inheritance and circumstances. With no obvious alternatives to replace the current system and China's historic lack of democratic traditions, including the rule of law, the initial steps in political liberalization will likely be driven by internal Party forces at the local level, responding to the pressures of a rising and more urbanized middle class.

Factors Shaping Views on China

There is no simple explanation for why China generates such a wide range of views and emotions, creating a conundrum that makes it difficult for even the most dispassionate observer to see the country in an ideologically neutral way. The consequence is that far too often, conventional wisdom about its economy is wrong. China now generates such visceral feelings that anyone criticizing China is accused of having a pro-Western agenda by commentators in China, and those conveying an optimistic message risk being labeled as an apologist for the regime by commentators in the West. Is it even possible to talk about China without being boxed into a simplistic notion of what is clearly a complex reality?

Individually, we see China through our own self-prescribed lens. Emotions often come into play because of the lack of transparency in the economic and political system and the biases that come from mistrust and increasing geopolitical tensions. The various factors shaping such perceptions can be loosely grouped under two themes: the former affects perceptions more generally and the latter affects those who have a more serious interest in China's economic system. One relates to China's size and complexity, which comes from its regional diversity along with choice of comparators. The other comes from the lack of an agreed-upon analytical framework driven by being a transitional economy with differing institutions and incentive structures.

In many instances, judgments are faulty because micro-examples or one-dimensional indicators are used to derive conclusions when a more holistic view, including recognition of the importance of spatial factors such as urbanization, is warranted. As this book argues, many of the popular perceptions that the general public or even informed China observers have about China are misplaced or wrong, and thus the policy prescriptions that emanate from these beliefs are flawed.

GEOPOLITICAL TENSIONS AND MISTRUST

Global perceptions about China are becoming increasingly hawkish because its political and economic initiatives are threatening the position of the dominant global power (see Chapters 7–9). Such concerns are also shared in Europe and elsewhere because China's societal values and political traditions differ so much from those in the West. China's foreign-policy intentions are often seen as incompatible with the principles upon which the existing international order was established, but these frictions emanate from insecurities on both sides. The dominant power fears losing its place and the rising power lacks the experience and capacity to maneuver effectively on the world stage.

Differing national economic aspirations can drive envy and raise concerns, but their resolution need not be a zero-sum game. Hence, China frequently characterizes foreign trade and investment interactions as potential win-win opportunities, although rising protectionism in the United States and Europe has undermined this argument. However, a realignment of global power and security relations is often considered a zero-sum game, and thus likely to flare tensions and warp perceptions. The election of President Trump and consolidation of authority of President Xi has only sharpened these differences.

China is an easy and inevitable target from a Western perspective because of its human rights record and the authoritarian nature of its actions. For the average citizen in the United States or Europe, the concern may not be who is ahead economically but who will win the battle to shape mankind's values. Thus, for a significant segment of the public in the West or even elsewhere, no amount of factual evidence or analytical reasoning is enough to shake the belief that China's political and economic systems are destined to fail—it is, for them, inevitable because the alternative is unimaginable or unpalatable.

Coverage of China is so extensive that every week there is likely to be a provocative article from notable figures in academia, politics, or the media arguing for either a more cooperative or more combative approach.

On the more cooperative side, Nobel Laureate in economics, Joseph Stiglitz cautions:

> Now China is the world's No. 1 economic power. Why should we care? On one level, we actually shouldn't. The world economy is not a zero-sum game, where China's growth must necessarily come at the expense of ours. In fact, its growth is complementary to ours . . . If we see China's gains as coming at our expense, we will strive for "containment," . . . These actions will ultimately prove futile but will nonetheless undermine confidence in the U.S. and its position of leadership. . . China won't be able to accept the global system simply as it is, with

rules that have been set by the West, to benefit the West . . . We will have to cooperate, like it or not—and we should want to.[11]

In contrast, both sides of the political spectrum in the 2016 US presidential campaign came down hard on China. Such views by now are deeply rooted in America's political psyche. China's currency manipulation is a favorite topic among lawmakers in both parties. Senator Charles Grassley, a Republican from Iowa, said in 2015 that "China has manipulated its currency for a long time . . . Administrations under both Democrat and Republican presidents have been too timid about taking action."[12] Senator Chuck Schumer, a Democrat from New York, is quoted as saying, "For years, China has rigged and played games with its currency, leaving American workers out to dry."[13]

Academics and diplomats have contributed to this debate. In their 2015 report prepared for the Council on Foreign Relations, Ashley Tellis and Robert Blackwill state:

> Because the American effort to "integrate" China into the liberal international order has now generated new threats to U.S. primacy in Asia . . . Washington needs a new grand strategy toward China that centers on balancing the rise of Chinese power rather than continuing to assist its ascendancy . . . Congress should . . . substantially increase the U.S. defense budget . . . Washington should intensify a consistent U.S. naval and air presence in the South and East China Seas . . . The United States should . . . develop a coordinated approach to constrict China's access to all technologies . . . and should build up the power-political capabilities of its friends and allies on China's periphery.[14]

A more collaborative view is expressed by China security specialist Michael Swaine:

> Chinese leaders today are not trying to carve out an exclusionary sphere of influence, especially in hard-power terms; they are trying to reduce their considerable vulnerability and increase their political, diplomatic, and economic leverage in their own backyard . . . It does not necessarily threaten vital U.S. or allied interests, and it can and should be met with understanding rather than defensive aggressiveness . . . Trying to sustain such predominance, therefore, is actually the quickest route to instability, practically guaranteeing an arms race, increased regional polarization, and reduced cooperation between Washington and Beijing.[15]

Such debates have cycles of their own. Back in 2007, when tensions were also increasing, there was a heated debate between reporter James Mann, who wrote about the "unduly optimistic" assumptions of those writing about China's rise, and David Lampton, a respected China scholar, who has written on the need to engage China but with awareness of the complexities involved.[16] Lampton's views are reflected in a recent speech:

> Beijing and Washington need something like a "Fourth Communiqué" laying out such a vision . . . The first things to say would be that the world has changed, the distribution of power is changed, balance and stability is our joint objective, and that the primacy of any one nation is insufficient to achieve balanced stability. Second, such a document should say that the two countries will work with each other, and others, to build and adjust current economic and security institutions to reflect the new realities. [17]

Fundamentally, the debate between containing or accommodating China's rise is spurred by the *lack of trust* regarding long-term intentions between the United States and China spawned by the wide chasm in values and beliefs. This applies at both their leadership levels and among their ordinary citizens, many of whom believe that some form of a confrontation is inevitable. Some will argue that if there is a solution, it lies in building stronger people-to-people relationships. Among the many agreements signed by President Xi during his October 2015 visit to the United States, the relatively unnoticed announcement of 2016 as the year of US–China tourism may turn out to have a greater long-term impact on lowering tensions than any formal security arrangement.

BIASES DRIVEN BY CHINA'S SIZE, COMPLEXITY, AND WHERE ONE SITS

Where one is located shapes the environment that has led to such contrasting perceptions about China's economic rise, prospects, and impact on others. Because China's political system and values often clash with Western norms, the perception from Western capitals will be fundamentally different from that in Beijing. The Chinese people overwhelmingly feel that their economic circumstances have improved, but they have also become more concerned about where their society is heading. They are increasingly pressing for more accountability in the administrative system but do not necessarily share the same conviction as their American and European counterparts that election-based democratic systems are the answer. On the other hand, policy makers in Beijing are reluctant to acknowledge that a rapidly changing economic and social landscape is pressuring the governance system to adjust in ways that will push China closer to Western approaches. On both sides, entrenched interests and strongly held political beliefs make it difficult for China watchers to change their views, regardless of the evidence.

China's size and regional diversity thwarts efforts to convey an easily digestible yet accurate and balanced message for audiences both in China and abroad. China is simply too big, with more varied economic and social conditions than other major economies. Spatial factors are as important as key macro-indicators in shaping economic trends. The population of the city of Chongqing, at thirty million, is roughly the same as the country of Malaysia. Shanghai is four times more populous than Singapore. Lesser known provinces such as Henan and Shandong have populations of over ninety-five million, larger than any country in the EU. Qinghai province is larger than Germany in its land mass, but its per-capita incomes are closer to African than Southeast Asian levels. The result is that it is harder to judge whether anecdotal examples are just that, or if they are truly characteristic of the country more generally.

Moreover, *the pace of China's transformation* is unprecedented, compounding the impact of its size. No country has grown so rapidly with such dramatic shifts in the composition of its production, making it difficult if not impossible for affected countries to adjust easily without significant social consequences. Thus, while the loss of labor-intensive jobs from the United States and Europe to lower cost producers in the developing world was inevitable, China's entry into the global market sharply accelerated the process. Similarly, in key but contrasting sectors such as steel production and solar energy equipment, China became a dominant player in just a few years, when normally it would have taken a decade or more to gain such prominence.

For many typical indicators, China is often the *extreme example, with either seemingly negative or positive connotations*. It has the highest investment share of GDP (seemingly good) but also the lowest share of consumption (seemingly bad). Growth in labor productivity has been the highest of any country (seemingly good), but its ratio of per-capita urban to rural incomes is probably the highest in the world (seemingly bad). China is the largest exporting nation but also the biggest emitter of greenhouse gases. It produced the largest initial public offering with Alibaba but also the longest traffic jam, running sixty-two miles and lasting twelve days. The impression on global psyches conveyed by each of these examples can be deceiving. A more thoughtful view requires a heavy investment of time and an enduring on-site presence. The wisest of experts is often the one that is humbled by the realization that, even after years if not decades of scrutiny, China remains largely a mystery.

DIFFERING ANALYTICAL FRAMEWORKS AND INSTITUTIONS

Many critics with impeccable credentials make the *mistake of assuming that China's economy will follow the same growth path* as other countries. China is neither a true socialist nor capitalist system. It also cannot be easily characterized as a developing or developed economy. This makes the choice of appropriate comparators difficult. Comparing China to the United States makes little sense, even though many choose to. Others turn to the BRICS, in particular Brazil or India, which also does not work given the differing structure of their economies and alternative growth paths. Looking at other East Asian export-driven cases has merit, but many make the mistake of choosing late 1990s Japan because of debt similarities—when a 1970s Japan would be more appropriate in terms of income and technological levels, Or they choose South Korea in the late 1990s when the relevant period is the early 1980s in terms of growth potential. That China is not easy to typecast does not vitiate application of traditional economic reasoning, but more caution is needed in interpreting the context and making the right assumptions.

China's mixed and decentralized economic system is especially difficult to decipher because it *does not fit the analytical frameworks* that economists and financial experts are most comfortable with. Analysis of a country's debt problem, for example, typically assumes that the key financial relationships involve private agents. The implications become less obvious when almost all of the major actors are state owned or controlled. The importance given to interest rates to promote efficient outcomes—a standard principle in traditional financial analysis—is significantly reduced when resources are allocated in accordance with planning guidelines. Shadow banking—a common feature in most market-driven economies—was absent in China until a broad-based private property market emerged only a decade ago, and its role has been misunderstood during its debt surge. In contrast to market-based systems, China's financial and fiscal systems are more interlinked. Thus its debt problem is viewed by most China financial watchers as a banking issue rather than a fiscal problem.

Americans and Europeans, accustomed to arguing that government interventions can only mess things up, may find it hard to accept that China's state-driven system can deliver impressive results at key junctures because this mixed system has found alternative ways to promote efficiency. But market forces have become increasingly more dominant over time, making it now even more important for the role of the state to be redefined—scaled back in some areas but strengthened in others.

Revisiting the major long-term economic assessments of China prepared every decade or so by the World Bank, one can see a pattern of actual achievements turning out to be better than the original predictions. The explanation lies in the tendency to underestimate the potential productivity benefits that can come with reforms or the power of collective actions.

The major governance difference between China and other countries—even those with federalist systems—is its *regionally decentralized administrative system* which has profound implications for how the country operates both politically and economically. This system not only ensures that the regions are politically in tune with the intentions of the Chinese Communist Party but also the source of state-driven competitive pressures that have nurtured China's impressive economic achievements over the past three decades.

Differing views also come from an *incomplete understanding of the nature of China's economic relationships* and the tendency to favor premises that support politically convenient sentiments, as illustrated in the way that US–China trade links, the role of exchange rates, and foreign investment policies are typically cast in public discourse in the West. Regardless of the evidence and analytical arguments that have been made that trade balances should be seen from a multilateral and not bilateral perspective and that China's currency is not the major factor driving US trade deficits, popular impressions have not shifted significantly. This fallacy comes through again in discussions of the unbalanced nature of China's growth process, which is almost always depicted as a problem based on the usual macroeconomic criteria but actually symbolizes a broadly successful growth path if spatial factors, specifically the rural to urban migration, are properly understood.

A generation from now, scholars will be in a better position to assess China's performance given the *evolution of its institutions and policy responses*. Much of the criticism of China's policies and performance reflects an idealized vision of what it should eventually be rather than what it is today and where it came from. A successful developing country is one whose structure and institutions evolve as it moves from a low- to middle- to high-income status, which many would argue has been the case for China. Failure comes from not responding to shifting economic circumstances. And it is this aspect that is creating concern among even the more optimistic China observers.

The challenge of making appropriate judgments is also illustrated by how one should judge the *many distortions in prices, incentives, and governance* in China's economic system relative to other countries. It is easy to build a case that, with such glaring distortions, China's economy is headed for disaster. Paradoxically, the existence of such distortions also can be seen positively as a source for productivity increases if resolved. The great irony is that relatively efficient but stagnant economies have limited upward potential since it is much harder to identify reforms that would have a quick and significant growth impact—Japan's current situation being a case in point.

Nor has China's reform path been built on what economists call "first-best" solutions. Instead, a *succession of "second-best" actions*, arguably more appropriate for a mixed economy and phased in over time, has been the norm. This has been China's means of overcoming vested interests—to co-opt or get around such interests rather than spend years if not decades trying to develop a consensus on what might be an optimal but politically infeasible solution.

More generally, getting a good reading on what is going on in China's economy has been a problem given the *lack of transparency* and the reluctance of policymakers to communicate as openly as would be the norm for a major economy. The problem is made worse by the widespread perceptions that China's statistics are manipulated for political objectives (see Appendix B). Much of the confusion reflects the limited understanding of how GDP indicators are formulated and the evolution of the methodology as China moves away from a socialist system. There are studies by credible institutions and experts that indicate that there is no systematic bias to inflate national outcomes even if some of the numbers at local levels are flawed. The reality is that China's GDP has been larger, not smaller, than reported over the past several decades, but this may not be of any help to investors or commodity-driven speculators whose fortunes are linked to a narrower set of physical indicators that the GDP concept was never intended to represent.

China, the Abnormal Economic Power

While markets continue to fret over how much further China's economy will fall, China's more aggressive posture on the foreign-policy front has leaders across the world on edge. Many might argue that China's more forceful external policies are typical of a great power, although the nature of its ascendancy and how its policies are executed are not. These seemingly contradictory elements are part of the China conundrum.[18]

Normal in the economic sense means that China's double-digit growth rates are moderating to something more representative of a upper middle-income country, and it will also become more vulnerable to global market fluctuations— including capital movements. With the increasing dominance of the private sector, the economy will no longer be immune to business cycles and rising debt ratios. Part of the cost of becoming a more normal market-based economy is increased vulnerability to cross-border financial flows and the "Keynesian" risk of lack of demand. Increasing productivity needs to displace increasing capacity as the priority, since Beijing can no longer count on ratcheting up activity with massive state-led investments. Nor can it ensure stability by controlling interest and exchange rates as these key prices are being freed up.[19] In this context, internationalizing the renminbi may convey the prestige that Beijing seeks, but it will also restrict macro-policy options.

The challenge that the leadership now faces is that weakening state control over the economy can no longer provide the certain outcomes that it could a decade ago. In a more normal economy, the state's role is not to manage everything but to establish the necessary market-friendly regulatory agencies. Beijing still has much to learn about establishing and running such institutions. Its economy is simply becoming too complex to respond to political decrees and the whims of local officials.

Meanwhile, President Xi has broken with the passive foreign-policy position advocated by Deng Xiaoping and followed by his immediate predecessors. This has signaled the advent of a more assertive China at a time when globalization is being questioned in the West. Some would argue that in this sense China is the same as the other great powers in exercising its increasing clout.

Yet Beijing's ability to exercise influence on the global stage is more limited and its experience in dealing with sensitive issues lags well behind its economic achievements. China's command of soft power is often ineffective, as are its alliances, placing it at a disadvantage in negotiating with other major powers. And thus far, its efforts to promote Confucianism abroad as a set of core values have found little support in the international community.

China is an abnormal great power compared with the historic rise of European nations and the United States, in part because it was in the distant past so dominant economically and is just now finding its footing again. Even in 2016, after three decades of double-digit growth, its share of the global economy is still only about half of what it was two centuries ago. Nor are its prospects of making it to developed status a foregone conclusion. It is the first developing country to become a great power and the first to grow old before becoming rich.

With a proud history to live up to and numerous domestic problems to overcome, China attempts to balance its internal tensions with an evolving international order. To the outside world, China is seen as more threatening, no longer a passive rule taker in a system largely established by the Western powers in the aftermath of World War II. It will be a rule challenger, maneuvering to reshape the balance of power especially regarding territorial interests that affect its regional influence.

China's formerly reactive approach was to moderate tensions that might constrain its potential to develop. The concept of "peaceful rise" is now being questioned in a world where America's rebalancing in Asia is viewed by many as a containment strategy. The sentiments expressed by some policymakers in Washington to secure support for the TPP and perceptions that the United States was against the creation of a Beijing-led AIIB reinforce such sentiments.

It is wishful thinking to believe that China will ultimately embrace the norms of the West. It will continue to develop its own set of political, cultural, and ethical values that will shape domestic and foreign policies. President Xi's tightening control over the political and administrative system may be a step backward in the eyes of many China watchers, but years from now such actions might be judged as a consolidation phase for more ambitious reforms to come.

China may be unhappy with the global status quo, but it will push for change in a manner that does not jeopardize arrangements that it has benefited from. But unlike the other great powers, it is not aligned with any set of countries or issues. Beijing's selection of partners, its fluid alliances, and its intentions vary depending on the concern at hand and evolving circumstances. Thus how it views itself and how others view it regarding global power relations and influence depends on the context.

First, China sees itself as a still relatively poor, developing country in contrast with the wealth and traditions of the West. Second, it shares many but not all of the defining interests of the third world and thus was an observer to and broad supporter of the non-aligned movement, though not a member. Third, it is an emerging power that along with the other BRICS countries is pushing for more influence and a global role as an alternative to the G7. Fourth, China's position as a permanent member of the Security Council of the United Nations and a leader of the G20 in the World Bank and IMF gives it a stake in the existing global power structures, with all the accompanying responsibilities.

Finally, a decade ago, some US policymakers played with the concept of a G2 given the centrality of China in driving Asia as a region—a concept that China at that time deemed to be premature. More realistically, China will act primarily as a regional power, although with President Xi's more activist approach, it is now moving closer to a bipolar view in the context of proposing a "new kind of great power relations" with the United States. With the possible fracturing of the EU with Brexit, this concept may gain greater weight internationally over the coming decades.

This is a world of evolving, intersecting, and often issue-specific relationships. Efforts to typecast China often fail, and views of this abnormal great power differ sharply depending on one's perspective. President's Xi's China Dream and OBOR initiatives are as much about finding pragmatic solutions as establishing a comprehensive approach. For the West, a more collaborative, integrationist view based on recognizing the reality of China's increased global presence and that it will be "peaceful and harmonious"—while also taking the precautions to hedge against more extremist tendencies—would seem to be the best option. This would create the political space for China to find its place in an increasingly globalized world. But the prospects for a more harmonious US-China relationship may have diminished given the potential clash between President's Trump objective of "Make America Great Again" and President's Xi's vision of China's destiny.

As a regional power that currently feels constrained by US actions, a more confident China with expanded core interests will continue to generate the tensions and uncertainties that have defined its resurgence. In doing so, the middle kingdom will continue to defy typical classifications, behave unpredictability, and play the unique role that makes it so hard for views to coalesce. Cracking the China conundrum is an initial step in understanding what is transpiring and laying the basis for forging more constructive outcomes.

Appendix A

ELABORATION OF CHINA'S DEVELOPMENT EXPERIENCE

There are a plethora of studies on China's growth experience in the Deng era up to the GFC.[1] This appendix provides a fuller discussion of aspects related to themes in this book. The general consensus is that China success was due to reforms that were

- Implemented pragmatically and gradually and based on discovering what worked from experimentation.
- Sequenced in line with institutional capabilities and evolving conditions.
- Geared to access foreign expertise and exploit advantages of backwardness.
- Motivated by the desire to maintain stability both economically and politically.
- Designed to avoid major economic downturns which would have weakened commitment to reforms.
- Influenced by aversion to global financial risks and unforeseen events.
- Seen as part of a long-term transition spanning decades rather than years.

Context

China's growth performance was the result of a series of pragmatic reforms which made use of the country's natural advantages and were sequenced to reflect evolving institutional capabilities and market opportunities. What was different was the process that China used to reform its economy rather than the policies themselves, since the reforms broadly adhered to mainstream prescriptions including liberalizing markets, diversifying ownership, and maintaining stable macroeconomic conditions. By pursuing reforms in a gradual, experimental way and providing incentives for local governments, the authorities were able to discover workable transitional institutions at each stage of development. China also grew rapidly because it was able to sustain its reforms over long periods of time and was not diverted by swings in either economic or political cycles. Part of its success has been its ability to develop the domestic capacity to design home-grown reforms suited to local conditions over three phases in China's transformation.

First, China reallocated labor from low-productivity agriculture to higher-productivity services and industry. The sector shift in the labor force went hand in hand with rapid urbanization, which is remarkable in light of the household registration system that discouraged rural residents moving to the city. Second, China rapidly opened up its closed economy, moving to one with 70 percent of GDP in trade on the eve of the GFC, which is exceptionally high for a country of its size. Third, China's economy transformed from one dominated by SOEs and collective farms to more diversified entities (private, diversified shareholding companies; TVEs; and foreign-invested firms).

China's planning system was not eliminated in one go. Instead, the economy was allowed to "grow out of the plan." This preserved the level of existing production while giving strong incentives to households and enterprises to grow outside the system. While this approach preserved some of the inherent inefficiencies, it was politically acceptable and introduced gains from market-induced competition throughout the economy.

Pragmatic Approach under Special Initial Conditions

China's success compared with other transitional economies was made possible by differing initial conditions and a gradual approach. It did not have to deal with the complications of a political disintegration that totally distracted the former Soviet Union Republics and was thus able to focus on its economic transformation. By taking a trial-and-error approach, it was able to avoid the political dissensions that could have stalled the process. This allowed the leadership to find practical alternatives unencumbered by whether it was ideologically correct or theoretically optimal.

The dual-track system for growing out of the planned economy was a major feature of the transition process.[2] It allowed continuation of the administered system, which avoided the collapse of production that would likely have occurred if resources had been allocated based solely on market-driven mechanisms. By the time of the abolition of most material planning in the mid-1990s, administered and market-based prices had been largely aligned.

This gradual reform process worked only because commitment to reform was so strong. The signals began with Deng Xiaoping's early statements on the reform process and the administrative system followed through with actions. Incentives were reinforced with the rewards that officials received for delivering on reform goals: growth, attracting FDI, generating employment, and maintaining social stability. Experience in the regions also counted heavily for promotions, which provided the most talented with the incentives to demonstrate their capacity to spur growth.[3]

China's vast size and regional differences meant that decentralization was an effective means for local governments to experiment and champion specific reforms within the parameters established by central authorities. This allowed the transformation of the structure of agriculture- and enterprise-based production to fit the needs of a socialist market economy while the centrally guided institutional basis for managing the economy—involving the fiscal and financial systems and the trade and exchange-rate regimes—were still being shaped.

At various stages, issuance of key policy reform statements such as those protecting property rights and opening up Party membership for private entrepreneurs solidified the position of the private economy. But the decentralized, experimental reforms did not always work and worked better for some purposes than for others. As discussed later, economy-wide reforms such as those affecting intergovernmental fiscal relations and the functioning of the exchange-rate regime have proven to be more difficult to handle as macro-management became more complicated for a government that preferred stability. This has arguably led in some instances to prolonging systems that had outlived their usefulness.

Reviving Growth and Emerging Production Structures

The result is that China was able to avoid the economic setbacks that hampered the reform process in other countries. Not only has economic growth averaged nearly 10 percent annually for decades, but it has been remarkably stable.

Agrarian reforms drove the initial surge in production. Growth increased sharply in the first half of the 1980s with the new household responsibility system. Land leases also emerged, which shifted user rights from collectives to households. By simply allowing farmers to sell their surplus on the market, increasing procurement prices, and reducing state-mandated quotas, rural per-capita incomes tripled during the 1978–1984 period. This contributed to a surge in the GDP growth rate to 14 percent by the mid-1980s. Continued agrarian reforms, notably the overhaul of China's food-grain marketing system in the mid-1990s, led to another surge in rural incomes. These reforms paved the way for rapid changes in technology and crop diversification, which over the subsequent decades brought yields in line with other high-performing countries.Together these reforms helped push GDP growth rates well into the double digits during the first half of the 1990s. Further liberalization of the agrarian economy was inspired by the 2001 WTO trade-related reforms, which eliminated any remaining pricing biases against agriculture and encouraged a shift in the cropping mix in favor of crops more in line with China's comparative advantages. This has been reinforced in recent years with a wholesale reduction in agriculture taxes and fees which uplifted agrarian incomes and helped moderate regional disparities.

By the late 1980s, when the momentum from the initial agrarian reforms was petering out, growth was given a new impetus from the emergence of rural-based TVEs. TVEs were an enterprise form that operated outside the plan but drew on the support of local governments in collaboration with emerging private interests across rural China. These enterprises were highly successful in expanding production and creating employment, even though their ownership form did not fit the norm. But they served a useful purpose in expanding industrial activities where private property was still frowned upon.[4] As market processes deepened, TVEs started to falter, and eventually most of them were overtaken by private and foreign-invested companies as the main source of growth and job creation.

TVEs were part of the process of industrial agglomeration that influenced the nature of China's transition from a planned to a market economy. The transition was supported initially by a dual-track reform agenda and an open-door policy that strengthened the investment climate along the coastal provinces before becoming national. The open-door policy began with the establishment of the first SEZs in 1980. These SEZs led to a general improvement in China's investment climate and laid the foundations for ratcheting up investment rates.

Fiscal System and Decentralization

The fiscal system was instrumental in aligning subnational government incentives with those of the center. Fiscal reforms introduced in 1980 represented a de facto tax-contracting system with high revenue retention rates for local governments to provide incentives to pursue growth and promote a market economy. Subnational governments had large discretionary powers to grant tax privileges and strong incentives to retain revenues to allow localities to support its enterprises in competing with those in other regions. These actions selectively provided coastal provinces with revenue incentives to experiment with reforms and thereby improve their investment climate.

The fiscal capacity of local governments reflected closely their resource availabilities. To keep resources within their control, local governments avoided sharing their revenues with the central government. Central government revenues as a share of total government revenues declined from 55 percent in 1980 to 31 percent in 1989 and to 22 percent in 1993. Fiscal devolution, on the one hand, contributed to rapid economic growth by effectively enhancing incentives of local governments. On the other hand, it limited the central government's ability to use tax and expenditure policy instruments to narrow regional fiscal disparities and support delivery of basic public services in poor localities.

The tax-contracting system also provided strong incentives for local governments to generate extra-budgetary funds largely outside the control of the central government. Extra-budgetary funds became as large as budgetary funds (and over the past decade have been augmented with land sales and property development, which have contributed to the current property bubble). Although formal budget deficits remained small, quasi-fiscal operations through the banking system were substantial (mirroring the situation even today). Relying on the banking system for policy purposes created a growing amount of nonperforming loans in the banking system.

The poor performance of many state enterprises during the early years resulted in a structural decline in the ratio of total government revenue to GDP and in central government revenues relative to total government revenues. The ratio of total government revenues to GDP declined from 26 percent in 1980, to 16 percent in 1989, and to 12 percent in 1995. The system also encouraged fiscal disparities to widen between the relatively better-off coastal provinces and the poorer inland areas.

With the major tax reform of 1994, this discretion-based revenue-sharing system was replaced with a more rule-based fiscal assignment system allowing the central authorities to use fiscal policy more actively for redistribution.[5] The reform package brought China's intergovernmental fiscal system much closer to international practice and paved the way for a surge in the ratio of government revenues to GDP in the second half of the 1990s. Before the reforms, the share of central government expenditures was commensurate with its share of revenues. After the reform, the share of central government revenues to total government revenues more than doubled from 22 percent in 1993 to 56 percent in 1994, and has hovered around 50 percent in recent years. Over the same period the share of central government expenditures to total government expenditures remained at about 30 percent.

The centralization of the fiscal system strengthened the central government's capacity to redistribute in favor of poorer inland provinces. After a decade of decline under the fiscal contracting system, the share of total fixed-asset investment that went to the inland region versus coastal region increased gradually from the mid-1990s onward. Nevertheless, its redistributive impact in providing more equitable access to public services is still modest because of the way expenditure assignments are pushed down to local levels without providing commensurate funding and in part because of the structure of revenue sharing. These consequences are more significant in the poorer inland provinces and partially explain why urban-to-rural disparities are greater there relative to the coastal areas.

Trade and Investment Policies

China reformed its trade and investment policies in its characteristic gradual manner, over time as well as across geographical space. At the outset, China was a closed economy, with very limited trade and financial interaction with the rest of the world, and with self-sufficiency as the proclaimed policy goal. With the open-door policy, China has become one of the most trade-oriented countries in the world. It has also been very successful in attracting FDI, accounting for about 10 percent of global totals. The reforms that achieved this consisted of: (1) a gradual liberalization of the trade system, (2) reforms in the exchange and payments system, and (3) opening up to foreign investment.

Over the past thirty years, foreign trade management was freed up from being the exclusive responsibility of a dozen foreign trade companies and then a concession for SEZs to being virtually available to all trading companies upon application. Tariff reductions were less significant in trade liberalization during the first decade and a half; average tariffs had been cut from 56 percent in the early 1980s to 43 percent by 1992. But the run-up to WTO accession in December 2001 saw a major reduction in tariffs as well as other barriers, with average rates falling from over 40 to 15 percent, and subsequently to 10 percent by the middle of the last decade. Along with tax rebates and unification of the exchange rate in 1994, China became more firmly integrated into the global trade networks. In addition to tariff reductions, financial and trade liberalization as well as better IPR protection have been moving forward gradually over the past decade.

The second leg of China's opening-up was the gradual reforms in the exchange-rate regime, which today remains the most contentious issue regarding China's perceived impact on global trade imbalances. Initially, the Bank of China was the only bank that was allowed to conduct foreign currency business. By 1986, all domestic banks were allowed to do so. Initially, domestic firms had to surrender all their foreign exchange but over time retention quotas were established which allowed them to import products with prior approval. The share of foreign exchange retention quota was gradually increased and then abolished by the end of 1993.

A dual exchange-rate system was also used to motivate firms to generate foreign exchange earnings. The various rates were unified and fixed at 8.27 in 1997, remaining fixed until the country moved to a managed float from 2005 to

2008 and again in 2010, which together have resulted in a real appreciation of nearly 50 percent. The government's general preference to maintain exchange-rate stability has been an important consideration in maintaining incentives for exporters. But this posture has been seen as contributing to macroeconomic imbalances as China's export performance accelerated following WTO entry in 2001, and the US trade deficit surged in line with its increasing fiscal deficits.

The SEZs made up the third pillar of China's opening-up policy. Enterprises in those zones enjoyed tax exemptions and reductions as well as better infrastructure and often better government services. In 1980, the first SEZs were established in four coastal cities and then in the provinces of Guangdong and Fujian. These zones were allowed to offer special advantages to attract foreign investors. Within four years (1981–1984), the trade volume of Shenzhen SEZ, for example, increased by sixtyfold. To capitalize on the success of these zones, Beijing extended them to 14 coastal cities, the major deltas, another 140 coastal cities and counties, and then nationwide. Meanwhile, foreign-invested enterprises outside SEZs enjoyed more advantages over domestic enterprises, including concessional income tax rates and lower prices for land granted by local governments eager to attract FDI. Thus much of China's success in exports is due to foreign-invested firms, whose share in exports rose from 1 percent in 1985 to more than 50 percent by 2015.[6]

State-Enterprise Reforms

Until 1993, state-enterprise reforms focused on increasing efficiency within the existing system of state ownership. Thus, reforms became a matter of expanding "enterprise rights" beginning with giving firms more autonomy in production and personnel appointments and the right to retain and use some of their profits through various forms of contracting and linkage of the wage bill to profitability. Although the reforms to increase enterprise autonomy showed some success, inefficiencies in the enterprise system continued, and losses increased. Thus, the reforms launched in 1993 shifted emphasis to institutional innovation and developing a "modern enterprise system" with clearly established property rights, well-defined powers and responsibilities, and separation of the enterprise from the government. But the outcome was altogether disappointing, as most involved enterprises merely turned themselves into shareholding companies with the same owners and made little change to management practices.

It was only in 1999 that a broader program of reforms began, and it included diversification of shareholders' ownership, selloffs, management buyouts of smaller firms, and the breakup of monopolies. Supporting reforms in the banking system allowed for debt-equity conversion, whereas social obligations were gradually shifted off the books. Finally, the State Assets Supervision and Administration Commission was established to enhance and regulate the role of the state as the owner.

In the decade up to the GFC, profitability of SOEs rose sharply. But interference from the state remains an issue for the larger SOEs, notably in the managerial appointments. Many SOEs remain active in competitive industries, and they continue to be major creditors of bank loans, even though their share in production has shrunk considerably. Returns on assets for SOEs fell precipitously after the GFC, raising new concerns about what is needed to turn them around and to promote a larger role for the private sector.

Financial-Sector Reforms

China's financial-sector reforms came relatively late in the reform process. Before reforms, China's financial system was typical of other Soviet-style economies. China's central bank—Peoples' Bank of China (PBOC)—was the only bank in the planned system. The bulk of fixed-asset investment was paid for by the budget, whereas the banking system predominantly provided working capital "loans." China's reforms initially focused on the breakup of the mono-bank system and creation of four specialized commercial banks: (1) the Agricultural Bank of China; (2) the People's Construction Bank of China, specializing in investment financing; (3) the Bank of China, handling international transactions; and (4v) the Industrial and Commercial Bank of China, dealing with working capital financing.

The big four SOCBs remain the pillar of the banking system, but their market share has gradually declined from around 70 percent in the mid-1980s to around 40 percent today. This resulted from the entry of private and foreign banks, the growth of rural cooperatives and city banks, and the creation of state-owned policy banks (Agricultural Development Bank of China, China Development Bank, and Export-Import Bank), which, in principle, served to relieve the commercial banks from their policy function.

In the early stages of reforms, the credit plan remained the dominant policy instrument. The plan allocated individual credit according to centrally determined priorities, at controlled interest rates that varied per sector, leaving little discretion to the banks. The credit plan gradually was relaxed. After reforms in the mid-1990s, banks were in principle free to lend to whomever they wanted. China's reforms allowed for a gradual increase in the type and number of banks combined with a relaxation, and then abolition, of most restrictions on lending. In practice, however, local government influence on banks remained significant. As a result, banks continued to build up nonperforming loans.

It was not until the AFC that the authorities realized the importance of re-forming the financial sector. Reforms were made easier by the progress in state-enterprise reforms which reduced the necessity to keep lending going to ensure social stability. Newly created policy banks also could take over more of the directed lending from the commercial banks. By 1998, major financial-sector reforms started to take shape: state-owned banks embarked on financial and operational restructuring, shutting down branches, centralizing lending author-ity, and shifting bad assets to newly created asset management companies. Weak nonbank financial institutions were closed and resolved. Banks recapitalized on several occasions, in part by making use of China's bulging international re-serves, and in part by issuing state bonds to the asset management companies.

In contrast to the situation in the mid-1990s, by the year 2000, China had the budget resources to absorb the costs of financial-sector reforms. Interest-rate liberalization allowed for a return to profitability of the banks. In addition, com-petitive pressures from the WTO accession helped accelerate banking restruc-turing. The most notable aspects included the IPOs for the major banks which brought in strategic partners and the creation of the China Banking Regulatory Commission, which has strengthened supervision and risk management.

In the aftermath of the GFC and the surge in lending coming from the stimu-lus program, concerns have risen anew about the potential quality of the out-standing loans, even though official numbers for nonperforming loans are still less than 2 percent. Recent reforms have largely eliminated the ceiling on lend-ing and allowed some flexibility in setting deposit rates. As a result, the share of lending to the private sector has surged, with some estimates suggesting that as much as a quarter or half of recent loans have gone to households and private commercial borrowers.

Macroeconomic Management

Macroeconomic policy management has become more complex with the changing global and domestic environment. Strong fluctuations in economic growth and inflation have occurred during the past three decades with the af-termath of the AFC and GFC adding to vulnerabilities, even though China has been partially protected by its strict controls on capital movements. With each cycle, the system has introduced countercyclical policies—expansionary credit and fiscal policies followed by tightening—with varying degrees of success in achieving a "soft landing." The creation of a government bond market allowed the government to pursue a more active fiscal policy and seek noninflationary means of financing the deficit. This proved useful in mobilizing a fiscal stimulus in the aftermath of the Asian crisis, but the mega-stimulus of 2008–2009 drew more on financial rather than fiscal channels for supporting expenditures.

Monetary policy has gained in importance through the gradual liberalization of interest rates beginning in the mid-1990s, and their levels are gradually being freed up to market forces. Even so, interest-rate movements probably still play less of a role in influencing economic activity than in most emerging market economies given the tendency of state-owned banks to respond to the needs of SOEs and local authorities.

Despite progress in establishing market-based instruments for managing the economy, China still relies in part on administrative measures to manage demand. Recent experience suggests that the discretionary tools that were relatively effective a decade ago are becoming less effective over time as activities become increasingly driven by private agents and the emergence of shadow banking. Also, the government's capacity to rein in credit expansion and influence public expenditures at the local levels appears to be much weaker because of the role played by LGFVs.

Lending through more diversified and informal channels facilitated by interest-rate ceilings may have distorted intentions and created unknown risks. China's capacity to manage these issues has been hindered by its tight management of exchange-rate policy. The consequence is that monetary policy is partly determined by the balance-of-payments fluctuations. Rising domestic liquidity has fed into an investment boom and fostered a potential bubble in property prices. Until recently, successive increases in reserve requirements and interest rates have been used to absorb liquidity and curb demand given inflation concerns. But with recent deflationary pressures, the reverse is now happening.

Agglomeration, Urbanization, and Labor Migration

China's success in building a more competitive economy came from transforming its industrial sector through investments, which ratcheted up productivity by securing the benefits of agglomeration—economies of scale and specialization. Economic reforms allowed market signals and globalization to play a more important role in encouraging industries with an export orientation to locate along the coast.[7] As reforms deepened, a process of rapid urbanization and industrial specialization evolved.

Several factors supported this process. First, integrated national markets provided labor and capital mobility, while cross-provincial commodity exchanges encouraged industrial development in line with locational advantages. Second, external market integration as part of globalization encouraged concentration of more dynamic activities in the coastal region. As the coastal cities became linked to the global economy, the benefits became obvious, exemplified by rapid employment creation, pressures on enterprises to restructure to compete, and a much-improved domestic and external financial position. This provided the basis for broad-based political support for WTO membership and trade liberalization more generally. And it promoted more flexible wage markets, which began to reflect quality differences with the consequence that labor skill premiums rose sharply.

All this was facilitated by major improvements in transportation and communication networks. This allowed competitive forces to reshape interprovincial industrial structures and link domestic and global markets. Internal transport and logistics costs have fallen significantly, and interprovincial output prices—which varied widely in the past—have converged. The progress that China has made over the past few decades is impressive. According to the rankings based on the World Bank's Logistics Performance Index, China ranks first among middle-income countries.

China's urbanization and labor migration pressures accelerated when the introduction of TVEs drew workers out of farm production and facilitated migration. China is now officially 56 percent urban, although this ratio needs to be discounted by the number of urban migrant workers who lack formal residency rights and thus are unable to access the usual range of social services and employment benefits. The large migrant labor population now totals over 250 million and is heavily concentrated in the major commercial centers along the coast.

For many migrants, economic security is typically linked to their rural *hukou* or residency rights in their home province. Functioning land markets would permit existing land owners to sell or lease use rights to others and migrate to the city if they found employment. As addressed in many studies, perhaps the most effective instrument to deal with rural-urban disparities would be to reform the *hukou* system to give migrant workers better access to social services and equal employment rights. The Third Plenum reforms include actions to liberalize residency rights and to make it easier for rural household to migrate, although the actions fall short of needs.

Income Disparities

Regional income disparities now show up in two ways: widening income differentials between the coastal and inland provinces and between urban and rural areas. Some would call these disparities "good disparities," since they are not the result of stagnant growth in certain segments of society or regions but rather the consequence of unusually high and sustained growth in urban areas and along the coast. The Gini coefficient has increased by about 50 percent, from around .30 to over .45 over the past twenty-five years. Currently, the ratio of urban-to-rural per-capita income is over 3, and per-capita GDP in the coastal region is more than twice that in the western region, registering among the highest spatial disparities in the world.

The shifts in the urban-to-rural income ratio as well as the Gini coefficient are largely explained by performance in the rural economy. Rural incomes have been increasing by 4–5 percent over the past twenty-five years—which is remarkable by international standards—but this is only about half of the rate of growth in urban incomes. As a result, the trend lines for disparity indicators either level off or reverse during periods of sharply rising rural incomes.

Studies vary in attributing inequalities to either regional differences or intra provincial factors, but the key point is that urban-to-rural disparities tend to be much greater in the poorer provinces than along the richer coastal areas.[8] Thus a large part of the inequality between regions is in fact associated with the differences between their respective rural areas and is related to the uneven degree of urbanization across provinces. Inequality within provinces, rural areas, and especially urban areas has accounted for a larger share of total inequality over time. Regional factors also matter, however, since the larger urban-rural differences in the western provinces are structural. Ecological conditions militate against higher agriculture productivity in the western region and its lower level of urbanization and isolated communities raises the cost of providing public services.

How much of the recent convergence in regional growth rates is due to the government's regional development initiatives, notably the "Go West" program launched in 1999, the "Revive the Northeast" strategy in 2003, and the more recent "Center Rising" themes is unclear. But the shift in investment priorities toward the interior has led to visible improvements in its infrastructure services in the period up to the GFC and arguably has probably been even excessive given the costs involved. Since 2008, investment as a share of provincial GDP has ratcheted up sharply in the western region but stayed relatively constant along the coast. This is related to the mega-stimulus taken in response to the financial crisis that promoted infrastructure projects in the interior.

Some of the convergence may also be due to the trade and agriculture-related reforms that removed distortions affecting agriculture and disseminated the benefits of an improved incentive regime more evenly across regions. More recent efforts to reduce rural-urban disparities by trying to increase agriculture productivity to levels that are actually higher than in the developed economies may prove to be wasteful and also environmentally damaging.

China's performance as measured by non-income or social indicators has been favorable, with achievements exceeding what would be predicted in relation to income levels. Its Human Development Index ranking, as measured by the UN, has risen continuously over the past quarter-century. However, disparities in social indicators between regions and rural and urban areas are substantial. The proportion in rural areas with no education is about three times that in urban areas. Child and maternal mortality indicators are much worse in rural areas than in the cities. Moreover, non-income disparities between urban and rural areas appear to be greater in the poorer provinces, particularly in the west. With the increased attention to regional differences, inter-regional differences at the primary educational levels have narrowed. However, urban-rural disparities in health indicators have widened since the late-1990s due to unrelenting income inequalities and slow development of rural health-care insurance systems.

The persistence of such disparities in welfare indicators illustrates how much further fiscal policies need to go to moderate trends. While the equalization grant—established in 1995 to ease the widening regional disparities—has increased, it is still relatively modest. Operating funds per primary school student in urban districts are 50 percent higher than in rural counties. Less-developed provinces do not systematically receive more total central transfers in per-capita terms. Solutions lie not only in deepening the distributional impact of centralized transfers but also reforming how social expenditures are assigned to local levels.

Appendix B

ARE CHINA'S STATISTICS MANIPULATED?

Whether one feels positive or negative about China's economic prospects, everyone seems to believe that its economic statistics are manipulated to meet political objectives.[1] A *Wall Street Journal* poll of sixty-four market analysts reported that 96 percent of them thought that China's growth rates have been regularly overstated.[2]

Reported distortions affect two key policy concerns that dominate public attention. One has to do with the purportedly overstated GDP growth rates based on production figures. The other involves measurement of GDP based on expenditures, and this has driven perceptions that China's growth is exceptionally unbalanced as reflected in its extremely low consumption share of GDP and high investment share.

On the first issue, there is a widespread belief that provincial GDP numbers have been falsified and thus the national GDP numbers are too optimistic. There are in fact many examples of flawed regional data. But the national GDP estimates are put together based not just on provincial estimates, which are adjusted to eliminate double-counting and inconsistencies, but also on alternative indicators.

These concerns have intensified with the current economic slowdown. Many commentators suggest that GDP growth rates might actually be 3–4 percent or even lower. They typically point out in support of this argument that growth rates for some indicators of economic activity, such as power generation and freight traffic, have been in the range of 1–2 percent or even negative at times compared with the official GDP growth rates of around 6–7 percent. But the more informed realize that using electricity sales, for example, as a proxy for GDP growth is inappropriate. Energy use normally declines more sharply than GDP during economic slowdowns but increases more rapidly during periods of expansion because of the differing intensities in energy use across industries during business cycles.

Heavy industries such as steel production are very energy intensive, and with cutbacks in production, electricity generation numbers have fallen sharply. But the impact on GDP is not as significant since value added in steel production is relatively low compared with services and light industries, which are less energy intensive. Similarly, freight traffic in China is closely linked to movement of coal, which is not a good proxy for economic activity given the shift to gas and renewables and increasing energy efficiency in economic activity.

In the last several years, industrial production has stagnated given the slowdown in construction and exports. But since services now account for the bulk of GDP, what matters more is growth in services, which has remained strong given continued strong growth in personal incomes.

Some analysts have constructed their own proxies for GDP growth, but such exercises are not actually measuring GDP as it is defined; they are relying on alternative measurements of economic activity. The Conference Board, for example, has created its own GDP series using an alternative methodology. Their numbers suggest that annual GDP growth rates over the past three decades were closer to 7.5 percent than the reported 10 percent.[3] But their methodology assumes little or no improvement in the quality of China's industrial production, which for most countries is a significant factor in determining GDP growth. If the Conference Board numbers were correct, China's economy today would be about half of what it is reported to be. Or its economy decades ago was twice as large as it was reported to be then. Neither case seems logical, as others have noted.[4]

More significant are the discrepancies originating from China's central-planning days when a "material balance approach" was the basis for deriving GDP rather than the standard UN system of national accounts. China has adopted the UN system, but its statistics have not been fully cleansed of its former socialist bias in favor of industrial production relative to services and neglect of informal private activities. This means that the size of its economy is systematically underestimated given the increasingly prominent role that services play as a country develops.

This has been borne out by periodic "benchmark revisions" undertaken with international assistance to revise the magnitude and composition of GDP.[5] The last two rebasing exercises were done in 1993, which increased the nominal size of the service sector by 32 percent and GDP by 10 percent, and in 2004, which led to another large increase in the share of services in GDP and increased the annual economic growth rate from 9.2 percent to 9.9 percent for the previous decade. Ironically, the government was not enthused about these upward adjustments, since they weakened China's case for favorable treatment in international trade and aid negotiations.

On the second issue of the expenditure shares in GDP, there is also much debate about whether China's consumption and investment shares of GDP are really so extreme. There are statistical problems in the way that these numbers are estimated. Consumption growth rates in most economies closely follow other proxies, such as retail sales. Until the recent economic slowdown, the news for China was all about double-digit growth rates in sales of luxury goods, autos, and home furnishings. How can one reconcile sales figures that were growing at 15–20 percent a year for a decade with GDP numbers that suggest single-digit growth in personal consumption? This raises suspicions that something is amiss, quite possibly that consumption is seriously understated.[6] A 2008 Morgan Stanley study estimated that Chinese GDP was about 30 percent higher than official figures, and per-capita consumption was as much as 80 percent higher. Some research surveys show that household income has been understated by some 20–30 percent of GDP.

There is official support for such views. The head of the national accounts department at China's National Bureau of Statistics (NBS) acknowledged on the NBS website in 2009 that its household consumption figures are deficient. The statistics are based on an obsolete, thirty-year-old sample survey; do not take full account of cash transactions; do not include fully indirect payments for social services; and have not been adjusted to reflect the market values for housing services, which is based largely on estimated construction costs and miss the surge in property values. Moreover, as a result of high sales taxes, businesses often do not issue receipts leading to household purchases being underreported.

These conclusions have been given more credence by two Shanghai-based professors, Jun Zhang and Tian Zhu, who concluded that personal consumption was significantly underestimated by as much as 15 percentage points of GDP.[7] This is due to underreporting of housing expenses, company-provided consumption benefits, and informal household income.

By implication, estimates of the share of investment in GDP are inflated. This stems partly from the practice among many companies and government agencies to classify consumption-type expenditures as investment because of the belief in a socialist economy that consumption is bad and investment is good. In addition, GDP estimates of investment have not been adequately adjusted for the rising cost of land—which has soared in recent years. This has led to an upward bias in some indicators of investment.

Overall, the personal consumption-to-GDP ratio might be around 45 percent rather the reported 35 percent, and the investment ratio about 38 percent instead of 48 percent. If so, then China's consumption and investment ratios are in line with its Asian peers such as Japan and South Korea during their comparable stage of development.

There are many flaws and inconsistencies in China's statistics but there is no systematic intention to distort the results in one direction or another. Carsten Holz, one of few experts familiar with how such accounts are constructed in China, has concluded that while China's statistics have methodological problems, they are nevertheless not being deliberately manipulated to yield higher growth rates.[8] Even the US Federal Reserve came to this conclusion in their own study of China's GDP statistics.[9]

NOTES

Chapter 1

1. Joseph Stiglitz, "The Chinese Century," *Vanity Fair*, January 2015.
2. See the commentary on Professor Rogoff's views in Andrew Ross Sirkin, "A Warning on China Seems Prescient," *International New York Times*, August 24, 2015.
3. George Magnus, *Uprising: Will Emerging Markets Shake or Shape the World Economy* (West Sussex, UK: John Wiley, 2010).
4. See, for example, Stephen Roach, "False Alarm on China," *Project Syndicate*, January 26, 2016.
5. See Danny Quah, "Chinese Lessons: Singapore's Epic Regression to the Mean," *World Bank Future Development Blog*, November 10, 2014.
6. The concept of a "middle-income trap" was developed by Indermit Gill and Homi Kharas, *An East Asian Renaissance: Ideas for Economic Growth* (Washington DC: World Bank, 2007). The concept is that developing countries have been relatively successful in moving from low- to middle-income levels, but for a variety of reasons—notably the inability to shift to higher-valued production—only a few middle-income countries have been able to move up to high-income levels.
7. Congressional-Executive Commission on China, "2016 Annual Report," October 6, 2016.

Chapter 2

1. The Washington Consensus encapsulates a number of neoliberal economic beliefs, dominant in the 1980s and 1990s, put forward by John Williamson that reflected the views of the IMF, World Bank and US Treasury. These stressed the role of market forces in shaping prices including interest and exchange rates, fiscal and financial discipline, trade

liberalization, competition, property rights and privatization of SOEs. In contrast, a British official, Joshua Cooper Ramos coined the term "the Beijing Consensus," which over time and as embellished by others introduced several key Chinese characteristics, including incremental reform, soft authoritarianism, and a heavy role for state capitalism. Over time, some have noted that the defining factor is the relative importance of the state in shaping policies and outcomes.

2. One would not have foreseen then that the euphoria surrounding unification would eventually be displaced by potentially destabilizing demonstrations in Hong Kong. Coupled with generally depressed sentiments in Taiwan where real wages have stagnated, the younger generation in both localities feels that increasing ties with mainland China have not created the same benefits that the wealthier business community has realized. More generally, the issue of inequality within China and the impact of China's rise on the incomes of its neighbors is a study of contrasts and misperceptions that are explored in Chapters 6 and 7.

3. World Bank, *China 2020: Development Challenges in the New Century* (Washington, DC: World Bank, 1997).

4. Gordon Chang, *The Coming Collapse of China* (New York: Random House, 2001).

5. The Pew Global Attitudes Survey showed favorability ratings for China at 63 percent in the Philippines in 2002 compared with 38 percent today. For Indonesia and Malaysia, favorability ratings for China were at 70–80 percent in 2002 compared with 60–70 percent today.

6. Ian Storey, *Southeast Asia and the Rise of China* (London and New York: Routledge, 2011).

7. Michael Pettis, *The Great Rebalancing: Trade, Conflict, and the Perilous Road Ahead for the World Economy* (Princeton, NJ: Princeton University Press, 2013); Nicholas R. Lardy, *Sustaining China's Economic Growth after the Global Financial Crisis* (Washington, DC: Peterson Institute for International Economics, 2012). Pettis and Lardy argue that China's low household consumption relative to GDP, rising debt levels, and increasing inequality are manifestations of an unbalanced economic growth model which favors industry and exports at the expense of households. Low interest rates and an undervalued exchange rate are seen as driving this process.

8. Ben S. Bernanke, "The Global Savings Glut and the U.S. Account Deficit," remarks at the Sandridge Lecture, Virginia Association of Economists, Richmond, Virginia, March 2005.

9. IMF, *Rebalancing Growth in Asia: Economic Dimensions for China* (Washington, DC: IMF, 2011), and *China's Economy in Transition: From*

External to Internal Rebalancing (Washington, DC: IMF, 2013). These are collections of articles that see China's unbalanced growth as a risk.

10. Press releases of US-China Strategic and Economic Dialogues from US Treasury website: https://www.treasury.gov/press-center/press-releases/Pages/jl0484.aspx.

11. Martin Jacques, *When China Rules the World* (New York: Penguin Press, 2009).

12. Arvind Subramanian, "The Inevitable Superpower," *Foreign Affairs*, September/October 2011.

13. Derek Scissors and Arvind Subramanian, "The Great China Debate: Will China Rule the World?," *Foreign Affairs*, January/February 2012.

14. Michael Pettis, *Avoiding the Fall: China's Economic Restructuring* (Washington, DC: Carnegie Endowment for International Peace, 2013).

15. Gordon Chang, "The Coming Collapse of China: 2012 Edition," *Foreign Policy*, December 2011.

16. Shiyin Chen, "China on a Treadmill to Hell amid Bubble, Chanos Says," *Bloomberg*, August 8, 2010.

17. "China Credit-Bubble Call Pits Fitch's Chu against S&P," *Bloomberg*, May 29, 2013.

18. Pew Global Attitudes survey, Gallup and national polls, various years were used for this section.

19. Discussion of the perceptions in the United States in particular and other aspects are discussed in Yukon Huang, "China's Most Dangerous Enemy Is Global Public Opinion," *The National Interest*, May 4, 2016.

20. This same sentiment shows up in the annual Pew surveys, except that the positions were reversed in 2016 because China's growth slowdown has altered sentiments.

21. In 2016, the first time since the GFC, Pew surveys indicated that Europe also saw the United States rather than China as the world's leading economic power.

22. Rankings produced by the UN, World Bank, and IMF generally place China around 85 in purchasing power terms and around 75 in nominal dollars in 2015.

23. The Uighur Islamic community is the dominant minority in Xinjiang where ethnic and religious tensions are strong and incidents of terrorism are on the rise. The Chinese artist and dissident Ai Wei Wei's family connections have fanned negative sentiments toward China's human rights policies.

24. Pew Research Center, "Global Opposition to U.S. Surveillance and Drones, but Limited Harm to America's Image: Many in Asia Worry about Conflict with China," Pew Global Attitudes Research, 2014, chapter 2.

25. Accordingly, in a recent survey across nine African countries, respondents are on average "satisfied" with Chinese companies that work on large projects in their respective countries, with a majority further observing that China's policies in the continent are "somewhat beneficial" overall. Barry Sautman and Hairong Yan Hairong, "African Perspectives on China-Africa Links," *The China Quarterly*, September 2009, 728–59.

26. Alexander Gadzela and Marek Hanusch, "African Perspectives on China-Africa: Gauging Popular Perceptions and Their Economic and Political Determinants," Afrobarometer Working Paper 1117, January 2010.

27. Zan Tao, "An Alternative Partner to the West? Turkey's Growing Relations with China," The Middle East Institute, October 15, 2013.

Chapter 3

1. See Dani Rodrik, "When Ideas Trump Interests: Preferences, Worldviews, and Policy Innovations," *Journal of Economic Perspectives* 28, no. 1 (2015): 189–208.

2. See Annex A for a summary of China development experience.

3. Some of his alleged statements have been questioned in terms of authenticity or precise meaning in translation.

4. See Chenggang Xu, "The Fundamental Institutions of China's Reforms and Development," *Journal of Economic Literature* 49, no. 4 (2011): 1076–151. Xu calls this a "regionally decentralized authoritarian system." My focus is on the incentives for competition that the structure created.

5. For a fuller discussion, see Yukon Huang, "Reinterpreting China's Success through the New Economic Geography," Carnegie Endowment for International Peace, Asia Program, Number 115, November 2010.

6. Yao Yang, "The Political Economy of Government Policies toward Regional Inequality in China," in *Reshaping Economic Geography in East Asia*, eds. Yukon Huang and Alessandro Magnoli Bocchi (Washington, DC: World Bank, 2009).

7. These theories were the basis of a Nobel Prize in Economics awarded to W. Arthur Lewis in 1979 and Paul Krugman in 2008.

8. Agglomeration economies are the dynamic benefits coming from the interaction of firms, labor, and knowledge-related activities when economic agents are concentrated in a specific locality.

9. This focus on the coast is highlighted in Yukon Huang, "Eye China's coast not its currency," *Financial Times*, August 10, 2010.

10. A more technical treatment of these issues is in Yukon Huang and Xubei Luo, "Reshaping Economic Geography in China."

11. World Bank, "China Transport Survey," 2007, unpublished.

12. There are many views on the role of the state in shaping governance and institutions at the local level and implications for China's development see Dali Yang, *Remaking the Chinese Leviathan: Market Transition and the Politics of Governance in China* (Stanford, CA: Stanford University Press, 2004).

13. Chenggang Xu, "The Fundamental Institutions of China's Reforms and Development," *Journal of Economic Literature* 49, no. 4 (2011): 1076–151.

14. Yang Yao, "The End of the Beijing Consensus," *Foreign Affairs*, February 2, 2010.

15. Geng Xiao, Zhang Yansheng, Law Cheung Kwok, and Dominic Meagher, "China's Evolving Growth Model: The Foshan Story," Asia Global Institute, University of Hong Kong, May 11, 2015.

16. Zhu Rongji served as the first vice premier in charge of the economy from 1993 to 1998 and then premier from 1998 to 2003. He was also earlier governor of the People's Bank of China and mayor of Shanghai.

17. James Miles, "A Dragon out of puff," *The Economist*, June 13, 2002.

18. Deepak Bhattasalli, Shantong Li, and Will Martin, eds., *China and the WTO* (Washington, DC: World Bank, 2004).

19. Shi Li, Hiroshi Sato, and Terry Sicular, eds., *Rising Inequality in China: Challenges to a Harmonious Society* (New York: Cambridge University Press, 2013).

20. See Yang Li and Xiaojing Zhang, "China's Sovereign Balance Sheet Risks and Implications for Financial Stability," in *China's Road to Greater Financial Stability: Some Policy Perspectives*, eds. Udaibir S. Das, Jonathan Fiechter and Tao Sun (Washington, DC: IMF, 2013); Arthur Kroeber, "Why Financial Reform Is Crucial for China's Growth," Brookings Research Paper, March 19, 2012.

Chapter 4

1. US Treasury Department, Office of Public Affairs, Fact Sheet, June 7, 2016.

2. See summary of the book on back cover of Anoop Singh, Malhar Nabar, and Papa N'Diaye, eds., *China's Economy in Transition: From External to Internal Rebalancing* (Washington, DC: IMF, 2013); and Vivek Arora and Roberto Cardarelli, eds., *Rebalancing Growth in Asia: Economic Dimensions for China* (Washington, DC: IMF, 2011).

3. See for example, Nicholas Lardy, "China: Toward a Consumption-Driven Growth Path," Institute for International Economics Policy Brief 06-6, October 2006; Michael Pettis, *The Great Rebalancing: Trade, Conflict, and the Perilous Road Ahead for the World Economy* (Princeton, NJ: Princeton

University Press, 2013); Guonan Ma, R. McCauley, and L. Lam, "The Roles of Saving, Investment and the Renminbi in Rebalancing the Chinese Economy," *Review of International Economics* 21, no. 1 (2013): 72–84.

4. Ettore Dorrucci, Gabor Pula, and Daniel Santabarbara, "China's Economic Growth and Rebalancing," European Central Bank, Occasional Paper Series No. 141, February 2013.

5. The discussion of unbalanced growth in this chapter elaborates on my earlier research on this topic. See Yukon Huang and Clare Lynch, "Unbalanced but in a Good Way," *China Economic Quarterly*, September 2013; Yukon Huang, "Understanding China's Unbalanced Growth," *Financial Times (Alphaville)*, September 4, 2013; and Yukon Huang, "How China's Consumption Matters," *Wall Street Journal*, August 31, 2015.

6. As reported by Xinhua news outlets on March 16, 2007.

7. Jahangir Aziz and Li Cui, "Explaining China's Low Consumption: The Neglected Role of Household Income," IMF Working Paper 07/181, 2007.

8. That low interest rates would encourage more investment seems plausible and also consistent with economic theory. But the rationale for the argument that low interest rates curbs consumption is less obvious. Economic theory suggests that low interest rates would normally lead to lower savings since households might be tempted to spend more if their savings are not being rewarded with attractive interest rates. But the counterargument being made for China is that households have a target for how much they want to earn from savings accounts and if interest rates are low they have to save more to achieve their target.

9. Joe Studwell, *How Asia Works* (London: Profile Books, 2013). That practically all developing countries have interest rates structures indicative of financial repression while advanced economies do not is elaborated in Juli Escola, Anna Shabunina, and Jaejoon Woo, "The Puzzle of Persistently Negative Interest Rate-Growth Differential: Financial Repression or Income Catch-up?," IMF Working Paper WP/11/260, 2011.

10. Julian Gruin, "Asset or Liability?: The Role of the Financial System in the Political Economy of China's Rebalancing," *Journal of Current Chinese Affairs* 42, no. 4 (2013): 73–104.

11. W. Arthur Lewis, "Economic Development with Unlimited Supplies of Labour," *The Manchester School* 22, no. 2 (May 1954): 139–91.

12. Cai Fang, "Demographic Transition, Demographic Dividend, and Lewis Turning Point in China," *China Economic Journal* 3, no. 2 (2010): 107–19; Cai Fang and Wang Meiyan, "Chinese Wages and the Turning Point in the Chinese Economy," East Asia Forum, January 29, 2011.

13. To get total consumption, one would have to calculate what percent of the revenues from selling the iPod goes to managers and other workers

and then add their consumption. In total, perhaps 35 to 50 percent of the total industrial production is consumed compared with 70 percent for agriculture.

14. Chong-en Bai and Zhengjie Qian, "The Factor Income Distribution in China: 1978–2007," *China Economic Review* 21, no. 1 (2010): 650–70.

15. Some studies have noted these regional differences but did not relate them to the issue of overall macro imbalances. See Il Houng Lee, Murtaza Syed, and Xueyan Liu, "China's Path to Consumer-Based Growth: Reorienting Investment and Enhancing Efficiency," IMF Working Paper WP/13/83, 2013; and M. K. Tang, "Investment Efficiency in China: What Does Provincial Differentiation Suggest?," Goldman and Sachs, June 13, 2013.

16. Although developing the interior priority began building up around the mid-1990s, the formal Develop the West Program was launched in June of 1999. This program provided financial and fiscal support covering twelve western provinces, all of which were relatively less developed.

17. This is based on data from the National Bureau of Statistics for eight eastern provinces and special administrative areas and the twelve focal provinces and autonomous regions eligible for the "Develop the West" initiative.

18. See Lee, Syed, and Xuyan, 8.

19. That urbanization is the primary reason why consumption has fallen as a share of GDP is also the conclusion of the joint World Bank and Chinese Government report. See World Bank and Development Research Center, *Urban China* (Washington DC: World Bank, 2014).

20. Marcos Chamon and Eswar Prasad, "Why Are Savings Rates of Urban Households in China Rising?," *American Economic Journal: Macroeconomics* 2, no. 1 (2010): 93–130.

21. See, for example, Shang-Jin Wei and Xiaobo Zhang, "The Competitive Saving Motive: Evidence from Rising Sex Ratios and Savings Rates in China," NBER Working Paper 15093, June 2009.

22. Binkai Chen, Ming Lu, and Ninghua Zhong, "Hukou and Consumption Heterogeneity: Migrants' Expenditure Is Depressed by Institutional Constraints in Urban China" (Shanghai: Fudan University, 2012). They use cross-provincial data to show that migrant households save substantially more than other households. Various other household budget studies for major cities along the coast have also indicated that migrant households save considerably more than established residents. Some of this savings is remitted to their families back home, which moderates the overall increase in savings rate for the combined households.

23. Yanrui Wu, "Has China Invested Too Much? A Study of Capital Efficiency and its Determinants," Discussion Paper 36, China Policy Institute, University of Nottingham, 2008.

24. The ICOR—or incremental capital to output ratio—indicates how much output is generated per unit increase in the capital stock (or investment). The lower is the number, the higher returns to investment.

25. Total factor productivity is a measurement of the contribution to growth not accounted for by increases in investment and labor. It serves as a proxy for factors such innovation, technological progress, and general productivity gains.

26. See Kharas and Gill, *An East Asian Renaissance*.

27. Yukon Huang and Clare Lynch, "Unbalanced but in a Good Way."

28. See Meng Xin, "Harnessing China's Untapped Labor Supply," *Paulson Policy Memorandum*, Paulson Institute, 2015.

29. Nabar and Yan note that low productivity increases in services is part of the reason for China's low consumption share. See Malhar Nabar and Kai Yan, "Sector-level Productivity, Structural Change and Rebalancing in China," IMF Working Paper WP/13/240, 2013.

30. See Yukon Huang, "How Consumption Matters," *Wall Street Journal*, September 1, 2015.

31. A rough estimate by the World Bank is that consumption as a share of GDP might be nearly 2 percentage points higher. See World Bank and Development Research Center, *China 2030: Building a Modern, Harmonious, and Creative Society* (Washington, DC: World Bank, 2013), 109.

32. There are many studies on whether capital is being efficiently allocated in China. Methodological approaches range from cross-country and time-series studies on investment and GDP growth to analysis of firm-level rates of return by sector, size, and ownership. Some studies conclude that rates of return are lower for state versus private enterprises. Other studies show that long-term returns and investment efficiency in China are either higher than or comparable to other developing countries. There is also evidence of a decline in returns following the GFC due to the surge in expenditures as part of the stimulus program—which is consistent with the experiences of most other countries affected by the growth slowdowns. See Gavekal Dragonomics, "China's Surprisingly Efficient Allocation of Capital," January 10, 2013, for evidence that returns in China are relatively high contrary to popular perceptions. World Bank and other studies generally show that total factor productivity and incremental capital output ratios for China have been above average for most of the past several decades but are declining toward the norm more recently. See World Bank and Development Research Center, *China 2030*; Barry Bosworth and Susan Collins, "Accounting for Growth: Comparing

China and India," *Journal of Economic Perspectives* 22, no. 1 (2008): 45–66; and Louis Kuijs and Jianwu He, "Rebalancing China's Economy—Modeling a Policy Package," World Bank China Research Paper no. 7, (2007).

33. Gavekal Dragonomics, "Urbanization's Winners and Losers," February 20, 2014.

34. Yukon Huang and Xubei Luo, "Reshaping Economic Geography in China," 196–217, in *Reshaping Economic Geography in East Asia*, ed. Yukon Huang and Alessandro Magnoli Bocchi (Washington, DC: World Bank, 2009).

35. Taking a different approach in looking at when economies slow down after rapid periods of growth, Eichengreen et al. calculate that China's slowdown is likely to occur around 2016. However, because China still has a large rural population and undeveloped interior, he notes that there is still an untapped potential for continued productivity increases and timing of the slowdown could be later. See Barry Eichengreen, Donghun Park, and Kwanho Shin, "When Fast Growing Economies Slow Down: International Evidence and Implications for China," NBER Working Paper 16919, 2011.

36. Mitali Das and Papa N'Diaye, "Chronicle of a Decline Foretold: Has China Reached the Lewis Turning Point?," in *China's Economy in Transition: From External to Internal Rebalancing*, eds. Anoop Singh, Malhar Nabar, and Papa N'Diaye (Washington, DC: IMF, 2013): 157–79.

Chapter 5

1. IMF, "People's Republic of China: Staff Report for the Article IV Consultation," August 2016.

2. "The Coming Debt Bust," *The Economist*, May 7, 2016.

3. David Dollar and Bert Hofman, "Intergovernmental Fiscal Reforms, Expenditure Assignment, and Governance," in *Public Finance in China: Reform and Growth for a Harmonious Society*, eds. Lou Jiwei and Shulin Wang (Washington, DC: World Bank, 2008).

4. For a fuller discussion of China's debt issues, see Yukon Huang and Canyon Bosler, "China's Debt Dilemma—Deleveraging while Generating Growth," Carnegie Endowment Policy Paper, September 2014.

5. Wang Tao, "Three Big Questions and the Most Important Chart," *UBS Macro Keys*, January 2014.

6. That China's debt is relatively high is not particularly surprising for a country with such a high savings rate and a bank-dominated financial system, both of which are traits associated with high debt.

7. Giovanni Dell'Ariccia, Deniz Igan, Luc Laeven, and Hui Tong, "Policies for Macro-financial Stability: Dealing with Credit Booms and Busts," IMF Staff Discussion Note 12/06, June 2012.

8. Martin Kessler and Arvind Subramanian, "Is the Renminbi Still Undervalued? Not According to New PPP Estimates," Peterson Institute for International Economics *Real Time Economic Issues Watch* (blog), May 2014.

9. Stijn Claessens, Simeon Djankov, and Lixin Colin Xu, "Corporate Performance in the East Asian Financial Crisis," *World Bank Research Observer*, February 2000.

10. Jay Bryson, "Does China Have a Debt Problem?," Wells Fargo Special Commentary, September 2013.

11. Mali Chivakul and W. Raphael Lam, "Assessing China's Corporate Sector Vulnerabilities," IMF Working Paper WP/15/72, March 2015.

12. Thomas Gatley, "How Big Is the Zombie Army," Gavekal Dragonomics, March 31, 2016.

13. China Council for International Cooperation on Environment and Development, "State Council Urges to Cut 80m Tons of Steel Capacity in 5 Years," October 25, 2013.

14. Ryan Rutkowski, "Will China Finally Tackle Overcapacity," *Peterson Institute for International Economics, China Economic Watch* (blog), April 2014.

15. Yukon Huang, "China's Productivity Challenge," *Wall Street Journal*, August 2013.

16. Kenneth Ho et al., "The China Credit Conundrum," Goldman and Sachs Portfolio Strategy Research, July 26, 2013.

17. Andrew Batson, "Fixing China's State Sector," Paulson Institute Policy Memoranda, January 2014.

18. Kenneth Ho et al., "The China Credit Conundrum."

19. The city of Xinyu, which receives 12 percent of its tax receipts from LDK Solar, arranged to pay off all $80 million of the solar firm's debt rather than allow it to default in 2013. Similarly, when the city of Wenzhou's vibrant underground financial system began to collapse a few years ago, the local government pressured state-owned banks to step in and bail out many of the private firms that had relied on informal lending markets rather than allow their bankruptcies to become a drag on the local economy.

20. "Bursting China's Credit Bubble," *Wall Street Journal*, April 19, 2016.

21. Thomas Gatley and Long Chen, "Defaults Are Coming—Where, When and How," Gavekal Dragonomics, April 2014.

22. Arthur Kroeber, "After the NPC: Xi Jinping's Roadmap for China," Brookings Institute, March 2014.

23. Andrew Batson, "Fixing China's State Sector."

24. Yinqiu Lu and Tao Sun, "Local Government Financing Platforms in China: A Fortune or Misfortune," IMF Working Paper WP/13/243, October 2013.

25. "The Decision on Major Issues Concerning Comprehensively Deepening Reforms in Brief," *China Daily*, November 16, 2013.

26. Shannon Tiezzi, "Re-evaluating Local Officials Key to China's Reforms," *Diplomat*, December 2013.

27. Yukon Huang, "Squaring the Circle: How the Reforms Can Work," *China Economic Quarterly*, December 2014.

28. Ideally shadow banking would be measured entirely from the asset side (trust loans, entrust loans, bankers' acceptance bills, etc.) or entirely from the liability side (WMPs, trust products, etc.) to ensure consistency and minimize double counting. However, data constraints make such an approach impractical and would end up omitting some relevant forms of credit extension through shadow banking. This is a conservative definition that allows for some double counting to ensure comprehensive coverage and is likely to be an overestimate.

29. Nikolaos Panigirtzoglou, Matthew Lehmann, and Jigar Vakharia, "How Scary Are China's Shadow Banks?," J. P. Morgan Global Asset Allocation, January 2014.

30. "Wealth Products Threaten China Banks on Ponzi-Scheme Risk," *Bloomberg News*, July 2013.

31. Suwatchai Songwanich, "Shadow-banking Poses Problems for China," NationMultimedia.com, March 2014.

32. Kenneth Ho et al., "The China Credit Conundrum."

33. Janet L. Yellen, "Interconnectedness and Systemic Risk: Lessons from the Financial Crisis and Policy Implications," speech at the American Economic Association/American Finance Association Joint Luncheon, San Diego, California, January 4, 2013.

34. Some studies using a narrower definition of shadow banking come up with higher percentages of risky assets but this is the result of excluding from the total the less risky components.

35. Bank for International Settlements, "Strengthening the Banking System in China: Issues and Experiences," BIS Policy Paper, 1999; Nicholas Lardy, *China's Unfinished Economic Revolution* (Washington, DC: Brookings Institute Press, 1998).

36. Guonan Ma, "Who Pays China's Bank Restructuring Bill?," *Asian Economic Papers*, January 2007.

37. "Asset-Management Companies in China: Lipstick on a Pig," *The Economist*, August 2013.

38. For example, McKinsey's recent study suggests that at the extreme, nonperforming loans might reach as high as 15 percent several years from

now but would be manageable. See McKinsey Global Institute, "China's Choice: Capturing the $5 Trillion Productivity Opportunity," June 2016.

39. Yukon Huang and Canyon Bosler, "China's Debt Dilemma."

40. IMF, *Global Financial Stability Report* (Washington, DC: IMF, 2016), 17.

41. IMF, "People's Republic of China: Staff Report for the Article IV Consultation," August 2016.

42. Chuin-Wei Yap, "China Tries to Choke Off Steel and Coal Loans," *Wall Street Journal*, April 21, 2016.

43. Wang Tao et al., "Bubble Trouble: Are We There Yet?," *UBS Global Research*, May 2014.

44. Yukon Huang, "Do Not Fear a Chinese Property Bubble," *Financial Times*, February 2014.

45. Wang Tao, Harrison Hu, Donna Kwok, and Ning Zhang, "What's New About China's New Urbanization Plan?," *UBS Global Research*, March 2014.

46. Li Gan, "Findings from China Household Finance Survey," January 2013.

47. The price rebound in 2016 has been supported in some localities by riskier forms of financing. Whether such activity will persist is unclear.

48. Li Gan, "Findings from China Household Finance Survey."

49. Nicholas Borst, "How Vulnerable Are Chinese Banks to a Real Estate Downturn?," Peterson Institute for International Economics *China Economic Watch* (blog), April 2014.

50. Although China's new urbanization plan anticipates slower migration to the cities than in the past decade, it intends to allow more migrants to register as urban residents, which would increase their demand for housing and other social services.

51. Michael Pettis, "Will the Reforms Speed Growth in China?," *China Financial Markets*, January 2014.

52. Charlene Chu, Chunling Wen, Hiddy He, and Jonathan Cornish, "Indebtedness Continues to Rise with No Deleveraging in Sight," *Fitch Ratings Special Report*, September 2013.

53. M. K. Tang, "Is Credit Losing Its Cyclical Growth Impact?," Goldman Sachs Emerging Markets Macro Daily, May 2013.

54. See Global Property Guide, www.globalpropertyguide.com/most-expensive-cities.

55. Many studies using the concept of total factor productivity have shown that productivity growth in China has been above normal for the decades leading up to the GFC but fell off sharply since 2010. See, for example, Martin Wolf, "China's Struggle for a New Normal," *Financial Times*, March 22, 2016.

56. For a capsule description of the themes of the Third Plenum, see Yukon Huang, "How to Make Comprehensively Deepening Reform in China," *Financial Times*, November 13, 2013.

57. Every Chinese citizen is given formal residency rights—*hukou*—usually according to where they were born. These rights provide access to public services such as education and health and grant eligibility for state-sponsored employment. Migrant workers who relocate to other localities for employment purposes are not usually accorded such rights and thus many do not bring their families with them since they would not have access to local social services and cannot buy a house, secure a driver's license, etc. Such residency rights can be granted by local authorities upon application, but the guidelines for doing so have been strict.

58. See Steve Barnett and Ray Brooks, "Does Government Spending in Health and Education Raise Consumption?," for analysis showing how increased budget support for social programs would also increase personal consumption of social services.

59. For more on all topics related to China's urbanization process, see the World Bank, *Urban China: Toward Efficient, Inclusive, and Sustainable Urbanization* (Washington, DC: World Bank, 2014).

60. Kai Guo and Papa N'Diaye, "Determinants of China's Private Consumption: An International Perspective," in *Rebalancing Growth in Asia*, eds. Vivek Arora and Robert Cardarelli (Washington, DC: IMF, 2011).

61. See World Bank and Development Research Center, *China 2030*, 91.

62. See for example, IMF, "People's Republic of China: Article IV Consultation," July 7, 2015.

Chapter 6

1. This chapter draws on research over many years. See Yukon Huang, "China's Conflict between Economic and Political Liberalization," *SAIS Review* 32, no. 2 (Summer–Fall 2012): 51–63; and Yukon Huang, "The Challenge for China's New Leaders," *Foreign Affairs*, March 7, 2012.

2. Daron Acemoglu and James Robinson, *Why Nations Fail: The Origins of Power, Prosperity, and Poverty* (New York: Crown Publishing Group, 2012).

3. Pew's 2011 survey shows China topping the other twenty-four countries in the degree its citizens are satisfied with the "direction that its economy is going" as well as how the current generation compares with their parents' standard of living. Comparisons across countries are questionable, but China was in the middle of the pack a decade ago and thus the degree of satisfaction clearly has increased.

4. The last official figures of incidents of mass unrest indicated some 87,000 in 2005. More recent estimates range as high as 160,000–180,000. See Tom Orlik, "Unrest Grows as Economy Booms," *Wall Street Journal*, September 26, 2011. The government stopped publishing data on incidents of mass unrest in 2006, but periodic estimates suggest that the numbers have continued to increase rapidly. See for example, Yangqi Tong and Shaohua Lei, "Large-scale Mass Incidents and Government Responses in China," *International Journal of China Studies* 1, no. 2 (2010): 487–508.

5. David Shambaugh, "The Coming Chinese Crackup," *Wall Street Journal*, March 6, 2015.

6. For a broad survey of the institutional factors shaping China's growth see Chenggang Xu, "The Fundamental Institutions of China's Reforms and Development," *Journal of Economic Literature* 49, no. 4 (2011): 1076–151.

7. This initiative was designed to liberalize the flow of capital and registration of businesses both domestic and foreign.

8. Each member of the Politburo, including its seven-person Standing Committee, as well as the state council which is similar to a cabinet, has assigned responsibilities over economic as well as security or political issues. These functions are also delineated along chains of responsibility down to the provinces and localities. See Susan V. Lawrence and Michael F. Martin, "Understanding China's Political System," Congressional Research Service, 2012.

9. Views on how authoritarian regimes handling of popular resistance can be either stabilizing or destabilizing are discussed in Yongshun Cai, "Power Structure and Regime Resilience: Contentious Politics in China," *B.J. Pol. S* 38 (2008): 411–32; and Elizabeth Perry and Mark Selden, eds., *Chinese Society: Change, Conflict and Resistance*, 2nd. ed. (New York: Routledge, 2003).

10. Some have suggested that China is the only country where local governments have played a leading role in increasing rates of growth. See Pranab Bardhan and Dilip Mookherjee, eds., *Decentralization and Local Governance in Developing Countries: A Comparative Perspective* (Cambridge, MA: MIT Press, 2006).

11. Yu Liu and Dingding Chen, "Why China Will Democratize," *The Washington Quarterly*, Winter 2012.

12. See Tong and Lei, "Large-scale Mass Incidents and Government Responses in China."

13. The Gini coefficient is a measure of inequality varying from 0 to 1. One means that all the income accrues to one individual and 0 means that incomes are distributed equally. Most countries fall in the .30–.60 range. China's Gini coefficient rose from around .25 to close to over .45 over

the past three decades. The magnitude is comparable to other successful economies such as Malaysia and Singapore, and also similar to the United States. But the speed of the increase is unprecedented.

14. World Bank, *China Poverty Assessment* (Washington, DC: World Bank, 2009).

15. Gabriel Wildau, "China's Income Inequality among the World's Worst," *Financial Times*, January 14, 2016.

16. See Martin King Whyte, "Myth of the Social Volcano: Popular Response to Rising Inequality in China," in *The People's Republic of China at 60*, ed. William C. Kirby (Cambridge, MA: Harvard University Asia Center, 2011).

17. Yukon Huang and Canyon Bosler, "China's Burgeoning Graduates—Too Much of a Good Thing?," *The National Interest*, January 7, 2014.

18. Yukon Huang, "Making Corruption Unsustainable in China," *Wall Street Journal*, March 26, 2015.

19. Ravi Kanbur and Xiaobo Zhang, "Fifty Years of Regional Inequality in China: a Journey through Central Planning, Reform and Openness," *Review of Development Economics* 9, no. 1 (2005): 87–106.

20. Christine Wong, *Financing Local Government in the People's Republic of China*, Asian Development Bank, 1997.

21. World Bank and Development Research Center of the State Council, People's Republic of China, *China 2030*.

22. In absolute terms, rural areas have benefited greatly from reduced agrarian taxes and improved infrastructure but until recently, growth in rural incomes has lagged well behind urban.

23. Yukon Huang, "China's New Challenge—Less Frugality," *Financial Times*, January 18, 2012.

24. Yukon Huang, "The Real Risks to China's Financial System," *Financial Times*, November 16, 2011.

25. Martin King Whyte, "The Paradoxes of Rural-Urban Inequality in Contemporary China," in *One Country, Two Societies*, ed. Martin King Whyte (Cambridge, MA: Harvard University Press, 2010).

26. The peak of around 270 million was reached in 2015 but there has been some reverse flow more recently.

27. These financial concerns can be addressed through fiscal reforms and more concentrated development of urban services. See World Bank and Development Research Center of the State Council, *Urban China*.

28. Migration reduces inequalities measured on a national or regional basis because migrants tend to be poorer than nonmigrants in sending areas. They earn and send back a portion of their increased earnings to relatives left behind. With *hukou* or formal residency rights, migrants have the

opportunity to earn and remit even more. But if their families choose to migrate with them, this frees up their land for those left behind whose incomes also increase. Overall this process uplifts the incomes of the poor relative to the better off on a per-capita basis. See Nong Zhu and Xubei Luo, "The Impact of Migration on Rural Poverty and Inequality: A Case Study in China," *Agricultural Economics* 41, no. 2(2010): 191–204.

29. Concerns that China's major cities are too large are in fact overblown. See Yukon Huang, "China Needs Beijing to Be Even Bigger," *Bloomberg*, September 9, 2013.

30. This discussion on corruption draws on Yukon Huang, The Truth about Chinese Corruption," *Diplomat*, May 29, 2015.

31. See for example, Andrew Wedeman, *Double Paradox: Rapid Growth and Rising Corruption in China* (Ithaca, NY: Cornell University Press, 2012).

32. Minxin Pei, *China's Crony Capitalism: The Dynamics of Regime Decay* (Cambridge, MA: Harvard University Press, 2016).

33. Acemoglu and Robinson, *Why Nations Fail: The Origins of Power, Prosperity, and Poverty*.

34. Carl E. Walter and Fraser J. T. Howie, *Red Capitalism: The Fragile Financial Foundation of China's Extraordinary Rise* (Singapore: John Wiley, 2011).

35. See for example, David Cohen, "What Wukan Really Meant," *Diplomat*, January 1, 2012.

36. Elizabeth Perry and Mark Selden, eds., *Chinese Society: Change, Conflict and Resistance*, 2nd ed. (New York: Routledge, 2003).

37. Pierre F. Landry, Deborah Davis, and Shiru Wang, "Elections in Rural China: Competition without Parties," *Comparative Political Studies, 2010*, 1–28.

38. More representative local processes can lead to better outcomes as discussed in Scott Rozelle, Jikun Huang, Renfu Luo, and Linxiu Zhang, "Village Elections, Public Goods Investments and Pork Barrel Politics, Chinese-style," mimeo, Stanford University, 2009.

39. Thus far, the senior leadership has signaled that the country is not yet ready to have more representative processes extended to higher levels of regional authority much less to national levels.

40. See Minxin Pei, "The Twilight of Communist Party Rule in China," *The American Interest*, November 12, 2015.

41. See for example, Larry Diamond and Gi-Wook Shin, eds., *New Challenges for Maturing Democracies in Korea and Taiwan* (Stanford, CA: Stanford University Press, 2014); Minxin Pei, "Creeping Democratization in China," *Journal of Democracy* 6, no. 4 (1995): 65–79.

42. See for example, John F. Hsieh, "Democratizing China," *Journal of Asian and African Studies* (2003): 377–91.

43. Evan Osnos, *Age of Ambition: Chasing Fortune, Truth, And Faith In The New China* (New York: Farrar, Straus, Giroux, 2014).

44. There is considerable literature on the persistence of authoritarianism. See for example, Andrew J. Nathan, "Authoritarian Resilience," *Journal of Democracy*, January 2003.

45. See Liu and Chen, "Why China Will Democratize," for a representative discussion of this topic.

46. Henry Rowen wrote in 1996 that China might become politically more democratic by 2015 and then later suggested that this might take place by 2025. See Henry S. Rowen, "When Will the Chinese People be Free?," *Journal of Democracy* 18, no. 3 (July 2007): 38–52.

47. Andrew Sheng and Xiao Geng, "The Night-Watchman's State's Last Shift," *Project Syndicate*, China-US Focus, June 5, 2013.

48. Andrew Sheng, *From Asian to Global Financial Crisis: An Asian Regulator's View of Unfettered Finance in the 1990 and 2000s* (London: Cambridge University Press, 2009).

Chapter 7

1. A major sell-off of US securities by China would cause interest rates to soar as security prices fall and also likely lead to a decline in the value of the US dollar. The decline in security prices and the value of the dollar would end up hitting the value of China's investments in the United States.

2. Benn Steil and Emma Smith, "The Trump-Sanders China Syndrome," *Wall Street Journal*, March 29, 2016.

3. A 2014 US-China Business Council Survey indicated that the primary objective of 91 percent of its respondents was to access the China market, up from 57 percent in 2006.

4. "U.S. Passes China to become the Most Favored Destination for Foreign Investment but Washington Could Imperil That," *Forbes*, February 4, 2014.

5. Alan Smart and Jinn-Yuh Hsu, "The Chinese Diaspora, Foreign Investment and Economic Development in China," *The Review of International Affairs* 3, no. 4 (Summer 2004): 544–66.

6. Willem Thorbecke, "Measuring the Competitiveness of China's Processes Exports," *China and World Economy* 23, no. 1 (2015): 78–100.

7. Prema-chandra Athukorala and Jayant Menon, "Global Production Sharing, Trade Patterns and Determinants of Trade Flows in East Asia," Asian Development Bank, January 2010.

8. Daniel Poon, "China's Development Trajectory: A Strategic Opening for Industrial Policy in the South," UNCTAD, December 2014.

9. Wayne Morrison, "China's Economic Rise, History, Trends, Challenges and Implications for the United States," Congressional Research Service, October 21, 2015.

10. Martin Feldstein, "End the Currency Manipulation Debate," *Financial Times*, May 15, 2014.

11. See Wayne Morrison, "China-U.S. Trade Issues," Congressional Research Service, January 4, 2017.

12. See for example, Tim Worstall, "The Effect of Apple's new iPhone on China's Exports, Trade Balance and GDP," *Forbes*, September 3, 2014.

13. The OECD and WTO estimate that the US trade deficit in China would be reduced by 25 percent if bilateral trade flows were measured according to value added. See OECD, "Measuring Trade in Value Added: An OECD-WTO Joint Initiative," 2015.

14. William Cline, "Renminbi Series Part 2: Is China's Currency Fairly Valued?," Peterson Institute for International Economics, *China Watch Series* (blog), March 23, 2016. In late 2015, China announced that it would no longer peg its exchange rate to the US dollar but to an unspecified basket of currencies.

15. Paul Hannon, "Why Weak Currencies Have a Smaller Effect on Export," *Wall Street Journal*, December 27, 2015.

16. Neil Irwin, "What Donald Trump Gets Pretty Much Right, and Completely Wrong about China," *Washington Post*, March 17, 2016.

17. David Autor, David Dorn, and Gordon Hanson, "The China Syndrome: Local Labour Market Effects of Import Competition in the United States," *American Economic Review* 103, no. 6 (2013): 2121–68.

18. Martin Wolf, "Donald Trump's tough talk will not bring US jobs back," *Financial Times*, January 21, 2017.

19. Yukon Huang, "America's Hammering China's RMB Makes Little Sense," The Forum Discussing International Affairs and Economics, Summer 2012.

20. Michael Schuman, "Is China Stealing Jobs, It May Be Losing Them Instead," *New York Times*, July 22, 2016.

21. Charles Wolf Jr., Xiao Wang, and Eric Warner, "China's Foreign Aid and Government-Sponsored Investment Activities," Rand Corporation, 2013.

22. A 2011 government white paper indicated that the total amount of aid extended from 1950 to 2009 was $41 billion, with half going to Africa and nearly a third to Asia, followed by Latin America and other regions. A 2014 white paper gave a figure of $5 billion annually for the period 2010–2012. Studies using a broad definition of aid, including debt relief, have come up with numbers ranging from $3–8 billion annually in recent years, while more narrow definitions yield estimates closer to $2 billion.

See Deborah Brautigam, *The Dragon's Gift: The Real Story of China in Africa* (New York: Oxford University Press, 2009).

23. Charles Wolf Jr. et al., "China's Foreign Aid and Government-Sponsored Investment Activities."

24. Unlike the World Bank and Inter-American Development Bank, Chinese banks do not regularly publish detailed figures regarding their loan activities, making it hard to calculate an exact amount. Gallagher's statistics were calculated by following Chinese and host-country press reports.

25. Charles Wolf Jr. et al., "China's Foreign Aid and Government-Sponsored Investment Activities."

26. Infrastructure Consortium for Africa. *Infrastructure Financing Trends in Africa: ICA Annual Report 2013.*

27. Catherin E. Dalpino, "Consequences of a Growing China," statement before the Senate Committee on Foreign Relations Subcommittee on East Asian and Pacific Affairs, June 7, 2005; Heritage Foundation, "Southeast Asia's Forgotten Tier: Burma, Cambodia and Laos," July 26, 2007; Marvin C. Ott, "Southeast Asian Security Challenges: America's Response?," *Strategic Forum*, October 1, 2006; Joshua Kurlantzick, "China's Charm Offensive in Southeast Asia," *Current History* 105, no. 692 (September 2006): 270–76.

28. Thomas Lum, Hannah Fischer, Julissa Gomez-Granger, and Anne Leland, "China's Foreign Aid Activities in Africa, Latin America and Southeast Asia," Congressional Research Service, February 2009.

29. Kevin P. Gallagher, Amos Irwin, and Katherine Koleski, "The New Banks in Town: Chinese Finance in Latin America," Global Development and Environment Institute at Tufts University, February 2012.

30. Ibid.

31. Jamil Anderlini, "China to Become One of the World's Biggest Investors by 2020," *Financial Times*, June 25, 2015.

32. According to the Ministry of Commerce's geographical breakdown of outbound investment flows in 2013, nearly 70 percent of China's outward FDI went to Asia, largely because Hong Kong captured 58 percent of total flows. When combined with the tax havens of the Cayman Islands and British Virgin Islands, this figure climbs to 70 percent of China's outward FDI flows. These two distortions undoubtedly skew recorded investment toward Asia and Latin America while making calculation of China's real FDI destinations hard to trace.

33. David Dollar, "United States-China Two-way Direct Investment," Brookings Institution, December 2014.

34. James Kynge, Tom Mitchell, and Arash Massoudi, "M&A: China's World of Debt," *Financial Times*, February 11, 2016.

Chapter 8

1. For an excellent discussion of these issues, see Caroline Pan, "Foreign Tech Companies: Alive in the Bitter Sea," *China Economic Quarterly*, Gavekal Dragonomics, September 15, 2016.

2. UNCTAD data provides comparable foreign investment numbers across countries but has not yet been updated for recent years. Some other reports suggest a surge in FDI going from China to the United States over the past year in part because of the desire of Chinese investors to diversify their holdings given the economic slowdown at home and appreciation of the US dollar. The EU has become less attractive given the sharp fall in the value of the euro and pound.

3. Thilo Hanemann and Mikko Huotari, "Chinese FDI in Europe and Germany: Preparing for a New Era of Chinese Capital," Rhodium Group, June 26, 2015.

4. David Dollar, "United States-China Two-way Direct Investment," Brookings Institution, 2015.

5. The US-China Business Council, "US Exports to China, by State, 2004–2013,"2014.

6. UBS, "Beyond Commodities," *China Focus*, June 26, 2014.

7. Eurostat and Bureau of Economic Analysis data, various years.

8. Compilation done by OECD and Deutsche Bank.

9. Christian Oliver and Michael Pooler, "Europe Splits over Whether to Grant China Market Economy Status," *Financial Times*, December 28, 2015.

10. Francois Godement and Angela Stanzel, "The European Interest in an Investment Treaty with China," European Council on Foreign Relations, February 2015.

11. Council on Foreign Relations, "Backgrounder: Foreign Ownership of U.S. Infrastructure," February 13, 2007.

12. David Dollar, "United States-China Two Way Direct Investment."

13. Wayne M. Morrison, "China—U.S. Trade Issues," Congressional Research Service, December 15, 2015.

14. Paul Mozur and Jane Perlez, "Concern Grows in U.S. over China's Drive to Make Chips," *New York Times*, February 4, 2016.

15. Peterson Institute for International Economics, *Toward a US-China Investment Treaty*, February 2015.

16. Shayndi Raice and William Mauldin, "Chinese Deal-Making Draws Scrutiny in Washington," *Wall Street Journal*, February 18, 2016.

17. The distinction between state and private companies can be unclear.

18. Cadwalader, Wickersham and Taft, "Investing in the United States: CIFIUS Concerns for Chinese Investors," mimeo, July 9, 2015.

19. Daniel Thomas, "Lord Browne to head Huawei's UK board," *Financial Times*, February 16, 2015.

20. BBC News, "Huawei and ZTE Row: Should the UK Be Worried about the Chinese Tech Firms?," October 11, 2012.

21. Sam Schechner, "Huawei Founder: Company Aims to Be Viewed as European," *Wall Street Journal*, May 2, 2014.

22. Ken Davies, "China Investment Policy: An Update," OECD Working Papers on International Investment, 2013/01.

23. World Bank, *Global Development Horizons 2011—Multipolarity: The New Global Economy* (Washington, DC: World Bank, 2011).

24. Eva Dou, "Cisco Unveils $10 Billion China Plan," *Wall Street Journal*, June 17, 2015.

25. IP Commission, "The Report on the Theft of American Intellectual Property," 1.

26. Ibid.

27. McKinsey Global Institute, "The China Effect on Global Innovation," July 2015.

28. Daniel H. Rosen, Thilo Hanemann, and Anna Snyder, "Chinese Participation in US Infrastructure," Rhodium Group, October 23, 2013.

29. A study done by the Peterson Institute showed that in 2005, wages of Chinese majority-owned firms were much higher than those of US-owned firms and even higher than the average of foreign firms operating in the United States with wages at $65,000 compared to $85,000 at Chinese companies. See Theodore Moran and Lindsay Oldenski, "Foreign Direct Investment in the United States: Benefits, Suspicions, and Risks with Special Attention to FDI from China," Peterson Institute for International Economics, 2013.

Chapter 9

1. There has been debate about whether the South China Sea is a "core" interest, but increasingly it has been seen as such given that territorial integrity is now deemed a defining factor.

2. For an interpretation of China's "counterbalance" to America's "rebalancing" strategy see Douglas Paal, "China, the U.S. and the Coming Taiwan Transition," *Diplomat*, December 29, 2015.

3. Daniel H. Rosen and Thilo Hanemann, "China's Reform Era and Outward Investment," Rhodium Group, December 2, 2013.

4. Spencer Lake, "China Set to Overtake the US as an Outward Investor," *Financial Times*, June 30, 2015.

5. Yukon Huang and Clara Lynch, "Does Internationalizing the RMB Make Sense for China?," *Cato Journal* 33, no.3 (Fall 2013): 571–85.

6. Greg Ip, "U.S. Influence Hinges on Value of the Dollar, Yuan," *Wall Street Journal*, April 15, 2015.

7. Carnegie round-table discussion with China think-tank scholars, 2015.

8. See for example, Peter Petri, Michael Plummer, and Fan Zhai, "The Trans-Pacific Partnership and Asia-Pacific Integration: A Quantitative Assessment," *Policy Analysis in International Economics* 98 (November 2012).

9. Simeon Djankov and Sean Miner, eds., "China's Belt and Road Initiative: Motives, Scope, and Challenges," Peterson Institute for International Economics, March 2016.

10. Asian Development Bank, *Infrastructure for a Seamless Asia* (Manila: Asian Development Bank, 2009).

11. As reported in the *South China Morning Post*, June 29, 2015. Fifty had already signed as of mid-summer 2015, and dozens more had expressed interest in joining.

12. Lingling Wei, "China-Led Development Bank AIIB Will Be Lean, Green and Clean Says its President," *Wall Street Journal*, January 22, 2016.

13. Alexander Cooley, "China's Changing Role in Central Asia and Implications for US Policy: From Trading Partner to Collective Goods Provider," remarks for "Looking West: China and Central Asia" US-China Economic and Security Review Commission, March 18, 2015.

14. Xinhuanet, "Xi pledges 'great renewal of Chinese nation,'" November 29, 2012. http://news.xinhuanet.com/english/china/2012-11/29/c_132008231.htm.

15. See, for example, Tom Miller, *China's Dream: Quiet Empire Building Along the New Silk Road* (London: Zed Books, 2017).

16. See Ian Storey, *Southeast Asia and the Rise of China* (London and New York: Routledge, 2011), for a discussion of China's relations with ASEAN during this period.

17. Ian Storey, *Southeast Asia and the Rise of China*, 65.

18. Joshua Kurlantzick, "China's Charm Offensive in Southeast Asia," *Current History* 105, no. 692 (September 2006): 270–76.

19. *The Economist*, "Whale and Spratlys," December 13, 2007.

20. International Crisis Group, "Stirring Up the South China Sea," Report Number 223, April 23, 2012.

21. Speech delivered by President Obama in Australia in 2011.

22. Council on Foreign Relations, "China's Maritime Disputes," A CFR InfoGuide Presentation.

23. International Crisis Group, "Dangerous Waters: China-Japan Relations on the Rocks," Asia Report no. 245, April 8, 2013.
24. Ibid.
25. See "Prisoner's Dilemma," *Wikipedia*, last modified February 6, 2017, https://en.wikipedia.org/wiki/Prisoner%27s_dilemma.
26. See Jeffrey A. Bader, "What the United States and China should do in the wake of the South China Sea ruling," Brookings Institution *Order from Chaos* (blog), July 13, 2016.
27. Graham Allison, "The Thucydides Trap: Are the U.S. and China Headed for War," *The Atlantic*, September 24, 2015.
28. Robert B. Zoellick, "Remarks to National Committee on US-China Relations," New York City, September 21, 2005.
29. I initially developed the concept of China as an abnormal power in my paper, "China, The Abnormal Great Power," Carnegie Endowment, March 5, 2013, and elaborated further in "China Becomes An Abnormal Great Power," *Wall Street Journal*, May 28, 2015.
30. Xinhua news, September 28, 2015. http://news.xinhuanet.com/english/2015-09/28/c_134668393.htm.
31. Zheng Bijian, "The Internal and External Environments of China's Development over the Next Five Years," in *East Asian Visions*, eds. Indermit Gill, Yukon Huang and Homi Kharas (Washington, DC: World Bank, 2007).
32. Douglas Paal, "China's Counterbalance to the American Rebalance," *Strategic Review*, October–December 2015.
33. Orville Schell, "China Strikes Back," *The New York Review of Books*, October 23, 2014.
34. Kevin Rudd, "How to Break the 'Mutually Assured Misperception' between the U.S. and China," *The World Post*, April 20, 2015.
35. US congressional approval was delayed to December 2015, giving China and other emerging market economies a greater share in the voting power in the IMF and World Bank. The original proposal was tabled in 2010.
36. Robert B. Zoellick, "Remarks to National Committee on US-China Relations."
37. Mark Magnier, "How China Plans to Run AIIB: Leaner with Veto," *Wall Street Journal*, June 8, 2015.
38. Reuters, "China Gives More Details on South China Sea Facilities," June 17, 2015.
39. Mark J. Valencia, "New Round of China-Bashing over the South China Sea," East Asia Forum, June 18, 2015.
40. Xinhuanet, "Xi Jinping—China to Further Friendly Relations with the Neighboring Countries," October 26, 2013.

41. Charles Clover and Lucy Hornby, "China's Great Game: Road to a New Empire," *Financial Times*, October 12, 2015.

42. Keith Bradsher, "China Plans a New Silk Road but Trade Partners Are War," *New York Times*, December 25, 2015; Simon Denyer, "China's Assertiveness Pushes Vietnam toward an Old Foe, the United States," *Washington Post*, December 28, 2015.

43. Ian Storey, *Southeast Asia and the Rise of China*, 95.

44. Jane Perlez, "Obama Faces a Tough Balancing Act over South China Sea," *New York Times*, March 29, 2016.

Chapter 10

1. Alexandra Stevenson, "Fears about China's Economy Fester at Davos," *New York Times*, January 22, 2016.

2. Lant Pritchett and Lawrence Summers, "Asiaphoria Meets Regression to the Mean," NBER Working Paper 20573, October 2014; UBS, "China Economic Perspectives," January 2015.

3. See Justin Yifu Lin, *Demystifying the Chinese Economy* (New York: Cambridge University Press, 2012). Professor Lin recent interviews indicate that he sees China's near-term future growth to be in the range of 7 percent.

4. Nicholas Lardy, "False Alarm on a Crisis in China," *New York Times*, August 26, 2015.

5. Francois Godement, "China's Slowdown and Europe's Leverage," European Council on Foreign Relations, February 12, 2016.

6. See World Bank, World Development Indicators, 2014.

7. Michael Pettis, *Avoiding the Fall: China's Economic Restructuring* (Washington, DC: Carnegie Endowment, 2013).

8. The more labor intensive services sector has been buoyed up by sustained high wage increases. Meanwhile, the sharp declines in commodity and producer prices after 2011 have reverberated negatively on the valuation of industrial production. See Yukon Huang, "Can China Get Its Rebalancing Right," *Financial Times*, February 5, 2016.

9. See Xiao Geng, Yansheng Zhang, Cheung Kwok Law, and Dominic Meagher, "China's Evolving Growth Model: The Foshan Story," Asia Global Institute, University of Hong Kong, May 11, 2015.

10. Ibid.

11. Joseph E. Stiglitz, "The Chinese Century," *Vanity Fair*, January 2015.

12. "Grassley on China's Latest Currency Devaluation," Senator Grassley's website, August 11, 2015, http://www.grassley.senate.gov/news/news-releases/grassley-china%E2%80%99s-latest-currency-devaluation.

13. Ana Swanson, "China's Devaluation of Yuan Prompts Outcry from U.S. Politicians on Both Sides," *Washington Post*, August 11, 2015.

14. Robert D. Blackwill and Ashley J. Tellis, "Revising U.S. Grand Strategy towards China," Council on Foreign Relations, Council Special Report, April 2015.

15. Michael Swaine, "The Real Challenge in the Pacific," *Foreign Affairs* 94, no. 3 (May/June 2015): 145–53.

16. See the exchange of views in "What's Your China Fantasy," *Foreign Policy*, May 15, 2007. See David Lampton and Richard Daniel Ewing, *U.S.-China Relations in a Post-September 11th World* (Washington, DC: The Nixon Center, 2002).

17. David M. Lampton, "A Tipping Point in U.S.-China Relations Is upon Us," as presented at the conference "China's Reform: Opportunities and Challenges," co-hosted by The Carter Center and the Shanghai Academy of Social Sciences, May 6–7, 2015.

18. This section draws on my article "China Becomes an Abnormal Great Power," *Wall Street Journal*, May 27, 2015.

19. Yukon Huang, "There's more Volatility to Come in China," *Wall Street Journal*, January 14, 2015.

Appendix A

1. This section draws extensively on several background papers authored respectively by Bert Hofman and Jingliang Wu, "Explaining China's Development and Reforms," for the World Bank's Growth Commission and Yukon Huang, "Background Note: China's Policy Reforms—Why They Worked," for the joint World Bank and Chinese Government, *China 2030* report and the World Bank, *China 2020: Development Challenges in the New Century* (Washington, DC: World Bank, 1997). The key sources for much of the historical analysis in those papers were Yifu Lin, Fang Cai, and Zhou Li, *The China Miracle: Development Strategy and Economic Reform* (Hong Kong: The China University Press, 2003); Barry Naughton, *Growing out of the Plan: Chinese Economic Reforms 1978–1993* (Cambridge: Cambridge University Press, 1995); Barry Naughton, *The Chinese Economy: Transitions and Growth* (Cambridge, MA: MIT Press, 2006); Jingliang Wu, *Understanding and Interpreting Chinese Economic Reforms* (Singapore: Texere Press, Thomson-South Western, 2005); Dwight Perkins, "Reforming China's Economic System," *Journal of Economic Literature* 26 (June 1988): 601–45; Yingyi Qian and Jingliang Wu, "China's Transition to a Market Economy: How Far

Across the River," in *How Far Across the River: Chinese Policy Reform at the Millennium,* eds. Nicholas Hope, Dennis Tao Yang, and Mu Yang Li (Stanford, CA: Stanford University Press, 2003).

2. Barry Naughton, *Growing Out of the Plan: Chinese Economic Reforms 1978–1993.*

3. Chenggang Xu, "The Fundamental Institutions of China's Reforms and Development."

4. Qian and Wu elaborate on how this system aligned the interests of the state and firms.

5. Jiwei Lou and Shulin Wang, eds., *Public Finance in China: Reform and Growth for a Harmonious Society* (Washington, DC: World Bank, 2008).

6. Nicholas Lardy, *China's Unfinished Economic Revolution* (Washington, DC: Brookings Institution, 2003).

7. Yukon Huang and Xubei Luo, "Reshaping Economic Geography in China," in *Reshaping Economic Geography in East Asia,* ed. Yukon Huang and Alessandro Magnoli Bocchi (Washington, DC: World Bank, 2009).

8. Martin Ravallion and Shaohua Chen, "China's Uneven Progress in Poverty Alleviation," Policy Research Working Paper WPS 4107, World Bank, 2004.

Appendix B

1. This appendix draws on my article, "China's Misleading Economic Indicators," *Financial Times,* August 28, 2014.

2. Jeffrey Sparshott, "Wall Street Journal Survey: China's Growth Statements Make U.S. Economists Skeptical," *Wall Street Journal,* September 11, 2015.

3. Henry Wu, "China's Growth and Productivity Performance Debate Revisited," Conference Board Working Paper 14-01, January 2014.

4. Arthur R. Kroeber, *China's Economy: What Everyone Needs to Know* (New York: Oxford University Press, 2016), appendix.

5. Based on the World Bank's discussion with China's National Bureau of Statistics.

6. These issues are drawn from my article, "Misinterpreting China's Economy," *Wall Street Journal,* August 25, 2011.

7. Jun Zhang and Tian Zhu, "Re-estimating China's Underestimated Consumption," draft, Shanghai, Fudan University, 2013.

8. Carsten A. Holz, "The Quality of China's GDP Statistics," *China Economic Review* 30 (2014): 309–38.

9. See Federal Reserve Bank of San Francisco, "On the Reliability of Chinese Output Figures," FRBSF Economic Letter, March 25, 2013.

REFERENCES

Acemoglu, Daron, and James Robinson. 2012. *Why Nations Fail: The Origins of Power, Prosperity, and Poverty*. New York: Crown Publishing Group.

Arora, Vivek, and Roberto Cardarelli. 2011. *Rebalancing Growth in Asia: Economic Dimensions for China*. Washington, DC: IMF.

Asian Development Bank. 2009. *Infrastructure for a Seamless Asia*. Manila: Asian Development Bank.

Athukorala, Prema-chandra, and Jayant Menon. 2010. "Global Production Sharing, Trade Patterns and Determinants of Trade Flows in East Asia." Asian Development Bank, Working Paper Series on Regional Economic Integration.

Autor, David, David Dorn, and Gordon Hanson. 2013. "The China Syndrome: Local Labour Market Effects of Import Competition in the United States." *American Economic Review* 103 (6): 2121–68.

Aziz, Jahangir, and Li Cui. 2007. "Explaining China's Low Consumption: The Neglected Role of Household Income." IMF Working Paper 07/181.

Bai, Chong-en, and Zhengjie Qian. 2010. "The Factor Income Distribution in China: 1978–2007." *China Economic Review* 21 (1): 650–70.

Bank for International Settlements. 1999. "Strengthening the Banking System in China: Issues and Experiences." Policy Paper.

Bardhan, Pranab, and Dilip Mookherjee, eds. 2006. *Decentralization and Local Governance in Developing Countries: A Comparative Perspective*. Cambridge: MIT Press.

Barnett, Steve, and Ray Brooks. 2011. "Does Government Spending on Health and Education Raise Consumption?" In *Rebalancing Growth in Asia: Economic Dimensions for China*, edited by Vivek Arora and Roberto Cardarelli. Washington, DC: International Monetary Fund.

Batson, Andrew. 2014. "Fixing China's State Sector." Paulson Institute Policy Memoranda.

Bhattasalli, Deepak, Li Shantong, and Will Martin, eds. 2004. *China and the WTO*. Washington, DC: World Bank.

Blackwill, Robert D., and Ashley J. Tellis. 2015. "Revising U.S. Grand Strategy towards China." Council on Foreign Relations, Council Special Report, March.

Borst, Nicholas. 2014. "How Vulnerable Are Chinese Banks to a Real Estate Downturn?" Peterson Institute for International Economics, China Economic Watch, April.

Bosworth, Barry, and Susan Collins. 2008. "Accounting for Growth: Comparing China and India." *Journal of Economic Perspectives* 22 (1): 45–66.

Brautigam, Deborah. 2010. *The Dragon's Gift: The Real Story of China in Africa*. New York: Oxford University Press.

Bryson, Jay. 2013. "Does China Have a Debt Problem?" *Wells Fargo Special Commentary*, September.

Cai, Yongshun. 2008. "Power Structure and Regime Resilience: Contentious Politics in China." *British Journal of Political Science* 38 (3): 411–32.

Chamon, Marcos, and Eswar Prasad. 2010. "Why Are Savings Rates of Urban Households in China Rising?" *American Economic Journal: Macroeconomics* 2, (1): 93–130.

Chang, Gordon. 2001. *The Coming Collapse of China*. New York: Random House.

Chang, Gordon. 2011. "The Coming Collapse of China: 2012 Edition." *Foreign Policy*, December.

Chivakul, Malil, and W. Raphael Lam. 2015. "Assessing China's Corporate Sector Vulnerabilities." IMF Working Paper 15/72.

Chen, Binkai, Lu Ming, and Zhong Ninghua. 2012. "Hukou and Consumption Heterogeneity: Migrants' Expenditure Is Depressed by Institutional Constraints in Urban China." Fudan University.

Chu, Charlene, Chunling Wen, Hiddy He, and Jonathan Cornish. 2013. "Indebtedness Continues to Rise with No Deleveraging in Sight." Fitch Ratings Special Report, September.

Claessens, Stijn, and Simeon Djankov, and Lixin Colin Xu. 2000. "Corporate Performance in the East Asian Financial Crisis." *World Bank Research Observer*, February.

Cline, William. 2016. "Renminbi Series Part 2: Is China's Currency Fairly Valued?" Peterson Institute for International Economics, China Watch Series, March 23.

Council on Foreign Relations. 2007. "Backgrounder: Foreign Ownership of U.S. Infrastructure." February 13.

Council on Foreign Relations. n.d. "China's Maritime Disputes." CFR InfoGuide Presentation.

Das, Mitali, and Papa N'Diaye. 2013. "Chronicle of a Decline Foretold: Has China Reached the Lewis Turning Point?" In *China's Economy in Transition: From External to Internal Rebalancing*, edited by Anoop Singh, Malhar Nabar, and Papa N'Diaye. Washington, DC: IMF.

Davies, Ken. 2013. "China Investment Policy: An Update." Organization for Economic Cooperation and Development, Working Papers on International Investment 2013/01.

Dell'Ariccia, Giovanni, Deniz Igan, Luc Laeven, and Hui Tong. 2012. "Policies for Macro-financial Stability: Dealing with Credit Booms and Busts." IMF Staff Discussion Note 12/06, June.

Diamond, Larry, and Gi-Wook Shin, eds. 2014. *New Challenges for Maturing Democracies in Korea and Taiwan*. Stanford, CA: Stanford University Press.

Djankov, Simeon, and Sean Miner, eds. 2016. *China's Belt and Road Initiative: Motives, Scope, and Challenges*. Washington, DC: Peterson Institute for International Economics.

Dollar, David. 2015. "United States-China Two-way Direct Investment." Brookings Institution.

Dollar, David, and Bert Hofman. 2008. "Intergovernmental Fiscal Reforms, Expenditure Assignment, and Governance." In *Public Finance in China: Reform and Growth for a Harmonious Society*, edited by Lou Jiwei and Wang Shulin. Washington, DC: World Bank.

Dorrucci, Ettore, Gabor Pula, and Daniel Santabarbara. 2013. "China's Economic Growth and Rebalancing." European Central Bank, Occasional Paper Series no. 142.

Eichengreen, Barry, Donghun Park, and Kwanho Shin. 2013. "Growth Slowdowns Redux: New Evidence on the Middle-Income Trap." NBER Working Paper 18673.

Escolan, Juli, Anna Shabunina, and Jaejoon Woo. 2011. "The Puzzle of Persistently Negative Interest Rate-Growth Differential: Financial Repression or Income Catch-up?" IMF Working Paper 11/260.

Federal Reserve Bank of San Francisco. 2013. "On the Reliability of Chinese Output Figures." FRBSF Economic Letter, March 25.

Gadzela, Alexander, and Marek Hanusch. 2010. "African Perspectives on China-Africa: Gauging Popular Perceptions and Their Economic and Political Determinants." Afrobarometer. Working Paper 1117, January.

Gallagher, Kevin P., Amos Irwin, and Katherine Koleski. 2012. "The New Banks in Town: Chinese Finance in Latin America." Global Development and Environment Institute at Tufts University. February.

Gatley, Thomas. 2016. "How Big Is the Zombie Army." Gavekal Dragonomics. March.

Gatley, Thomas, and Long Chen. 2014. "Defaults Are Coming—Where, When and How." Gavekal Dragonomics. April.

Geng Xiao, Zhang Yansheng, Law Cheung Kwok, and Dominic Meagher. 2015. "China's Evolving Growth Model: The Foshan Story." Asia Global Institute, University of Hong Kong. May 11.

Gill, Indermit, and Homi Kharas. 2007. *An East Asian Renaissance: Ideas for Economic Growth.* Washington, DC: World Bank.

Gill, Indermit, Yukon Huang, and Homi Kharas, eds. 2007. *East Asian Visions: Perspectives on Economic Development.* Washington DC: World Bank and Institute of Policy Studies.

GK Dragonomics. 2013. "China's Surprisingly Efficient Allocation of Capital." January 10.

GK Dragonomics. 2014. "Urbanization's Winners and Losers." February 20.

Godement, Francois. 2016. "China's Slowdown and Europe's Leverage." European Council on Foreign Relations. February 12.

Godement, Francois, and Angela Stanzel. 2015. "The European Interest in an Investment Treaty with China." European Council on Foreign Relations. February.

Gruin, Julian. 2013. "Asset or Liability?: The Role of the Financial System in the Political Economy of China's Rebalancing." *Journal of Current Chinese Affairs* 42 (4): 73–104.

Guo, Kai, and Papa N'Diaye. 2011. "Determinants of China's Private Consumption: An International Perspective." In *Rebalancing Growth in Asia: Economic Dimensions for China*, edited by Vivek Arora and Roberto Cardarelli. Washington, DC: International Monetary Fund.

Hanemann, Thilo, and Mikko Huotari. 2015. "Chinese FDI in Europe and Germany: Preparing for a New Era of Chinese Capital." Rhodium Group. June 26.

Heritage Foundation. 2007. "Southeast Asia's Forgotten Tier: Burma, Cambodia and Laos." July 26.

Ho, Kenneth, et al. 2013. "The China Credit Conundrum." Goldman Sachs Global Economics, Commodities and Strategy Research. July 26.

Hofman, Bert, and Wu Jingliang. n. d. "Explaining China's Development and Reforms." Paper prepared for the World Bank's Growth Commission.

Holz, Carsten A. 2014. "The Quality of China's GDP Statistics." *China Economic Review* 30: 309–338.

Hsieh, John F. 2003. "Democratizing China." *Journal of Asian and African Studies* 38 (4–5): 377–91.

Huang, Jikun, Renfu Luo, Scott Rozelle, and Linxiu Zhang. 2009. "Village Elections, Public Goods Investments and Pork Barrel Politics, Chinese-style." Stanford University.

Huang, Yukon. 2010. "Reinterpreting China's Success through the New Economic Geography." Carnegie Endowment for International Peace. Asia Program Paper No. 115, November.

Huang, Yukon. 2011. "The Real Risks to China's Financial System." *Financial Times*, November 16.

Huang, Yukon. 2012a. "America's Hammering China's Renminbi Makes Little Sense." *The Forum Discussing International Affairs and Economics.* Summer.

Huang, Yukon. 2012b. "The Challenge for China's New Leaders." *Foreign Affairs*, March 7.

Huang, Yukon. 2012c. "China's Conflict between Economic and Political Liberalization." *SAIS Review* 32 (2): 51–63.

Huang, Yukon. 2013a. "How to Make Comprehensively Deepening Reform in China." *Financial Times*, November 13.

Huang, Yukon. 2013b. "China Needs Beijing to Be Even Bigger." *Bloomberg*, September.

Huang, Yukon. 2013c. "China's Productivity Challenge." *Wall Street Journal*, August.

Huang, Yukon. 2014a. "Squaring The Circle: How the Reforms Can Work." *China Economic Quarterly*, December.

Huang, Yukon. 2014b. "Do Not Fear a Chinese Property Bubble." *Financial Times*, February.

Huang, Yukon. 2014c. "China's Interest Rates Are Too High, not Too Low." *Financial Times*, January 7.

Huang, Yukon. 2015a. "How Consumption Matters." *Wall Street Journal*, September 1.

Huang, Yukon. 2015b. "Arresting Corruption in China." *Diplomat*, March 30.

Huang, Yukon. 2015c. "Making Corruption Unsustainable in China." *Wall Street Journal*, March 26.

Huang, Yukon. 2015d. "There's More Volatility to Come in China." *Wall Street Journal*, January 14.

Huang, Yukon. 2016a. "China's Most Dangerous Enemy is Global Public Opinion." *National Interest*, May 2

Huang, Yukon. 2016b. "Can China Get Its Rebalancing Right." *Financial Times*, February 5.

Huang, Yukon, and Alessandro Magnoli Bocchi, eds. 2009. *Reshaping Economic Geography in East Asia*. Washington, DC: World Bank.

Huang, Yukon, and Canyon Bosler. 2014a. "China's Burgeoning Graduates—Too Much of a Good Thing?" *The National Interest*, January 7.

Huang, Yukon, and Canyon Bosler. 2014b. "China's Debt Dilemma—Deleveraging While Generating Growth." Carnegie Endowment for International Peace. Policy Paper, September.

Huang, Yukon, and Clare Lynch. 2013a. "Does Internationalizing the RMB Make Sense for China?" *Cato Journal* 33 (3): 571–85.

Huang, Yukon, and Clare Lynch. 2013b. "Unbalanced, but in a Good Way." *China Economic Quarterly* 17 (3): 35–40.

Huang, Yukon, and Luo Xubei. 2009. "Reshaping Economic Geography in China." In *Reshaping Economic Geography in East Asia*, edited by Yukon Huang and Alessandro Magnoli Bocchi. Washington, DC: World Bank.

IMF. 2011. *Rebalancing Growth in Asia: Economic Dimensions for China*. Washington, DC: IMF.

IMF. 2013. *China's Economy in Transition: From External to Internal Rebalancing*. Washington, DC: IMF.

IMF. 2016a. *Global Financial Stability Report*. Washington, DC: IMF.

IMF. 2016b. "People's Republic of China: Staff Report for the Article IV Consultation." August 2016.

Infrastructure Consortium for Africa. 2014. *Infrastructure Financing Trends in Africa: ICA Annual Report 2013*.

International Crisis Group. 2013. "Dangerous Waters: China-Japan Relations on the Rocks." Asia Report no. 245, April 8.

IP Commission. 2013. "The Report on the Theft of American Intellectual Property." National Bureau of Asian Research.

Jacques, Martin. 2009. *When China Rules the World*. New York: Penguin Press.

Kanbur, Ravi, and Zhang Xiaobo. 2005. "Fifty Years of Regional Inequality in China: a Journey through Central Planning, Reform and Openness." *Review of Development Economics* 9 (1): 87–106.

Kessler, Martin, and Arvind Subramanian. 2014. "Is the Renminbi Still Undervalued? Not According to New PPP Estimates." Peterson Institute for International Economics. Real Time Economic Issues Watch, May.

Kroeber, Arthur. 2012. "Why Financial Reform Is Crucial for China's Growth." Brookings Research Paper. March 19.

Kroeber, Arthur. 2014. "After the NPC: Xi Jinping's Roadmap for China." Brookings Institution. March.

Kroeber, Arthur. 2016. *China's Economy: What Everyone Needs to Know*. New York: Oxford University Press.

Kuijs, Louis, and He Jianwu. 2007. "Rebalancing China's Economy—Modeling a Policy Package." World Bank. China Research Paper no. 7.

Kurlantzick, Joshua. 2006. "China's Charm Offensive in Southeast Asia." *Current History* 105 (692): 270–76.

Lampton, David M., and Richard Daniel Ewing. 2002. *U.S.-China Relations in a Post-September 11th World*. Washington, DC: The Nixon Center.

Landry, Pierre F., Deborah Davis, and Shiru Wang. 2010. "Elections in Rural China: Competition Without Parties." *Comparative Political Studies* 43 (6): 763–90.

Lardy, Nicholas R. 1998. "China and the Asian Contagion." *Foreign Affairs*, July/August.

Lardy, Nicholas R. 2003. *China's Unfinished Economic Revolution*. Washington, DC: Brookings Institution Press.

Lardy, Nicholas R. 2006. "China: Toward a Consumption-Driven Growth Path." Institute for International Economics. Policy Brief no. 06-6, October.

Lardy, Nicholas R. 2012. *Sustaining China's Economic Growth after the Global Financial Crisis.* Washington, DC: Peterson Institute for International Economics.

Lawrence, Susan V., and Michael F. Martin. 2012. "Understanding China's Political System." Congressional Research Service.

Lee, Il Houng, Murtaza Syed, and Xueyan Liu. 2013. "China's Path to Consumer-Based Growth: Reorienting Investment and Enhancing Efficiency." IMF Working Paper 13/83.

Lewis, W. Arthur. 1954. "Economic Development with Unlimited Supplies of Labour." *The Manchester School of Economics and Social Studies* 22 (2): 139–91.

Li Gan. 2013. "Findings from China Household Finance Survey." Unpublished, January.

Li, Shi, Hiroshi Sato, and Terry Sicular, eds. 2013. *Rising Inequality in China: Challenges to a Harmonious Society.* New York: Cambridge University Press.

Li, Taocai, and Shi Chen. 2009. "Crack the Mystery of China's Consumption Share Decline." Unpublished: Center for China in the World Economy. Tsinghua University School of Economics and Management.

Li, Yang, and Zhang Xiaojing. 2013. "China's Sovereign Balance Sheet Risks and Implications for Financial Stability." In *China's Road to Greater Financial Stability: Some Policy Perspectives,* edited by Udaibir S. Das, Jonathan Fiechter, and Tao Sun. Washington, DC: IMF.

Lin, Justin Yifu. 2012. *Demystifying the Chinese Economy.* New York: Cambridge University Press.

Lin, Yifu, Fang Cai, and Zhou Li. 2003. *The China Miracle: Development Strategy and Economic Reform.* Hong Kong: The Chinese University Press.

Liu, Yu, and Chen Dingding. 2012. "Why China Will Democratize." *The Washington Quarterly,* Winter.

Lou, Jiwei, and Shulin Wangn, eds. 2008. *Public Finance in China: Reform and Growth for a Harmonious Society.* Washington, DC: World Bank.

Lu, Yinqiu, and Tao Sun. 2013. "Local Government Financing Platforms in China: A Fortune or Misfortune." IMF Working Paper 13/243.

Lum, Thomas, Hannah Fischer, Julisaa Gomez-Granger, and Anne Leland. 2009. "China's Foreign Aid Activities in Africa, Latin America and Southeast Asia." Congressional Research Service. February.

Ma, Guonan, R. McCauley, and L. Lam. 2013. "The Roles of Saving, Investment and the Renminbi in Rebalancing the Chinese Economy." *Review of International Economics* 21 (1): 72–84.

Magnus, George. 2010. *Uprising: Will Emerging Markets Shake or Shape the World Economy.* West Sussex, UK: John Wiley and Sons.

McKinsey Global Institute. 2015. "The China Effect on Global Innovation." July.

Meng, Xin. 2015. "Harnessing China's Untapped Labor Supply." Paulson Institute. Paulson Policy Memorandum.

Miller, Tom. 2017. *China's Asian Dream: Quiet Empire Building Along the New Silk Road.* London: Zed Books.

Moran, Theodore, and Lindsay Oldenski. 2013. "Foreign Direct Investment in the United States: Benefits, Suspicions, and Risks with Special Attention to FDI from China." Peterson Institute of International Economics.

Morrison, Wayne M. 2015a. "China's Economic Rise, History, Trends, Challenges and Implications for the United States." Congressional Research Service. October 21.

Morrison, Wayne M. 2015b. "China—U.S. Trade Issues." Congressional Research Service. December 15.

Nabar, Malhar. 2013. "Interest Rates, Targets, and Household Saving in Urban China." In *China's Economy in Transition: From External to Internal Rebalancing,* edited by Anoop Singh, Malhar Nabar, and Papa N'Diaye. Washington, DC: IMF.

Nabar, Malhar, and Kai Yan. 2013. "Sector-level Productivity, Structural Change and Rebalancing in China." IMF Working Paper 13/240.

Nathan, Andrew J. 2003. "Authoritarian Resilience." *Journal of Democracy* 14 (1): 6–17.

Naughton, Barry. 1995. *Growing Out of the Plan: Chinese Economic Reforms 1978–1993.* Cambridge: Cambridge University Press.

Naughton, Barry. 2006. *The Chinese Economy: Transitions and Growth.* Cambridge, MA: MIT Press.

Osnos, Evan. 2014. *Age Of Ambition: Chasing Fortune, Truth, and Faith in The New China.* New York: Farrar, Straus, Giroux.

Ott, Marvin C. 2006. "Southeast Asian Security Challenges: America's Response?" *Strategic Forum,* October 1.

Paal, Douglas. 2015. "China's Counterbalance to the American Rebalance." *Strategic Review,* October–December.

Panigirtzoglou, Nikolaos, Matthew Lehmann, and Jigar Vakharia. 2014. "How Scary Are China's Shadow Banks?" *J.P. Morgan Global Asset Allocation.* January.

Pei, Minxin. 1995. "Creeping Democratization in China." *Journal of Democracy* 6 (4): 65–79.

Pei, Minxin. 2016. *China's Crony Capitalism: The Dynamics of Regime Decay.* Cambridge, MA: Harvard University Press.

Perkins, Dwight Harald. 1988. "Reforming China's Economic System." *Journal of Economic Literature* 26 (2): 601–45.

Perry, Elizabeth, and Mark Selden, eds. 2003. *Chinese Society: Change, Conflict and Resistance.* 2nd ed. New York: Routledge.

Peterson Institute for International Economics. 2015. *Toward a US-China Investment Treaty.* February.

Petri, Peter, Michael Plummer, and Fan Zhai. 2012. "The Trans-Pacific Partnership and Asia-Pacific Integration: A Quantitative Assessment." Peterson Institute, Policy Analysis in International Economics.

Pettis, Michael. 2013. *Avoiding the Fall: China's Economic Restructuring.* Washington, DC: Carnegie Endowment.

Pettis, Michael. 2013. *The Great Rebalancing: Trade, Conflict, and the Perilous Road Ahead for the World Economy.* Princeton, NJ: Princeton University Press.

Pettis, Michael. 2014. "Will the Reforms Speed Growth in China?" *China Financial Markets,* January.

Pew Research Center. 2014. "Global Opposition to U.S. Surveillance and Drones, but Limited Harm to America's Image: Many in Asia Worry about Conflict with China." Pew Global Attitudes Research.

Poon, Daniel. 2014. "China's Development Trajectory: A Strategic Opening for Industrial Policy in the South." UNCTAD. December.

Pritchett, Lant, and Lawrence Summers. 2014. "Asiaphoria Meets Regression to the Mean." NBER Working Paper 20573.

Qian, Yingyi, and Jingliang Wu. 2003. "China's Transition to a Market Economy: How Far Across the River." In *How Far Across the River: Chinese Policy Reform at the Millennium,* edited by Nicholas Hope, Dennis Tao Yang, and Mu Yang Li. Stanford, CA: Stanford University Press.

Quah, Danny. 2014. "Chinese Lessons: Singapore's Epic Regression to the Mean." World Bank Future Development Blog, November 10.

Ravallion, Martin, and Shaohua Chen. 2004. "China's Uneven Progress in Poverty Alleviation." World Bank. Policy Research Working Paper WPS 4107.

Rodrik, Dani. 2014. "When Ideas Trump Interests: Preferences, Worldviews, and Policy Innovations." *Journal of Economic Perspectives* 28 (1): 189–208.

Rosen, Daniel H., and Thilo Hanemann. 2013. "China's Reform Era and Outward Investment." Rhodium Group. December 2.

Rosen, Daniel H., Thilo Hanemann, and Anna Snyder. 2013. "Chinese Participation in US Infrastructure." Rhodium Group. October 23.

Rowen, Henry S. 2007. "When Will the Chinese People Be Free?" *Journal of Democracy* 18 (3): 38–52.

Rutkowski, Ryan. 2014. "Will China Finally Tackle Overcapacity?" *Peterson Institute for International Economics, China Economic Watch.* April.

Sautman, Barry, and Yan Hairong. 2009. "African Perspectives on China-Africa Links." *The China Quarterly* 199: 728–59.

Schell, Orville. 2014. "China Strikes Back." *The New York Review of Books*, October 23.

Scissors, Derek, and Arvind Subramanian. 2012. "The Great China Debate: Will China Rule the World?" *Foreign Affairs*, January/February.

Sheng, Andrew. 2009. *From Asian to Global Financial Crisis: An Asian Regulator's View of Unfettered Finance in the 1990 and 2000s.* London: Cambridge University Press.

Singh, Anoop, Malhar Nabar, and Papa N'Diaye, eds. 2013. *China's Economy in Transition: From External to Internal Rebalancing.* Washington, DC: IMF.

Smart, Alan, and Jinn-Yuh Hsu. 2004. "The Chinese Diaspora, Foreign Investment and Economic Development in China." *The Review of International Affairs* 3 (4): 544–66.

Storey, Ian. 2011. *Southeast Asia and the Rise of China.* London and New York: Routledge.

Studwell, Joe. 2013. *How Asia Works.* London: Profile Books.

Subramanian, Arvind. 2011. "The Inevitable Superpower." *Foreign Affairs*, September/October, 66–78.

Swaine, Michael. 2015. "The Real Challenge in the Pacific." *Foreign Affairs*, May/June, 145–53.

Tang, M. K. 2013. "Investment Efficiency in China: What Does Provincial Differentiation Suggest?" Goldman Sachs. June 13.

Tang, M. K. 2013. "Is Credit Losing Its Cyclical Growth Impact?" Goldman Sachs Emerging Markets Macro Daily, May.

Thorbecke, Willem. 2015. "Measuring the Competitiveness of China's Processes Exports." *China and World Economy* 23 (1): 78–100.

Tong, Yangqi, and Shaohua Lei. 2010. "Large-scale Mass Incidents and Government Responses in China." *International Journal of China Studies* 1 (2): 487–508.

Walter, Carl E., and Fraser J. T. Howie. 2011. *Red Capitalism: The Fragile Financial Foundation of China's Extraordinary Rise.* Singapore: John Wiley.

Wang, Tao, Harrison Hu, Donna Kwok, and Ning Zhang. 2014. "What's New about China's New Urbanization Plan?" *UBS Global Research*, March.

Wang, Tao, et al. 2014. "Bubble Trouble: Are We There Yet?" *UBS Global Research*, May.

Wedeman, Andrew. 2012. *Double Paradox: Rapid Growth and Rising Corruption in China.* Ithaca, NY: Cornell University Press.

Wei, Shang-Jin, and Xiaobo Zhang. 2009. "The Competitive Saving Motive: Evidence from Rising Sex Ratios and Savings Rates in China." NBER Working Paper 15093.

Whyte, Martin King, ed. 2010. *One Country, Two Societies.* Cambridge, MA: Harvard University Press.

Whyte, Martin King. 2011. "Myth of the Social Volcano: Popular Response to Rising Inequality in China." In *The People's Republic of China at 60*, edited by William C. Kirby. Cambridge, MA: Harvard University Asia Center.

Wolf, Charles Jr., Xiao Wang, and Eric Warner. 2013. "China's Foreign Aid and Government-Sponsored Investment Activities." Rand Corporation.

Wong, Christine. 1997. *Financing Local Government in the People's Republic of China.* Asian Development Bank.

World Bank. 1997. *China 2020: Development Challenges in the New Century.* Washington, DC: World Bank.

World Bank. 2007. *China Transport Sector Review.* Washington, DC: World Bank.

World Bank. 2009. *China Poverty Assessment.* Washington, DC: World Bank.

World Bank. 2011. *Global Development Horizons 2011—Multipolarity: The New Global Economy.* Washington, DC: World Bank.

World Bank. 2014. *Urban China: Toward Efficient, Inclusive, and Sustainable Urbanization.* Washington, DC: World Bank.

World Bank and Development Research Center of the State Council, People's Republic of China. 2013. *China 2030: Building a Modern, Harmonious, and Creative Society.* Washington, DC: World Bank.

Wu, Jingliang. 2005. *Understanding and Interpreting Chinese Economic Reforms.* Singapore: Texere Press, Thomson-South Western.

Wu, Yanrui. 2008. "Has China Invested Too Much? A Study of Capital Efficiency and its Determinants." Discussion Paper 36, China Policy Institute, University of Nottingham.

Xin, Meng. 2015. "Harnessing China's Untapped Labor Supply." Paulson Institute. Paulson Policy Memorandum.

Xu, Chenggang. 2011. "The Fundamental Institutions of China's Reforms and Development." *Journal of Economic Literature* 49 (4): 1076–151.

Yang, Dali. 2004. *Remaking the Chinese Leviathan: Market Transition and the Politics of Governance in China.* Stanford: Stanford University Press.

Yang, Yao. 2009. "The Political Economy of Government Policies toward Regional Inequality in China." In *Reshaping Economic Geography in East Asia,* edited by Yukon Huang and Alessandro Magnoli Bocchi. Washington, DC: World Bank.

Yang, Yao. 2010. "The End of the Beijing Consensus." *Foreign Affairs,* February 2.

Zan, Tao. 2013. "An Alternative Partner to the West? Turkey's Growing Relations with China." *The Middle East Institute,* October 15.

Zhang, Jun, and Tian Zhu. 2013. "Re-estimating China's Underestimated Consumption." Fudan University.

Zhu, Nong, and Luo Xubei. 2010. "The Impact of Migration on Rural Poverty and Inequality: A Case Study in China." *Agricultural Economics* 41 (2): 191–204.

Zoellick, Robert B. 2005. "Remarks to National Committee on U.S.-China Relations." New York City. September 21.

INDEX

Note: Page references followed by a "*t*" indicate table; "*f*" indicate figure.